Practical
Data Processing
Management

Louis Fried

Reston Publishing Company, Inc.
A Prentice-Hall Company
Reston, Virginia

PRACTICAL
DATA PROCESSING
MANAGEMENT

לחיה רחל, באהבה

Library of Congress Cataloging in Publication Data

Fried, Louis.
  Practical data processing management.

  Includes bibliographical references and index.
  1. Electronic data processing—Management.
I. Title.
QA76.9.M3F74   658'.05   79-10116
ISBN 0-8359-5589-3

© 1979 by Reston Publishing Company, Inc.
A Prentice-Hall Company
Reston, Virginia 22090

10 9 8 7 6 5 4 3 2

Printed in the United States of America

CONTENTS

PREFACE

This book presents solutions and alternative approaches to a range of common problem areas in the management of data processing. It is written for:

Executives with ultimate responsibility for the data processing function, as a management aid for guiding and controlling EDP activities.

Executives who are significant users of data processing resources, as an aid in understanding the EDP function and what level of service can be expected.

EDP Managers, as a guide to the solution of frequently encountered problems and as exposure to alternative approaches.

Future EDP Managers, as a method of gaining the perspective of the EDP Manager and top management.

Advanced students of data processing, as a text providing insight into EDP management problems and solutions.

The management of data processing has provided this author with the opportunity to experience most of the problems described in this book . . . and the challenge of finding workable, pragmatic solutions.

Altogether, it has been (and continues to be) an enjoyable career. Finding the answers to the management problems of data processing and information systems is both rewarding and satisfying.

ACKNOWLEDGMENTS

Many of the sections of this book are updated or modified versions of articles that were previously published under similar or different titles. The author wishes to acknowledge the publishers who have graciously given permission to use these articles.

From the AUERBACH Publishers series, "AUERBACH Data Processing Management," "AUERBACH Systems Development Management," and "AUERBACH Data Center Operations Management" the following portfolios were used:

Defining a Corporate Information Policy
Corporate Organization for System Development
Centralization: To Be or Not To Be
EDP Steering Committees
Estimating Time, Cost and Resource Requirements
Setting Application Priorities
Purchasing and Installing Software Packages
Objectives and Requirements of a Good Feasibility Study
Managing the Problems of Organization Change
Systems Specification Checklist
Performing Cost Benefit Analyses
Using Top Down and Structured Design Methodology
Long Range Planning for EDP

Minimizing DP Management Risks
How to Minimize Reruns
Recruiting Operations Personnel
Using a Consultant
Developing Personal Management Skills
Improving Cost Effectiveness in EDP

These portfolios are copyrighted by the AUERBACH Information Management Series, AUERBACH Publishers, Inc., Pennsauken, NJ 08109. Copyrights 1974, 1975, 1976, 1977, 1978.

The article "The Performance Evaluation Review" is reprinted from *Modern Data,* August 1974; and "Up the Data Processing Manager," from *Modern Data,* November 1974; both copyrighted in 1974 by *Modern Data* (now *Mini-Micro Systems*).

The article "Don't Smother Your Project in People" is reprinted from *Management Adviser,* March–April 1972, and is copyrighted in 1972 by the American Institute of Certified Public Accountants.

During the late 1950s and early 1960s the author spent the early years of his data processing and management career in the aerospace and electronics industries. Those were the halcyon days of cost-plus-fixed-fee (CPFF) contracts and considerable experimenting with what computers could be made to do for industry. Many of us learned how to do things better by making our mistakes in that environment. Acknowledgment is therefore gratefully added to the United States government and to the millions of taxpayers who contributed to our education at that time.

Practical
Data Processing
Management

INTRODUCTION

This book is written for the executive in charge of data processing, the data processing manager, the experienced professional in data processing with management aspirations, and the advanced student of data processing. This leads to the first point about the book: it is *not* intended for the novice in business data processing.

The book is also *not* a reference work containing soporific chapters of detailed models, formulae and statistical analyses. It is not intended to be a comprehensive or exhaustive volume on all aspects of data processing.

Instead, this book takes the perspective of the senior executive in charge of data processing and deals with those areas that will improve the ability of data processing to contribute to the profitability of the firm.

The various sections of this book originated in several ways. Some were suggested by the editors of publications in which they first appeared. Some were used as course material for data processing management courses at the University of California and other schools. But the majority found their origins in my need to find alternative solutions to problems that arose during the more than fifteen years that I have spent as a senior data processing manager.

As a result, this book is oriented toward real-world prob-

Chapter 1

lems and real-world solutions. While there are occasional technical terms, the book is primarily *management* directed—dealing with the problems of planning and use of corporate resources and people to achieve corporate goals and objectives.

Some years ago, as Director of Management Information Systems, I was asked by the Vice President of Finance (to whom I reported) to describe the goals of MIS. I prepared a carefully worded statement of objectives which concentrated on the idea of providing decision-making information to management for the lowest possible data processing cost.

I proudly presented this statement, only to be told that the real objective of MIS in the corporation is *to contribute to the profitability of the firm.* In that sense, the objectives of all parts of the corporation are the same. However, EDP (Electronic Data Processing) organizations have often lost sight of this primary objective.

Keeping it in mind can provide data processing managers with a perspective more closely aligned with that of top management. And this perspective leads to priorities and problem solutions that are practical in terms of management objectives rather than convenient for data processing.

Therefore, the emphasis of this book is on *practical* data processing management.

ORGANIZATION OF THE BOOK

This book is organized into five major chapters, each dealing with a substantive problem area in the management of data processing.

There is some overlap in the subject matter of chapters. This is consistent with the fact that management problems often span multiple areas of subject matter and solutions also tend to be multifaceted.

The first chapter addresses organizational issues including centralization and decentralization, the organization of the systems function, management control of the EDP function and the development of corporate information policy.

The second chapter deals with various aspects of project management such as estimating project costs, setting priorities, and the use of program "packages."

The third chapter deals with some of the more troublesome aspects of system development with concentration on cost/benefit analysis and systems design methodologies.

The fourth chapter is oriented toward management planning for the EDP function and toward achieving a cost/effective data processing operation.

The fifth and last chapter deals with the "people" side of data processing: recruiting, using consultants, the impact of change, the performance review, and the management skills necessary to get the most out of the data processing organization.

ORGANIZATIONAL MATTERS

In trying to organize the contents of this book, the author was faced with the problem of deciding on the relative priorities of the chapters. Somehow each chapter seemed to be important enough to merit the leading position in the book.

Organizational matters was ultimately selected because these are usually the first considerations demanding the attention of a newly appointed MIS manager.

Incidentally, the terms MIS (Management Information Systems) manager, EDP (Electronic Data Processing) manager and DP (Data Processing) manager are used interchangeably in this book. They all refer to the individual normally in charge of systems development, programming and computer operations (although other functions may be added).

Experience has taught most data processing people that each organization feels that its methods of operation and systems

Chapter 2

requirements are unique, while in fact there is a limited range of variety.

Similarly, most organizations feel that their organizational problems are unique. In fact, the problems are usually similar—it is the people in the organization who are unique.

As a result, in dealing with organizational matters, the sections in this chapter recognize the human component and the impact of emotions, prejudices and motivators on the organization.

In contrast to most other functional areas of the organization, the EDP function has some unusual characteristics derived from its technical nature, its position as a service organization, its mixture of development and production operations and its involvement with many of the functions of other departments. These aspects are also considered in this chapter.

SECTION 1 DEVELOPING A CORPORATE INFORMATION POLICY

Policies are established by corporations to provide guidelines for response to common situations and to establish a framework for responding to unusual situations. As such, their intent is to provide *standards* for operating the company in a uniform, predictable manner. They tend to minimize ad hoc decision-making and reduce the potential for poor decisions based on crisis decision-making.

During the past twenty-plus years, as data processing has grown to be an integral part of the life of most companies, the technology of the field has grown more complex, applications have become more sophisticated, company dependence on EDP has increased and crises have proliferated.

What could be a more suitable subject for the deliberative planning involved in the policy-making activity than the management of information and information processing?

This section addresses the policies that should be developed, their content, who should develop them and who should approve them.

Corporate EDP Policy Issues

As with all corporate policies, those relating to EDP express the strategy and philosophy of top management. Although this philosophy may seem to be predetermined by historical practice, it may change if an effort is made to identify and rethink the issues as they relate to information management.

Some of these issues are identified below. In many cases they are interrelated. The list is not comprehensive and other issues will become apparent for different companies. No attempt has been made to identify any priority for these issues, since that also would vary by company.

SCOPE OF INFORMATION MANAGEMENT

Of what does information management consist? Many companies are finding that limiting the role of the MIS manager to responsibility for EDP alone falls short of meeting the organization's needs in information management. This parochial view does not address some of the major issues such as ensuring the integration of data processing, administrative processing and office labor productivity programs.

The company must address the entire content of information management by assigning responsibility for review, control and improvement in such areas as:

• Office automation: word processing, dictating systems, interoffice/interpersonnel communications systems, recording devices, copiers, printing services, archival storage, filing systems, microfilming, and so forth.

• Communications: voice and data communications, facsimile transmission, TWX, Telex, internal and external mail, and the management problems of vertical and lateral transmission of information to those who need to know.

EMPHASIS

Many MIS managers have become ex-MIS managers by misinterpreting the emphasis of management or by failing to report their contribution toward management goals. For example, top management may express a desire to "reduce the cost of data processing." The manager who follows this dictum may reduce the cost at the expense of limiting services or resources available to users. When the users rebel, the manager finds little defense in pointing out that the management direction was followed. It is far better to address the issue more broadly. The real goal of the organization may be to maximize the return on investment from MIS or to maximize the ability of operating segments of the company to make a profit. This type of emphasis may really mean that MIS costs will actually increase, but in a controlled, well-justified framework supported by the users.

INFORMATION SYSTEMS

The broad category of information systems may be subdivided into two areas:

• Operational systems that provide information processing service for the functions of the company (order entry, material requirements planning, bank teller terminal functions, etc.).

• Management decision support systems that provide information to allow management to make reasoned decisions on problems and on planning for the future (accounting and budgeting systems, simulation and modeling methods, etc.).

At various stages of a corporation's EDP maturity the emphasis on these areas may change. This should be considered in setting the policy direction for MIS.

Responsibility for Development Projects. A number of studies have shown that the most successful system implementations are those which were requested and sponsored by the user rather than those initiated by the MIS organization. These studies simply verified what most of us already know about human nature. The corporation that assigns responsibility for initiating projects to MIS must do so with full knowledge of the risks.

Issues to be addressed in this area are the responsibility for:

- Project initiation.
- Project management.
- Successful installation.
- Project payback results.

The Business of Data Processing. Some corporations have successfully spun-off data processing to create a service bureau that provides services to outsiders as well as the corporation. This requires a level of resources and commitment far beyond providing internal support alone. However, the fact that it has been done successfully in the past indicates that it is an issue for discussion.

Long-Range Planning. Speaking of commitment, maintaining a consistent base of support for information management requires development of a long-range plan. In clerical or blue-collar trades where high levels of training are often not required, the work force may be permitted to fluctuate without substantial economic detriment to the company. In fact, as unions often point out, layoffs during slack periods generally work only to the company's advantage. However, data processing requires intensive training and there is generally a scarcity of qualified personnel. A company that permits the EDP work-force to fluctuate will encounter increasing difficulty in obtaining qualified people.

The long-range plan expresses the commitment of the company to maintaining a stable direction for MIS. It also, of course, enables the MIS organization to plan and develop resources for the future.

However, long-range planning itself requires time and resources which must be recognized and budgeted by top management.

State of the Art. Some top executives feel that it is important to their companies that the MIS function maintain a leading edge position in regard to the state of the art of data processing. Without commenting on the value of this concept, it is important for the MIS manager to be aware of management's thinking on this issue.

Research. Whether or not top management is interested in maintaining a leading technical position for data processing, there is certainly a value in being aware of the methods, equipment or technology that could be profitably applied within the company. In too many companies this need is ignored, resulting in the implementation of "new" systems using technology that does not gain the maximum benefit to the user. Top management should consider establishing a regular budget (not necessarily for separate personnel or a separate department) for applied research in the MIS department. This budget should include appropriate seminars, publications, and educational resources or consulting arrangements.

Centralization vs. Decentralization. This major issue requires considerable investigation and deliberation by management. The form of the corporation does not necessarily dictate the pattern with which information management should be approached. The direction is dictated by factors such as top management style, diversity of divisional business, economic and technical considerations and internal politics. Centralization or the reverse may apply to all MIS functions, to systems analysis alone, to hardware alone, or to independent use of centralized hardware.

This issue should be considered as a part of long-range planning, but it will influence or initiate corporate policy.

System Integration. Along with the issue of centralization, management should consider the advantages and disadvantages of system integration, possibly in the form of a centralized corporate data base. This issue has major consequences for information management and information processing. Many companies undertake to create corporate data bases with too little consideration of the costs and technical expertise required, or the benefits to be derived.

Impartial Service. A major user concern is equity in the allocation of the limited resources of the MIS organization. For example, it is often believed that a MIS manager who reports to the corporate vice president of finance will disproportionately allocate resources to serving accounting and financial systems. An organizational method, often in the form of a corporate MIS steering committee, must be established to avoid both the reality and the appearance of partiality in service to users.

Incentives for Top Performance. Although data processing epitomizes automation, it is one of the most labor intensive functions in the company. Furthermore, it is performed by highly trained, highly paid people whose actions or inactions can have substantial impact on the earnings of the company. Motivating these people to perform at their best is extremely important. Various reward or compensation schemes may be used, but even if they are not, a Management By Objectives program should be considered.

Action. A list of appropriate policy issues should be developed and distributed to senior management. These issues should be discussed in a meeting of the management team with the MIS manager. The conclusions and directions indicated by this group can provide the foundation for developing corporate information policy.

In the Beginning

Corporate information policy cannot be created in darkness and chaos. It must be developed within the context of overall corporate plans and objectives. And, in fact, if these change, information policy must adapt to the changes.

Certain specific corporate policy statements should precede the development and publication of those relating to information. These include:

• *Statement of corporate purpose.* This policy should expand on those elements of the corporate charter that identify the purpose of the corporation in terms of business objectives, social responsibilities and responsibilities to employees, stockholders and customers.

• *Strategic business plan.* While not a policy in the formal sense the strategic or long-range business plan establishes a framework and objectives for the operating arms of the company. Within these, the staff and support functions must address their ability to respond to the needs of operating units.

• *Policy publication.* This policy should identify the responsibilities relating to the development, approval, publication and distribution of corporate policies. Corporate policies may be developed by a "Policy and Procedures" group or by corporate functional units, but approval requirements for policies should be centralized to prevent conflicting policy statements.

In addition, a corporate tactical or short-range plan is helpful to identify the manner in which the strategic plan is being implemented and identify priorities, but it is not essential to setting policy.

From the above documents, and with a knowledge of the personalities of key corporate officials, the development of further policies may take place.

Two separate but overlapping policy areas must be considered. First, those policies dealing with the use and distribution of information itself must be defined. Second, policies must be developed to cover the responsibilities and operation of information processing: the MIS or EDP function.

In the following descriptions, where *development responsibility* is assigned, it may be in conjunction with (or with the support of) a policies and procedures department. Where approvals are indicated, these are coordinative approvals and do not eliminate the need for approval by the president or other assigned executive officer.

Information Policies

A Diebold Research Program report of the late 1970s indicates that top US corporations are groping in the dark because of a lack of an overall information policy. Nearly 84 percent of such firms surveyed by the Diebold Research Program indicated such a lack, and they are "only now beginning to get an inkling" that such a policy is necessary.

Only 26 percent of these companies had a central group or individual responsible for information policy. Companies surveyed were mostly financial and manufacturing organizations with sales of over $90 million annually.

Diebold said that some companies that reported having information policies turned out to have "relatively narrow statements" focusing on rules and records retention, access to classified data and certain specific security measures.

Many companies are unclear about what a comprehensive policy would be, according to the study. Diebold defined it as a broad, overall policy which would apply to all departments so that a series of local decisions can be avoided. The development of policies such as those described below should aid in filling this policy gap.

PRIVACY OF PERSONAL INFORMATION

Increasing emphasis on the right to privacy of personal information for employees requires that strong rules be developed to assure it. This policy should address responsibility for control of personal information, access to such information, and disclosure (both internally and externally). The policy should be developed by the employee relations or personnel department and approved by the managers of payroll and MIS.

CONFIDENTIALITY OF INFORMATION

This policy should address the explicit responsibility of all employees to maintain the confidentiality of corporate information. It should separately address technical and business information issues and identify the approvals required for the release of information to external parties or the disclosure of information within the company on a "need-to-know" basis. If nondisclosure agreements are required of employees, this policy should be the enabling document. This policy should be developed by the corporate attorney and approved by the managers of engineering, manufacturing, sales/marketing, finance and MIS.

SECURITY OF INFORMATION

If government work requiring security clearances is involved, this policy should specify the clearances required for various levels, the consequences of breach of security, and the responsibilities for maintaining security. It should be developed by the corporate security officer and approved by the corporate attorney and all key executives.

FORMS DESIGN AND CONTROL

This area may not, at first glance, be considered to fall under the umbrella of information policy. However, in a corporation, forms constitute one of the major vehicles for the transmission, storage and organization of information. Responsibility for the design, development and control of forms should be assigned. Approval mechanisms for internal forms and forms that will leave the company should be identified. Control of forms should include the charter to eliminate redundancy, establish and maintain a forms numbering system, and develop and maintain forms usage instructions. This policy should be developed by the manager to be responsible for forms control and approved by the controller and MIS manager.

FORMATS FOR INTERNAL AND EXTERNAL COMMUNICATION

Many companies feel that their communications represent the company image to customers and to employees. They may be quite concerned about the design and use of corporate logos and letterheads, formats, and copyright infringement. A policy setting forth the responsibility for approval of guidelines for the above items is often required. This should be developed by the marketing department and approved by the corporate attorney.

REPRODUCTION OF INFORMATION

A policy providing guidelines for, or restrictions on, reproduction of information should be developed. This may be in conjunction with policies on security and confidentiality. In some cases this policy may only be necessary to enable procedures that will help to control the use and cost of today's ubiquitous copying machines. This policy should be developed by the corporate controller with approval by the corporate attorney, security officer and manager of administration.

INFORMATION RETENTION

IRS regulations exist for specifying the length of time, form and content of accounting-related information that must be retained by a corporation. A policy should specifically authorize responsibility for defining records retention of this and other information and approving the disposal or destruction of records. This policy should be developed by the corporate attorney and approved by the managers of adminis-tration, finance, MIS, engineering, security and personnel.

Information Processing Policies

E. Kirby Warren, in his book, *Long-Range Planning—An Executive Viewpoint*, says:

> The need for longer-range planning is nothing more than a recog-nition that the economic lives of most decisions, today, are becom-ing shorter, and, at the same time, the complexity of making such decisions is becoming greater. Thus *more* decisions will have to be made with *less* time to correct them and making them will require more time and the coordination of more skills. This being true, the planning or preparation for the decision must start sooner and be oriented toward dealing with a more rapidly changing and, as such, less predictable future.

While this statement applies to long-range planning, it should also be kept in mind during the development of policies, since policies are, in a sense, an expression of long-range corporate plans.

The following policies are those which should be developed to enable implementation of a corporate information processing function. The first of these deals with the charter for the MIS function itself.

THE MIS CHARTER

The MIS Charter outlines the authority and responsibilities of the MIS manager. Depending on the organization, the areas of responsibil-ity may include:

- Development and maintence of data processing systems.
- Evaluation and selection of computers and computer-related equipment.
- Operation of the corporate data center.
- Operation of distributed data centers.
- Controlling data input and output.
- Distribution of output reports.

• Design and management of data communications networks or of all telecommunications.

• Operation of the forms control function.

• Development of policies and procedures.

• Development of office methods and procedures.

• Evaluation and selection of computer systems software and applications software.

• Conducting feasibility studies of potential new manual or automated systems.

• Allocating the cost of MIS to user departments or functions.

• Conducting research into potential systems, methods, or equipment that could improve cost-effectiveness or enhance corporate profits.

• Assuring the security of all data processing operations.

• Developing and implementing office automation systems.

• Reporting on the performance of the above areas of responsibility to top management on a specified periodic basis.

All of the above items should be briefly explained in the policy so that the functions are clearly understood. In some companies not all of these areas of responsibility will be applicable, while in others even more will be added.

Where responsibilities are split between MIS and other groups, the limits of responsibility should be outlined. For example, if both MIS and user groups have systems analysts, some clear designation of the extent of responsibilities for systems analysis, maintenance and liaison functions should be provided.

The authority of the MIS manager should be stated in regard to specific functions other than the usual administrative and personnel management functions common to all managers at the same level in the organization. Such explicit designation of authority may include:

• Approval of certain policies and procedures.

• Review and approval of data processing equipment acquisitions or external services and contracts throughout the corporation.

• Review and approval of systems development proposals.

• Review of, and concurrence with, divisional EDP budgets.

• Performance review of divisional EDP centers (if not directly administered by corporate EDP).

• Approval of specific purchase order or expenditure levels for operating supplies (these are often greater than the levels permitted for other managers to allow for the purchase of large forms orders or magnetic storage media).

- Approval of all form designs and orders.

Again, depending on the organization, some of the specific authority granted above may not be applicable, or others may be added. This policy should be developed by the MIS manager and approved by the EDP steering committee (if such exists) or by the controller or finance manager.

THE EDP STEERING COMMITTEE CHARTER

This policy should establish the EDP steering committee, name its chairman (by title) and name its members. The policy should, further, designate the duties of the steering committee to include at least the following:

- Approve the level of EDP expenditure and capability desired for the company.
- Approve specific proposals for major equipment acquisitions.
- Approve EDP long- and short-range plans.
- Determine project priorities.

This policy should be developed by the MIS manager and approved by the manager's immediate superior.

MIS AUDITING

Either within the context of the charter of the internal audit department or as a separate policy, there should be specific designation of the authority and responsibility of the internal audit department for the auditing of EDP. This may cover such audits as:

- Controls of input and output.
- Actual report utilization and need.
- Compliance of the EDP function with stated policies and procedures.
- Security of the EDP operation.
- System design review.
- System performance (accuracy and timeliness).
- Archival storage.
- Survey of user satisfaction.

In some organizations, where sufficient data processing audit talent exists, the internal audit department may also be responsible for periodic tests or code reviews of sensitive programs and for annual reviews of the performance of the EDP function. This policy should be developed by the manager of internal audit and approved by the MIS manager.

Cost Allocation. This document establishes the corporation's policy relating to absorption or allocation of the costs of data processing and data communications. It designates the responsibility for implementing the guidelines set by the policy and indicates whether or not EDP charges will be considered in measuring users' performance and profitability. Guidelines are provided to assure that internal charges do not exceed costs for equivalent service purchased externally. It also designates whether the EDP function will be viewed as a profit center or a cost recovery center. This policy should be developed by the MIS manager and approved by the Steering Committee.

Corporate Procedures

Policies in most companies are simply enabling documents that grant authority or assign responsibility. They must be implemented through documented *procedures* which establish in some detail the methods used to implement the policy and specifically assign responsibility within the organizations affected.

Procedures for MIS would include:

- How to request a project for the development of a new system.
- How to request a modification to an existing system.
- How to cancel or change the distribution of a report.
- How to request use of the computer resources (or terminal access).
- How to request and use office automation systems.
- Records retention rules and archival storage.
- How to use printing services.
- How to request and use communications services (mail, telephone, TWX, Telex, terminals).
- Procedures protecting the individual employee's privacy.
- Rules for use of remote terminals access to the computer facilities.
- How to request acquisition of computer equipment or use of external computer resources.
- Security rules for EDP systems.

The above listed procedures indicate a certain commonality. That is, a procedure is required for every activity in which members of other organization units interface with the MIS organization.

In addition to these, the MIS organization requires internal manuals to document policies, procedures and standards such as:

- *MIS Policies and Procedures*
  A manual setting forth the internal policies and procedures that apply to all MIS personnel or to those activities that cross internal organization lines.

- *Project Control Guidelines*
  A manual describing the entire process of project control for development and maintenance of systems. This manual covers systems requests, feasibility studies, the development process, progress reporting, estimating, implementation of systems, documentation standards for systems design and operation, and so on.

- *Programming Standards and Guidelines*
  A manual setting forth the standards to be followed for programming and providing tips and guidelines to improve productivity.

- *Controls and Operating Guidelines*
  A manual for the operation of the data center that sets forth standards for input-output controls, auditability, library control, inventory management, computer operations, and so forth.

- *Distributed Processing Guidelines*
  A manual for all distributed processing operations that describes corporatewide EDP standards, publications available from corporate MIS and how to request and use corporate MIS resources.

Summary

Most companies venture into data processing in a small way to meet the needs of the controller or engineering director. Over time, the size and scope of EDP grows until it not only represents a significant part of company costs, but the company is highly dependent upon the uninterrupted operation of EDP activities. In fact, many businesses today could not be operated without computers. For example, the banking business is so computer dependent that if some banks were to be without these services for three or four days, they would literally go out of business through their inability to reconcile and post accounts.

Recent court decisions tend to indicate that companies may incur liability as a result of improper operation of computers (as in privacy concerns or billing methods). Further, computer crime (which is simply using automation to accomplish fraud or theft) is on the increase.

Considering these factors, as well as those having to do with long-range planning and proper conduct of the business, the development and publication of policies and procedures for information management and information processing are a corporate necessity. If they do not now exist, a corporate-level project for their development should be initiated by the corporate chief operating executive.

SECTION 2 CORPORATE ORGANIZATION FOR SYSTEMS DEVELOPMENT

The functions of systems analysis and design started with the concepts of industrial engineering introduced by Frederick W. Taylor in the early 1900s. His philosophy of "scientific management" was expanded by Carl Barth, Henry L. Gantt, Frank and Lillian Gilbreth, and others. About the same time, F. W. Harris developed the first economic lot-size model for a simple situation in an early attempt at mathematical analysis. From that time, until the early 1950s, most analysis was performed by consultants, except among a few major corporations and the government.

With the advent of data processing equipment it became evident that the "scientific management" techniques could be applied to office and accounting problems. In this environment the need for an internal systems analysis and design function was identified. Most of the early systems analysis groups came into being as a part of the accounting departments of large corporations. The initial organization was rarely planned. It began where the need was first perceived—at corporate headquarters for corporate accounting, or at a major division for accounting or manufacturing applications. In many instances the analysis function was included with the total EDP operations. However, some large line organizations acquired their own analysts. This led to questions about the relative merits of "closed" and "open" shop computer operations in the early 1960s.

Since that time, the questions of *where* and *how* to organize the systems development function have arisen with increasing frequency. An understanding of the organizational concepts involved in establishing an ongoing, successful systems development function is important to both the systems development manager, who must utilize these concepts directly, and the systems analyst, who must work within the environment created by the organization.

Frequently, the success or failure of a project is directly related to the appropriateness of the organization for performing the project tasks. An inappropriate system development organization location or structure can impede the project through conflicts created by changing priorities, inadequate assignment of resources, internal corporate politics, and/or other factors mentioned below.

Locating the Systems Development Function

The first question is *where* the systems development function should be located within the corporation. Four options appear to be in use in various corporations. Each is shown in an organization chart and its advantages and disadvantages outlined.

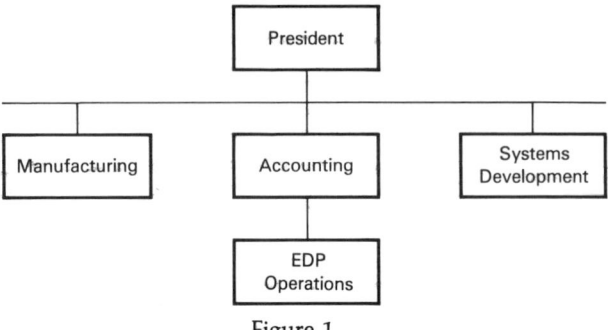

Figure 1.

Figure 1 shows an organization that contains centralized systems development and EDP operations functions, with systems development reporting directly to the president. EDP operations may report to accounting (as in the example) or to any other major function. This structure has the following advantages:

1. Reporting to the president increases the likelihood that systems development resources will be allocated most effectively for the corporation.

2. Decisions based on cost-benefit analysis will probably be made more rationally.

3. The systems development manager will have a greater influence on systems decisions.

4. The systems development manager, as a member of the senior management team, will have a greater insight into corporate plans and strategy. This enhances the manager's ability to develop short- and long-range plans for corporate systems.

5. Both the influences of the reporting relationship and the centralization permit control of systems development standards.

Disadvantages of this organization center around the separation from EDP operations:

1. Conflict over priorities for development or improvement of existing systems between systems development and EDP.

2. Conflict over adequacy of documentation for EDP operations.

3. Conflict over responsibility for maintenance and reruns.

4. These and other conflicts, which would normally be resolved *within* an integrated organization, may become visible at the highest level of management.

A variant of this structure with EDP operations integrated with the systems development group solves most of the problems listed above with

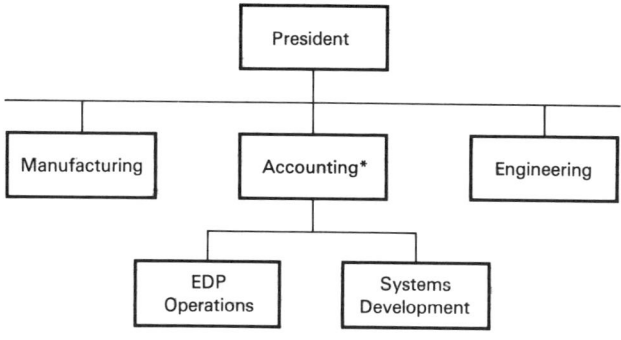

*or EDP Director   Figure 2.

a director of MIS reporting to the president.

The structure in Figure 2, with both systems development and EDP operations reporting to the same executive, retains the advantages of centralization for control of systems standards but may lose the insights available from reporting to the president if it does not report directly.

Disadvantages include:

1. Conflicts between systems development and EDP must be resolved by a senior executive who may not have the appropriate technical background.

2. EDP planning is more difficult since it would be the responsibility of the senior executive.

3. Decisions relating to allocation of systems development resources among line functions may be influenced by the individual to whom systems development and EDP report.

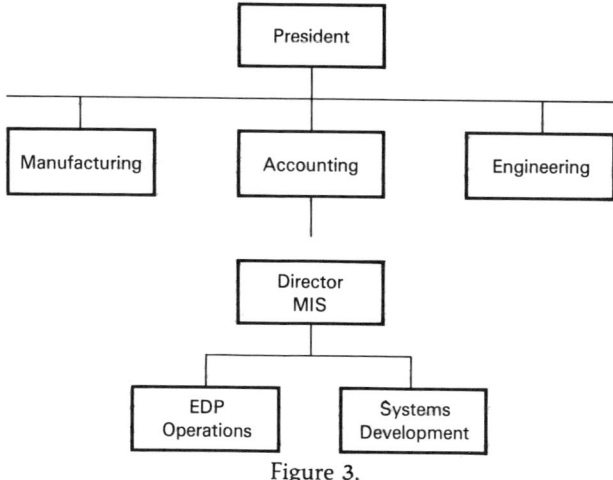

Figure 3.

4. Cost/benefit analyses may more easily be influenced by political considerations.

Figure 3 shows probably the most common organizational structure in use. The advantages and disadvantages may be readily deduced from preceding lists. It should be noted that the MIS director may report to a vice president of manufacturing or administration as opposed to the vice president of accounting (or finance).

Although it is still common for the MIS Director to report to the vice president of accounting or finance, two developments during the last decade have influenced this common structure. First, there has been a trend toward grouping staff functions such as building maintenance, supplies inventory, personnel, and EDP under a vice president of administration to provide for equitable and impartial allocation of resources. Second, the development of EDP steering committees, composed of senior executives who are users, has increased as a mechanism to resolve these problems of resource allocation.

Figure 4 illustrates a decentralized systems development function which is accompanied by a centralized EDP operation. This is frequently accompanied by the centralization of the programming function within EDP operations. This method has been recommended as a way of improving user satisfaction while retaining the benefits associated with centralized design and programming. In this concept, the user maintains a staff of analysts who define system requirements, establish user priorities, participate in acceptance testing, and direct users in implementation.

An American Management Association research study performed in 1968 indicates that large corporations tend to encourage divisions to maintain their own systems staffs whereas the programming staff is located with the hardware. Several other authorities in the EDP field indicate that this seems to be a frequently selected organization pattern. Some advantages of this method are:

1. User control of the staff permits local direction, flexibility and assignment of priorities.

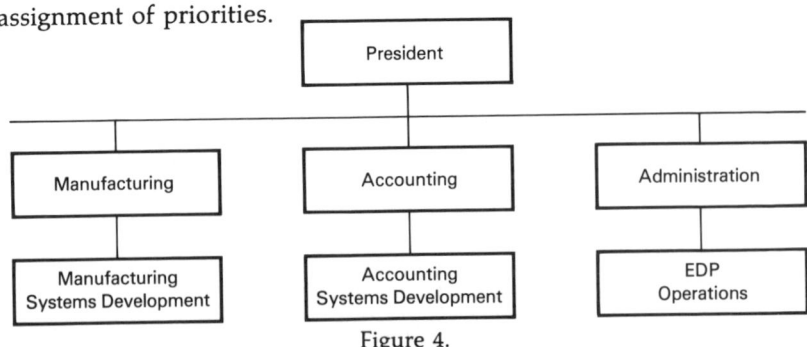

Figure 4.

2. Analysts are more responsive to the user who is their "boss."

3. Analysts become thoroughly familiar with user problems, personnel, and requirements.

4. Analysts protect the interests of the user.

5. Acceptance testing prior to implementation may be more rigorous.

6. User project managers may enhance visibility and control of EDP costs.

Disadvantages include:

1. Smaller staffs are more vulnerable to turnover and less likely to have technical expertise in certain areas.

2. Corporate documentation and design standards are more difficult to maintain.

3. Selection of projects may easily deviate from corporate return-on-investment guidelines.

4. Friction between the divisional analysts and central programmers and analysts may result from conflict over design criteria.

5. Control of applications design as it affects the economic utilization of hardware is difficult to maintain.

6. Divisions tend to invent their own solutions to problems rather than use corporatewide systems. This adds substantially to all EDP costs.

If the programming function is decentralized along with the analysis function, the advantages relating to user responsiveness are enhanced. However, acceptance testing and cost control of projects may suffer. The disadvantages relating to maintaining standards and avoiding system redundancy tend to become more intense.

While these models of organization structure have been displayed against the background of a centralized organization, it should be recognized that decentralization can occur by divisionalization as well as functional organization. For that matter, even large divisions face the same internal problems as separate corporations.

A divisionalized company may retain EDP operations as a centralized corporate function while decentralizing systems development, decentralizing both functions, or centralizing both.

Designing the Systems Development Organization

The remaining portions of this section address the problem of *how* to organize the systems development function. It is obvious that few managers have complete discretion in regard to organization. If the form of organization is not influenced by senior management, it must still respond to environmental influences and constraints.

CONSTRAINTS ON ORGANIZATION FORM

The first constraint on organizing the systems development function is contained in the charter of the organization. Responsibility under that charter may be for systems analysis and design alone or may include programming, operations research, policy and procedure development, forms control, scientific programming, and/or systems programming. There may even be a separation between design and development of systems and the continuing maintenance and enhancement of systems after implementation. It is apparent that the inclusion or exclusion of any of these responsibilities can result in a dramatically different organization.

Centralization or decentralization may affect organizational design through its impact on assigned responsibilities and group size. Group size (which may be a function of company size) may have an impact on the organization in several ways. Smaller groups may have less opportunity for specialization and may be more vulnerable to turnover. Generally fewer amenities are available (forms design service, librarian services, delegation of simpler tasks to junior personnel, etc.). Smaller companies may not recognize the need for continuing training of systems development personnel or know how to select and evaluate them. In fact, smaller companies may not be able to attract the personnel they desire.

The organization may also be constrained through other characteristics of available personnel. A manager taking over an existing department finds it staffed with personnel who may or may not be suitable for the kind of organization desired. For example, the group may be short of supervisory talent with no budget for acquiring such talent. Conversely, it may have too many supervisors who may object to being reorganized out of their positions. Training or education in certain skills or specialized areas of knowledge may be scarce or overabundant (too many programmers, not enough analysts). The knowledge of existing systems that is contained in the memories of present personnel may make drastic reorganizations or forced turnover impractical. Finally, the type of workload may dictate the organizational form. An organization primarily engaged in maintenance of existing systems may organize in a manner completely inappropriate to one engaged in major new systems development projects.

All these constraints must be evaluated when selecting the organization form for systems development.

PERSONNEL COMPOSING THE SYSTEMS GROUP

Since personnel are the raw material of any organization, it would be inappropriate to discuss organization without examining the specialized tasks of these people and the way in which they influence organizational form.

The following functions are those performed by most systems development organizations:

systems analysis and design

programming

documentation

library maintenance

procedure development

user training

forms design and control

In addition, the following functions may be included in the responsibilities of the systems development group:

operations research

systems programming

scientific programming

analyst and programmer training

data base management and administration

communications development

This section will place primary emphasis on the functions more usually found in the systems development group.·

Large organizations permit specialization of personnel so that functions frequently performed by analysts may be delegated to ancillary personnel.

• *Librarian.* Two types of position carry this title. The *departmental librarian* has responsibility for supervising the library of system and programming documentation, internal manuals and reference material. The *project librarian* has grown out of the "superprogrammer" team approach. He or she is responsible for maintaining project documentation sequence and integrity, ensuring the completion of all documentation segments, assisting in project correspondence, and frequently is also responsible for control of the JCL for the project. Organizations that do not perform the departmental librarian function in some manner will inevitably develop problems in system maintenance since documentation will be poorly organized and distributed among analysts and programmers, and not consistently updated.

• *Documentation Specialists.* Some large systems development organizations employ documentation specialists whose responsibility is to organize and formalize the documentation of systems projects. This function is usually performed by analysts or programmers, but if there is any intention of marketing the software product, the use of documentation specialists is recommended.

• *Procedures Analysts.* The failure to develop and document the manual interfaces and supporting procedures for EDP systems is a major cause of user dissatisfaction and system implementation failure. The procedures analyst specializes in analysis and documentation of office methods. His or her ability at writing understandable user procedures is usually superior to that of the EDP-oriented analyst. Procedures analysts frequently also design the forms to be used with systems for computer report and/or manual processes. If separate training personnel are not available, these analysts often conduct the user training for system implementation.

• *Training Specialists.* Two types of training specialists may be found in large systems development organizations. The *user* training specialist is usually associated with specific major projects implemented for large, decentralized user organizations. He or she prepares training materials, organizes training sessions, and conducts user training for system implementation. The *systems development* training specialist is responsible for organizing training programs, classes and seminars for analysts and programmers within the systems development group.

• *Systems Analysts, Programmers and Analyst/Programmers.* Discussion of these, the primary positions of the systems development organization, has been reserved until last in order to place appropriate emphasis on the organizational impact of the characteristics of these staff members.

In some companies the two highly skilled but intrinsically different professions of systems analyst and programmer have been combined. The rationale for this combination is generally a mixture of improved efficiency and lower system implementation cost. It is felt that combining these functions eliminates the communication interface between the systems analyst and the programmer. No program definition is needed because the analyst knows what has to be programmed. There is the additional advantage of removing a point of information transfer at which misunderstanding or error could occur. Eliminating these interfaces reduces the necessary documentation, reduces the total manhours from conception to implementation of a program and, by these means, reduces cost.

Despite these advantages, the practice of combining the analyst and programmer functions appears to be extremely shortsighted. The temporary gains achieved, if any, are overcome by long-range disadvantages. One must examine whether or not the claimed advantages really exist.

1. "Program definition can be eliminated." This is true if the analyst will write all programs in the system. If the system is of any size, obviously this would take too long. Other programmers would have to be called in to accomplish the project in a reasonable time, and they would require definitions.

2. "The analyst-programmer interface can be eliminated." This is not true for larger projects.

3. "Eliminating definitions reduces documentation." The documentation reduced is just that which is timesaving and helpful if the program must be maintained by another person sometime in the future.

4. "Total manhours from conception to implementation are reduced." Again, this applies to single programs or a few programs but not to larger systems. In fact, if the analyst writes some of the programs for a larger system, he or she may delay the implementation by not being available to consult with personnel who are writing the remaining programs in the system.

5. "Cost is reduced." Given the fact that an analyst-programmer is generally higher paid than the average programmer, if he or she is used on larger projects as a programmer only, costs will actually be higher.

A PROFILE OF THE PROGRAMMER

If the above arguments resulted in no decision for or against the combination of functions, there would still remain one overriding consideration: there are basic conflicts of interest between the analysis and programming functions. This can be better illustrated by first examining the differences between programmers and analysts as people within the context of a business (rather than a scientific) environment.

The business programmer is a highly skilled technician who works with logic as his basic tool. His primary qualification for the job is his talent for logical thought. He needs only a high school education or its equivalent, some training in programming and data processing concepts, and two to three years of experience to meet average productivity levels. Although many programmers today have acquired years of data processing experience (often as machine operators before becoming programmers), the qualifications stated above will suffice.

The expert programmer's technical specialization is so intense that he may have little or no time to devote outside his field. With the current pace of hardware (computers) and software (programming languages, operating systems, etc.) development, hardly a week passes without the announcement of some new technique, equipment or programming aid. Much of his time on and off the job is consumed in maintaining his knowledge of the current state of the art. He has to run as fast as he can just to stay in one place.

Not only is he busy maintaining his knowledge of the art, but also with learning about the place where he works. Robert Rosen of Computer Usage Education, Inc., at a seminar of the Association of Computing Machinery, pointed out that data processing personnel have the highest turnover rate in industry. Among programmers this rate is as high as 30 percent to 40 percent and reflects a lack of company loyalty and interest which is often complemented by an intense interest in programming expertise. The "programmer's programmer" is one who can design a program that will operate faster, using the least amount of memory, to produce a desired result. The programmer's interest is directed toward ultimate efficiency in the use of the computer. He is willing to spend an inordinate amount of effort, even on his own time, to find the "elegant" solution to a programming problem.

As might be expected from one drawn to a highly individual activity oriented toward abstract and machine-related problem solving, the programmer is generally introverted. He finds his best expression in dealing with situations that do not include human relationships. Programmers have frequently been accused by others of being prima donnas. This impression is conveyed by their lack of responsiveness to human relationships and often by an attitude of individualism which are outgrowths of introversion. Some other characteristics which distinguish programmers are their higher-than-average intelligence, their logical ability, and their patience in solving complex time-consuming problems.

A PROFILE OF THE SYSTEMS ANALYST

Due to the expansion of the data processing field, many of today's analysts are people who were, at one time, programmers. The normal progression through the ranks of business data processing encouraged such a path. It is generally true, however, that those who have become successful analysts have attained more than the minimum educational requirements and have acquired some business background. Many of those who made a successful transition to analyst were, at best, mediocre programmers since their profile of personal characteristics was not oriented to programming.

The systems analyst is a trained professional manager who works with people and equipment as his basic tools. His primary qualifications for the job are his abilities to manage resources in an economical manner, to communicate easily with other people and to visualize the organization's operation from the viewpoint of top management. He generally requires a bachelor's degree. If his degree is in one of the sciences, a master's in business administration is helpful. He needs a three-to-four year exposure to business systems and the operation of management to meet average productivity levels. His background should include training in data processing concepts and programming but he does not necessarily have to have been a programmer. Many successful analysts have been recruited from the operating departments of organizations after acquiring business experience at that level.

The analyst may be called the "Renaissance Man" of the organization. His role demands that he be a generalist, not a specialist. He must have a wide-ranging interest in every aspect of the organization's operations. Although he may concentrate his efforts in one particular field such as financial, production control or marketing systems, he must know how these systems relate to the rest of the operation.

The analyst also faces a time-consuming task of continual learning. He must be conversant with the latest state of the art in data processing equipment and techniques to communicate with the programmers and use the equipment to its full capacity. He must also maintain a current knowledge of developments in management techniques, accounting and control methods, the behavioral sciences, communications theory and practice, and any other area of use in the process of systems design and implementation. In addition, the analyst must be constantly aware of any expression by management of the goals of the organization and its plans for the future, as these may affect his systems designs.

The "systems analyst's analyst" is one who can design and implement a system that is appropriate to the problem, make the optimal use of the organization's resources, be integrally related to the other systems in the organization, and do the job intended. Ideally, he functions as an extension of the organization's management and provides the additional capabilities of his specialized training.

The analyst typically views the computer as a tool to be used in achieving management's goals, rather than a solution to all problems. He is keenly aware that all systems are run by people. His concern is centered around aligning the goals and activities of the people with the goals and activities of the system. Characteristically, the analyst is an extrovert. He is oriented toward interpersonal relationships. Like the programmer, he has above-average intelligence and logical ability. His background and training make him adopt the management viewpoint. (Many companies today are drawing management recruits from systems groups or having managers spend a year in a systems group.)

THEIR CONFLICTS OF INTEREST

Some organizations, new to the use of EDP, make the mistake of hiring a programmer to design and program their first computer system. Generally, these organizations are the most disappointed in the results of their installations. Their reasons are usually found in the design of the system. The training and education of the programmer hardly fits him for making the management decisions necessary in the design of the system. Furthermore, the programmer may inadvertently alienate some of the people who create the input (or who use the output of the system).

The programmer-designed system may be exceptionally efficient from the standpoint of computer operation, but it is often inefficient and awkward for the people who use it. The system designed by a systems analyst is oriented toward the needs, attitudes and efficiency of the users. The analyst will also spend time "selling" the system to new users and training them in the new procedures required. These differences point to the basic conflict of interest between analyst and programmer. If each does his conscientious best to perform in a proper professional manner, the programmer will strive to produce a system that optimizes use of the computer while the analyst strives to optimize the performance of the organization. The two goals are normally incompatible.

The major argument against combining the functions of analyst and programmer is this incompatibility of goals. In arriving at a compromise among the programming function, the machine function and the operation of the system, the performance of the organization will not be optimized. Furthermore, in making this compromise, the quality of programming will often suffer due to the analyst/programmer having to divide his interests and time.

The analyst/programmer's conflicts of interest render him less able to do an optimal job in either area. The best arrangement for most effective system development, implementation and performance is the complementary marriage of these two individuals to preserve their individuality. This marriage obtains for the organization the best combi-

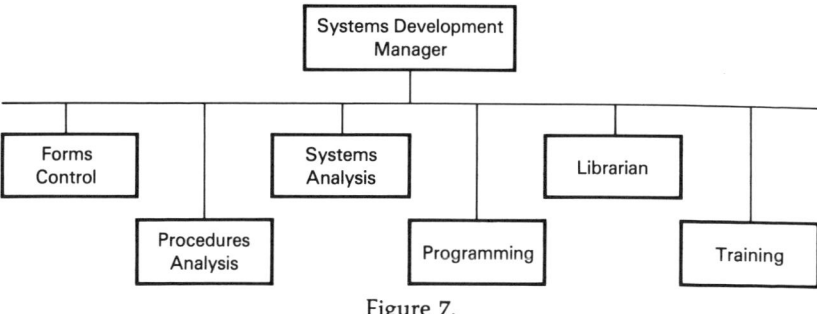

Figure 7.

Whereas Figure 6, in a sense, is a functional organization, another type of functional organization is represented by Figure 7. This organization is appropriate to the systems development groups that separate the analyst and programming functions. Each specialized functional section may be organized internally by system or by further functional classifications. Project development in this type of organization is performed through the use of "matrix management." This technique requires the appointment of a project manager, generally from the systems analysis section, who draws resource personnel from the other sections as required to form a project team.

There is considerable logic in including the forms control section in the systems development group. Separation of forms control from purchasing provides for better control. Most forms today are designed to interface with or support EDP systems. Forms are most effective when developed within the context of a system and supported by appropriate procedures. For these reasons it is recommended that the forms design and control function be a section within the systems development group in all organizations.

If the organization is decentralized, some method must be found to assure the enforcement of common standards and avoid the development of similar systems for different divisions (redundant development). This can be done by having all divisional systems development managers report directly to a corporate systems development

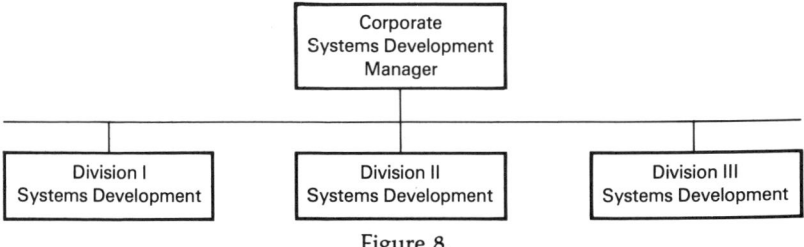

Figure 8.

manager or by having them report to division heads with technical and systems standards, approval for new systems projects, and quality control established and enforced by a corporate systems development manager. (See Figure 8.) This organization is appropriate for very large corporations with a decentralized organization pattern.

PROJECT DEVELOPMENT TEAMS

The concept of matrix management (Figure 9), previously mentioned, is critical to the success of systems development and implementation. Whatever the form of internal organization adopted by the systems development group, it is necessary to involve outside personnel (at a minimum, the user) in the project.

The project team is composed of personnel from various organizations. These "borrowed" people continue to report, for all company administrative and organizational purposes, to their home organization. For project purposes, they report to the project manager. The project manager has the task of coordinating their activities according to the project plan. In some cases, the project manager may have to integrate outside consultants into the project team. This is simply an extension of the use of matrix management.

In this regard, it is important to consider the relationship of consulting personnel to the total project. The major danger in the use of consulting personnel is that the experience and intimate knowledge of the system gained through its development and implementation may leave the organization at the end of the consulting contract. Even rigorous documentation cannot guard against some elements of this danger. Therefore, it is essential that systems development personnel from within the company participate with the consultants throughout the

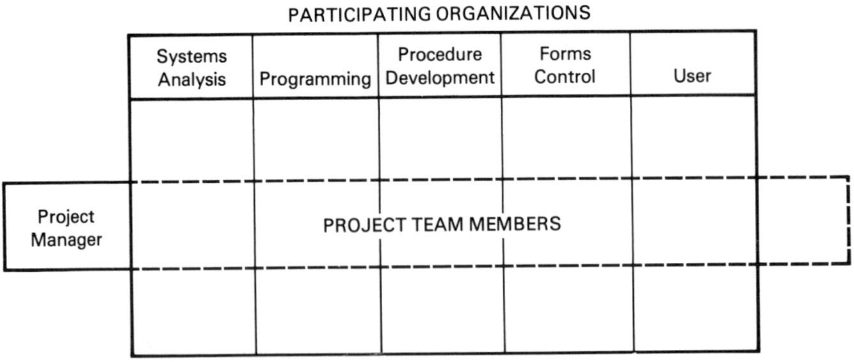

PARTICIPATING ORGANIZATIONS

	Systems Analysis	Programming	Procedure Development	Forms Control	User
Project Manager		PROJECT TEAM MEMBERS			

Figure 9.

project at a relatively detailed level. It is the duty of the project manager to assure that this takes place.

Another duty of the project manager is to assure adequate user participation in the project. This can be done in several ways, but the best methods are through co-opting user personnel for the project team and establishing a project steering committee containing user management.

Project steering committees composed of systems development group and user group managers aid the project manager by:

- Creating a sounding board for system concepts.

- Assuring adequate resources for project success.

- Providing faster decision-making.

- Monitoring project cost and progress.

- Resolving intergroup problems between users or between users and systems development.

Even with these techniques at the project level, continuing user liaison is a long-range problem that seems to have no solution without additional cost to the company. Two solutions that do seem to work are:

1. Assignment of a person with EDP experience to a division staff. Unless the EDP organization is lucky enough to have an analyst familiar with the user division and its problems (and can spare the analyst), it is difficult to find someone with knowledge of both worlds. This leaves two options: transfer an analyst from the EDP group (or hire one) and train that person in the needs of the division; or create an "internship" program whereby a person is transferred to the EDP organization for eighteen months to two years, after acquiring a thorough working knowledge of the user area. He is then transferred back to the user staff after he gains programming and analysis training and experience. The writer has used both techniques with substantial success.

2. Assignment of analysts within the EDP organization as "account managers" to specialize in the needs of, and communication with, a particular division or user function. While this method provides greater control by the EDP group, experience seems to indicate that it does not satisfy the user as well emotionally.

SELECTING THE ORGANIZATION FORM

In evaluating organization form for the systems development group one must carefully review the motivation for reorganizing. Reorganization is a traumatic experience for people on the staff and will disturb the flow of work for some period of time. The length of this period is probably closely related to the length of tenure of staff members in the present organization form.

There are several pressing reasons for considering reorganization:

1. The organization of systems development is inappropriate to the organization of the company.

2. The organization is not structured properly to meet its current goals and objectives.

3. Personnel who must be retained by the company do not function optimally in the existing organizational form.

4. Current tasks require substantial changes in the size of the organization.

Assuming that a substantial reason exists for reevaluating the organization form, the following checklist provides a guide to the form that should be considered.

Centralized company structure. Organizational form should depend on other factors.

Decentralized company structure. Consider decentralizing the systems development function to the divisions of the company while retaining central control of standards and project approval.

Systems development includes other related functions (forms control, procedures analysis, operations research, etc.). Consider functional organization by specialization. The analysis and programming groups within this structure may have systems-oriented structures internally.

Size of systems development group. A large systems group (over 50 people) should consider some specialization of functions such as training, documentation, procedure writing, forms design and control. This leads to a functional organization. Some elements of this may be desirable in smaller organizations. However, in organizations below fifteen or twenty people, the organization is almost forced to be system oriented. Such smaller organizations cannot afford specialization.

Preponderance of junior personnel on staff. This situation would suggest a system-oriented structure to spread the few senior people as far as possible over the organization.

Supervisory skills not available. In a large organization this situation can only be solved by acquiring the necessary skills from outside the organization. In a small organization senior people may report directly to the systems development manager for supervision.

Large development workload. Consider establishing a separate maintenance group for existing systems to obtain maximum performance from development project teams.

Large maintenance workload. Consider distributing maintenance work across all personnel to maximize productive use of man-hours available.

Analyst/Programmer functions combined. Any organization form may be used. This combined function may be necessary in small organizations to maximize use of personnel but it does not result in optimal systems design or programming.

Analyst function separate. Consider a functional organization overall with a system-oriented organization in the analyst group and utilization of matrix management concepts.

Summary

Reorganization should be approached carefully and only with substantial motivation. If possible, staff members should be apprised of the reasons for considering reorganization and the options available *before* such reorganization takes place. A consensus or participative management approach to reorganization may avoid a substantial amount of the trauma usually associated with change.

SECTION 3   CENTRALIZATION VS. DECENTRALIZATION

With substantial fanfare and articles in newspapers and trade magazines, First National City Bank of New York announced the decentralization of its computer operations. The bank, the second largest in the country, said that it was going to replace two large and six medium-sized computers with a host of small computers. They estimated reducing their annual $2.8 million data processing operation cost by about half.

This news was another indicator of the continuing effort to find an optimal solution to the "centralization vs. decentralization" controversy. Similar articles, claiming substantial savings, have appeared in the past and will appear in the future. Savings will be claimed for centralizing operations as well. (A vast project for centralizing all computer operations of North American Rockwell Corporation has been completed within the last several years.) As examples proliferate on either side, concerned managers ask, "What is the answer?" The question should be, "Is there an answer?" This section is intended to explore the latter question. It is most appropriate to start this by examining the objective reasons for both strategies of EDP organization.

Reasons for Centralization

ECONOMY OF SCALE

The reason most frequently used for centralization of operations is economy of scale. This economy results from several factors:

1. Decentralized small computers may have unused capacity. Centralization on a large computer could eliminate the cost of such unused capacity.

2. Individual small computers may be overloaded, generating pressure for upgrading of equipment or the purchase of expensive service bureau time. Centralization on a large computer could absorb this overload against the unused capacity of other small computers.

3. In terms of floor space, electricity, air conditioning and other facilities costs, a single large installation is less costly than multiple smaller installations.

4. The number of support personnel (operators, systems programmers, etc.) is lower for a large installation than for multiple small installations.

5. A single large installation would require fewer management and staff personnel than multiple smaller installations.

6. A larger computer is more cost effective than a small computer.

This last is normally the strongest argument advanced for economy of scale. It is derived from "Grosch's Law" advanced in the early 1950s. H. R. Grosch suggested that the performance of a computer increased as the square of its cost. That is to say, a computer that cost twice the amount of another should deliver four times the processing power. (Of course the reverse is implied also. One larger computer could do the work of four smaller machines at half the cost of four.)

Kenneth Knight tested Grosch's suggestion on the IBM 360 series using two different instruction sets, one scientific and one a commercial mix.[1] He discovered that economies were even greater than those predicted by the Law, especially for scientific work. (See Figure 10.)

Recently, with the dramatic improvements in microprocessor and large-scale integrated circuitry (LSI) technology, there have been claims that Grosch's Law is obsolete. This probably not true.

What is true is that new announcements of hardware are creating temporary discontinuities that appear to make the Law invalid. However, if one considers minicomputers alone, it will be found that

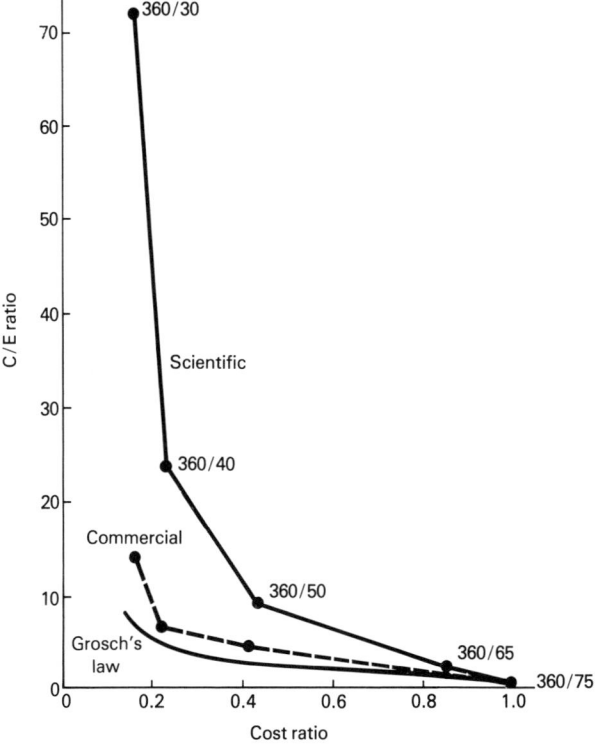

Figure 10.   Economies of scale as measured by Knight.

Grosch's Law is applicable within the minicomputer spectrum. In addition, as large mainframes adopt the LSI technology, the temporary discontinuities will disappear.

SOPHISTICATION OF APPLICATIONS

Large computers have other advantages beyond economy of scale. Higher internal speed, greater primary storage and higher channel capacity may make practical certain applications that are not feasible on smaller equipment. In some cases, even though it is technically possible to operate an application on a small computer, it would absorb a major part of the capacity. Some examples might include scientific computation, data base management systems, and the maintenance of and access to hierarchically structured files for manufacturing systems. In such cases, the application would justify the larger capacity computer, which would, in turn, justify the elimination of smaller computers in the organization to utilize the excess capacity of the large machine.

The trend toward increasing use of on-line access to large data base systems further emphasizes the need for a central operation that can provide this access to a common file to users throughout the organization. A decentralized operation inherently is incapable of providing this service without an extremely sophisticated network and distributed data base management software.

QUALITY OF SYSTEMS DEVELOPMENT

Empirical evidence lends weight to several reasons for centralization of the systems development and programming functions. Centralization permits design and use of common data bases (as indicated above). It permits use of common standards for data entry and validation of input. It can also enhance the ability to utilize development and project control techniques that result in specific benefits to the organization. Some of these are:

1. The ability to implement a data dictionary, saving considerable time in research for system modification.

2. The ability to establish and enforce systems documentation standards to insure future maintainability of systems and programs.

3. The ability to regulate standards for user documentation, reinforcing the ability to achieve the optimal benefits of the system.

4. The ability to establish and review proper programming techniques to minimize inefficient use of computer facilities.

5. The ability to evaluate development projects from an overall organization perspective, including establishing priorities, cost-benefit analysis, etc.

6. The ability to avoid redundant development of similar systems for different divisions of the organization.

7. The ability to apply good project control techniques, insuring the completion of projects on time and within estimated cost.

In addition, there are substantial differences between the abilities of large and small installations to attract and retain highly qualified technical personnel. The smaller installation will frequently suffer from a higher turnover rate as talented individuals outgrow the opportunities available. The retention of highly qualified personnel provides the centralized group with the ability to apply a higher level of expertise to the solution of problems. They are able to provide a greater range of alternative solutions to problems for evaluation by management. This results in a lower cost of development, operation, and future maintenance of the systems. Furthermore, a lower rate of turnover aids in reducing maintenance costs and risk exposure on systems.

Martin Solomon[2] has taken a "negative approach" by outlining the deficiencies of smaller installations. He indicates that smaller installations cannot provide the same quality of work as larger installations for the following reasons:

1. Limited supply of competent personnel.
2. Loss of continuity due to turnover.
3. Lack of task specialization.
4. Lack of standard procedures.
5. Inadequate doumentation.
6. Inability to integrate data and application.
7. Lack of professional EDP management.
8. Lack of exciting, employee-attracting work.
9. Lack of cross-fertilization.
10. Inability to direct overall use of computing.

CONTROL OF EDP EXPENSE

There remains a group of reasons for centralization that do not properly fit the general areas previously explored. Since most of these have to do with controlling the cost of EDP on an organizationwide basis, they are included below.

1. Decentralized installations are difficult to audit for operations or project development efficiency, effectiveness, and conformity to overall organizations standards. They may therefore be less visible (and perhaps more expensive) than a centralized installation.

2. Smaller installations generally do not have the skills and experience to perform a good job of equipment selection. They may rely on simply ordering from the current vendor or largest vendor of equipment. Frequently, the *equipment salesman* will develop the specifications.

3. Smaller installations generally do not have the negotiating power or experience to develop favorable contracts with hardware or software vendors. So-called national accounts, centrally controlled, frequently contract at better terms and prices than individual divisions could manage.

4. Centralization reduces the cost and improves the quality of personnel training. One current example is the use of video-assisted instruction by larger organizations.

5. Smaller installations generally lack sufficient overview to perform adequate advance planning. This may result in unexpected requirements for equipment or development.

6. Decentralization tends to obscure management visibility into the total cost of EDP for the entire organization. Decentralized data processing functions may record some of their costs in other organizational components (e.g., manufacturing or accounting). It is difficult for top management to apply measures of cost (such as EDP cost as a percentage of sales) or effectiveness to a decentralized EDP function.

Reasons for Decentralization

As a part of the continuing discussion that is almost as old as the computer field itself, there have been as many reasons developed for decentralization as for centralization. However, in contrast to the arguments for centralization, which center around *efficiency*, the arguments for decentralization center around *effectiveness*.

ECONOMIES

Until recently there has been little attempt to argue that decentralization of general purpose computers offers anything but added cost. In the last few years, with the advent of the minicomputer, there has become a potential for savings. A single purpose mini, programmed for a specific application, is extremely inexpensive. Furthermore, if it is used as an "office machine" it does not require the operator, programming, and technical support of a general purpose computer. Some minicomputers can provide on-line inquiry, saving the cost of telecommunications for this type of service. The high cost of telecommunications, the overhead associated with large general purpose computers, and the potential for underutilizing the capacity of a large centralized installation combine to mitigate the case against decentralization.

SOPHISTICATION OF APPLICATIONS

It is frequently proposed that the applications developed for a centralized operation are far more complex and costly than what is required to meet divisional needs. This results from the attempt to meet the needs of all divisions in a single common application. The application of a version of Parkinson's Law seems to take place in a large installation. Applications grow to take advantage of all available capability and capacity. A major problem that results is that maintenance to the system for one division could potentially affect all divisions. Similarly, if the central computer is disabled, all divisions are adversely affected.

Whereas the decentralized installation has only two areas of vulnerability—software and hardware—the centralized installation presents the divisional user with the following areas of vulnerability:

1. Central computer hardware.

2. Central computer software.

3. Communications lines (and or mail and delivery services).

4. Local RJE (remote job entry) or terminal hardware.

Not only are the risks increased but centralization forces divisions into a common mold that may be inappropriate to their needs. The specific hardware required for one user may be different from that required by another. These could be satisfied with far less complexity and cost by smaller installations.

The centralized installation creates a contention for machine time between users. Several jobs running concurrently on a single machine may delay response time to all users and invariably creates competition for priority of service.

QUALITY OF SYSTEMS DEVELOPMENT

Proponents of decentralization argue convincingly that local analysts are more attuned to local needs. They acquire an in-depth knowledge of divisional operations, managerial preferences, and organizational strengths and weaknesses. This gives them the ability to establish requirements specifications and design systems that are optimally suited for the local user. The local analyst can also respond more quickly to the emergencies and changes in priorities of local management. In contrast, setting priorities in a centralized environment places the division manager in contention with other users for the central systems development resources.

The closer association of the analyst and user created by the decentralized environment provides other benefits as well. The user becomes better educated in regard to the benefits and limitations of EDP. The user also has a tighter control of EDP personnel and the quality of their work in relation to the perceived needs.

CONTROL OF EDP EXPENSE

Even though most centralized installations allocate their costs to users in relation to the resources used, the division manager feels little responsibility for the total cost of EDP. The salaries paid to central personnel, the overhead rates, the choice of equipment, the time spent on projects, and the share of the resources used all seem to be out of the division manager's control. As a result, the allocations are viewed as "paper dollars." The manager's only incentive is to obtain as much service as he can from the centralized installation. In the long run, this drives up the cost of the installation. In contrast, if the EDP resource is local, the division manager has direct insight into all the elements of cost and a direct incentive to control those costs.

Motivations for EDP Organizational Design

The initial organization of the EDP function is rarely "planned." It begins where the need is first perceived—at corporate headquarters for corporate accounting or at a major division for accounting or manufacturing applications. Even computers installed for scientific purposes have been partially diverted to business applications. From these random beginnings an organization form for the EDP function grew within the firm. In the 1950s and early 1960s the options were limited. If data processing was required at a divisional location, an EDP facility was installed. If cost prohibited multiple installations, or if the firm could afford the time necessary to mail or ship data input and reports, the firm established a central EDP facility at headquarters. By the late 1960s technical options in the form of data transmission capabilities began to appear. Innovative EDP organizations recognized the potential for either centralization or decentralization inherent in data communications.

Given the opportunity to actualize alternatives, all that remained was motivation, and motivations existed in four areas:

Type of corporate organization

Economic considerations

Service considerations

Political considerations

TYPE OF ORGANIZATION

A 1968 survey of 108 large manufacturing companies indicated that 91 percent of the companies which were organizationally decentralized had computer facilities similarly divisionalized. In the same survey, 57 percent of the centralized companies had decentralized computer facilities.[3]

Since that time there may have been some change to this apparent correlation. In the 1968 booming business environment, divisions with substantial decision-making autonomy created their own EDP resources. With the economic crunch of the 1970s, however, many decentralized companies emphasized a stricter management of controllable expenses. An obvious target (often as great as two to three percent of sales) was EDP expenditures. As a result, while many other aspects of company operation remained decentralized, a tighter control was exercised on EDP. This has contributed to some emphasis on centralization of EDP to achieve better corporate visibility and control. In spite of this, there probably remains a significant correlation between the form of the EDP organization, the form of the corporate decision-making structure and the size of the company *and its divisions.*

ECONOMIC AND SERVICE CONSIDERATIONS

While these considerations have been addressed separately in the first two sections of this chapter, they must frequently be linked in any analysis of the EDP organization.

In describing the stages of EDP growth, Gibson and Nolan entitle the third stage "formalization." This is the point at which the initial explosive growth of EDP in an organization is over, there is a moratorium on new applications, and the emphasis is on control. It is at this point that the issue of centralization vs. decentralization arises:

> . . . because the company reaches a turning point in the way it uses the resource. As the EDP function evolves from the early cost-reduction applications of initiation and early growth toward projects aimed at improving operations, revenues, and the quality of unprogrammed and strategic decisions, the influence of the computer will begin to move up and spread out through the organization. The function may truly be called "MIS" instead of "EDP" from this stage forward.[4]

A part of the rationale for combining the economic and service considerations is the fallacy of isolating EDP cost from the other operating costs of the operation. Improvements in the service level to users may result in cost-savings efficiencies or profit-making effectiveness far in excess of the differential in EDP cost achieved by one EDP organization method over another. In other words, the company must accept the principle of subobtimization of certain functions in order to achieve overall optimization of company operations.

These concepts were summarized very effectively by Robert B. White, Executive Vice-President of First National City Bank, in an address before a Financial Systems Marketing Seminar conducted by NCR Corporation.[5] In describing the thinking behind the decentralization program referenced at the beginning of this chapter, Mr. White cited the following points. In regard to systems designed for the large-scale multiprogramming computer:

> First, such an approach is machine-efficient and people ineffi-cient . . .
> Second, this approach tends to require that systems be developed that homogenize user requirements . . .
> Third, the approach, because it is based on the principle of "econ-omy of scale," militates against the ability of the manager to solve the small-scale problems . . . where most of his short-term cost and quality opportunities lie.
> Fourth, functional systems tend to erect barriers that hinder the ac-countability system on which most business organizations are based . . .
> Fifth, . . . this approach encourages (indeed, demands) the optimi-zation of specific functions, usually the data processing activity, at the expense of all other functions—when the issue is really opti-mization of the complete system.

In regard to using large scale computers, White goes on to say:

> First, the large-scale computer assumes a level of business under-standing that most businesses today simply do not possess . . .
> Second, the long lead time needed to integrate systems in order to take advantage of the sheer scale of these computers is out of all proportion to business needs . . .
> Third, it is often necessary to practically rebuild our buildings to establish facilities for the large-scale computers . . .
> Basically, we end up grasping for technical solutions to what are fundamentally business problems.

While these views represent a justification for a decentralized ap-proach and the use of minicomputers located at the user site, there is considerable merit in the arguments. There is even greater merit in the consideration of EDP and non-EDP costs together. Depending upon immediate circumstances, the combination of these factors could serve to justify moves toward either centralization or decentralization on the basis of total economic and service factors.

POLITICAL CONSIDERATIONS

It would indeed be foolish to assume that organizational, economic and service considerations were always considered in an objective, dispassionate manner. This is probably the exception rather than the rule. Almost every attempt at reorganization brings forth advocates for each position. Vested interests, and territorial imperatives are challenged.

Larger divisions having a greater contribution to corporate profits may push for decentralization of EDP to extend their autonomy of operation. Smaller divisions may "gang up" to oppose decentralization as a threat to their ability to obtain a share of the more sophisticated centralized resources. The incumbent members of an existing EDP organization may fight proposals that threaten their positions or reduce their authority as a result of reorganization. Divisions may claim they obtain inadequate service. Corporate management may protest that they will lose control and the ability to coordinate efforts and direct priorities based on the greatest return to the overall organization. In fact, almost all of the other considerations may become weapons in the political struggle.

It is essential to remember that any proposal for organizational change will become politicized, that even if the "best" decision is reached, it will not be reached in a completely rational and objective manner and, that because of political factionalism, the final decision must be made at the highest organizational level (chief operating executive) to assure the maximum opportunity for success.

The Problems of Control

A critical concern of corporate management is control of EDP in the areas of cost, use of resources, and effectiveness. Therefore, regardless of the form of EDP organization, most companies feel that a top EDP executive is required at the corporate level. This executive's minimum responsibilities include coordination of EDP activities between divisions and corporate headquarters, overall planning and monitoring of EDP costs and resources, insuring effective use of resources and providing technical advice to top management. These responsibilities may be addressed by viewing the specific functions in terms of planning and control.

PLANNING

The prerequisite to control is planning. To this end it is necessary to provide corporate management with an overall annual and long-range plan. This involves the basic steps of:

1. Maintaining a concise description of the current status of EDP systems, hardware, personnel and costs.

2. Gathering corporate and divisional systems requirements and priorities.

3. Developing, in coordination with users, an annual systems plan consistent with the resources available to accomplish the desired projects.

4. Reviewing the systems plan for potential impact on hardware capacity and staffing.

5. Advising top management of the alternatives available for achieving planned objectives.

These plans must be developed with consideration of recent trends in the EDP field which impose constraints or add complexity to the systems design function. For example, constraints arise through the use of common systems by several divisions, through the need for divisional systems to interface with corporate systems, and through the use of large, standardized data bases.

The complexity and variety of solutions available in hardware, software, and telecommunications makes overall system design more difficult. The range of responsibilities includes: remote job entry to a centralized computer; intelligent terminals; distributed processing on small or medium-sized computers; specialized applications on single-purpose minicomputers; and the development of networks for communications and processing, to name a few. This is further complicated by the acquisition of equipment from various vendors and by the rent, lease, or purchase options.

CONTROL

The almost bewildering proliferation of alternatives leads to the need for control. The tasks relating to control are considered necessary in either form of organization. They include:

1. Monitoring budgets and performance against budgets for all EDP activities.

2. Reviewing and approving the purchase of equipment, software and outside services.

3. Applying management guidelines to the selection of major projects (in terms of cost/benefit analysis and return on investment).

4. Establishing and maintaining standards for operating procedures, project development, programming methods and documentation.

5. Auditing progress and performance on major projects.

6. Maintaining a specialized staff to provide services (such as technical advice on hardware, communications, or sophisticated systems or applications software) to the applications development or operating groups throughout the company.

The strength of these control functions is contingent upon the management style of the corporation's top management. A strong top executive who desires centralized control of EDP costs and use of resources may impose this type of control through the corporate EDP executive even if the EDP functions are decentralized. On the other hand, even a centralized EDP function probably will not work well if the top executive desires divisional autonomy in the selection and operation of systems.

Organizational Options

The range of options for organizing the EDP function can best be analyzed by recognizing that the systems development and operations functions are not constrained to take identical organizational paths. In fact, there exists a matrix of options that may be illustrated by the diagram below. It is simply a way of indicating that there are a large number of possible organizational structures and combinations that may be viable. Since every possible combination cannot be examined, this

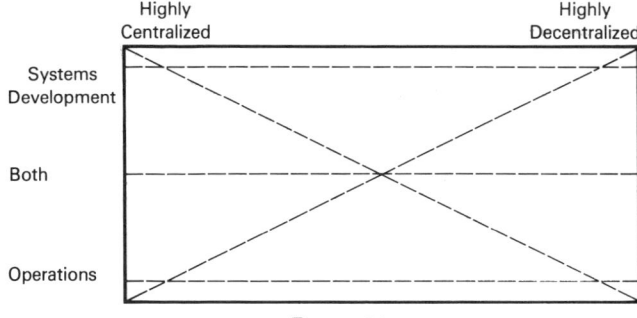

Figure 11.

chapter will concentrate on the more obvious alternatives for operations and systems development separately.

EDP OPERATIONS

Distributed Input and Control Techniques. These have existed since the beginning of commercial data processing. In its simplest form, this means that the user has the responsibility for controlling input and converting input to machine-readable form. Users may have their own data entry equipment (keypunches or key to magnetic media) or contract the work to outside vendors. This approach has several advantages:

1. The user feels more responsibility for and "ownership" of the system.

2. Data entry costs are not a part of the EDP organizational budget.

3. The EDP control costs are lowered by users controlling input and validating output.

4. Data entry problems can be corrected by direct user involvement.

5. Personnel costs may be reduced by using data entry employees for clerical and control tasks at the user site.

Disadvantages may be:

1. Higher equipment costs due to decentralization and the resultant inability to fully utilize equipment capacity.

2. Depending on the size of installation, there may be need for additional supervisory employees.

Some developments of the last few years have made this approach increasingly attractive. Data communications techniques have reduced the time of transmitting the data before and after processing. On-line and key-to-disk data entry permits extensive editing and validation of data prior to processing. (This not only results in local correction of data quickly, but frequently saves the cost of processing incorrect or incomplete data.) Where central computer capacity is available, on-line data entry also makes the resultant files immediately ready for processing or can provide for on-line update of data bases.

Distributed Processing. This term has become a new "buzzword" in the EDP industry. Very simply, this means that data is processed at separate computer installations which are able to transmit data to each other.

With fanfare almost equal to that of the First National City Bank, the Bank of America announced the development of a "distributive" processing system to meet its requirement of having current information on more than ten million accounts accessible around the clock from more than 1,000 statewide branch locations. They claimed that this approach became inevitable when a feasibility study showed a single integrated large-scale data base system wouldn't handle that kind of load with the reliability the bank had to have.

The number of files, the size of the corporate data base, the volume of activity and time constraints were cited as factors that ruled out the single large mainframe approach. The bank also foresaw a hazard in depending on a single mainframe, even if software could be found to support the required workload.

The system was described as having hardware modules which are linked through standard communications interfaces, simplifying the transfer of information among the specialized processors and the end users. Beyond that, all parts of each system are duplicated to protect the bank against failure anywhere in the system.

Each of these segmented distributive systems could communicate with all the others so that when an inquiry or transaction against a different part of the data base came in, it would be handled automatically.

The linkage extends between the bank's two data centers—one in San Francisco and one in Los Angeles—as well as between systems in the individual centers. Initially these systems are intended to support inquiries and data capture on checking and savings accounts. Close to four million transactions must be posted to the ten million accounts overnight, and these are handled by a mainframe-based batch processing system. In its turn, the batch system passes a copy of the updated data base to the distributive systems each morning so the inquiries and transactions coming in that day are matched against current information.

Bank of America personnel call this a "distributive" system since the entire data base is still retained for batch processing on central mainframes, but the processing work of inquiry and transaction posting is distributed.

It becomes obvious that there are permutations of the technique which can fall into the general classification of distributed systems. These may include partially or completely distributed data bases. One company maintains its inventory records through the use of minicomputer-based on-line systems in all locations. Summarized inventory status is periodically transmitted to corporate headquarters for updating central files. All invoicing, order entry and inventory related accounting is done on the minicomputer locally. Some of the advantages of distributed processing are:

1. "Safety in numbers." The entire operation is not dependent on one main computer. Downtime affects only the immediate local operation.

2. Users feel greater system responsibility and believe the system is more responsive to their demands.

3. Costs may not be substantially greater than remote job entry since the central installation may be able to operate with a less powerful computer.

Disadvantages include:

1. There may be less corporate visibility into local operations.

2. Divisions may tend to build up their own data processing departments and move to larger equipment.

Remote Job Entry (RJE). This is a well-established method of processing that permits use of a central computer (or time on a service bureau computer) by a local station having a minimum of transmission capability, tape or card input/output devices and a printer. Some advantages are:

1. Speed of transmitting input and output.

2. Extending the use of existing central computer capability at low cost.

3. Users feel increased responsiveness of systems.

Some disadvantages are:

1. Users can create or modify central programs from the RJE terminal. This reduces control over the program library.

2. Heavy RJE use can force the central installation into larger equipment. Users are difficult to control.

3. Since the RJE terminal provides all the capability of a large computer, users may tend to develop their own data processing department.

Finally, there are the *centralized installation* and the completely *decentralized installations* at the extreme ends of the range. The advantages and disadvantages of these have been described near the beginning of this chapter.

SYSTEMS DEVELOPMENT OPTIONS

Since the extreme ends of the centralization/decentralization spectrum are well known and have been explored earlier, this section will address several variations in use.

User Group Liaison. This is a continuing problem in almost all EDP organizations. There does not appear to be any way to solve this problem without additional cost to the company. (See earlier discussion under "Project Development Teams.")

Decentralized Analysis. This method has been recommended as a way of improving user satisfaction while retaining the benefits associated with centralized design and programming. In this concept the user maintains a staff of analysts who define system requirements, establish user priorities, participate in acceptance testing and provide user direction of implementation.

Although previously stated, the advantages and disadvantages of this approach are worth repeating in this context. Some advantages of this method are:

1. User "control" of the staff permits local direction, flexibility and assignment of priorities.

2. Analysts are more responsive to the user, who is their "boss."

3. Analysts become thoroughly familiar with user problems, personnel, and requirements.

4. Analysts protect the interests of the user.

5. Acceptance testing prior to implementation may be more rigorous.

6. User project managers may enhance visibility and control of EDP costs.

Disadvantages include:

1. Smaller staffs are more vulnerable to turnover and less likely to contain certain areas of technical expertise.

2. Corporate documentation and design standards are more difficult to assure.

3. Selection of projects may easily deviate from corporate return-on-investment guidelines.

4. Friction between the divisional analysts and central programmers and analysts may result from conflict over design criteria.

5. Control of applications design as it affects the economic utilization of hardware is difficult to maintain.

6. Divisions tend to invent their own solutions to problems rather than use corporatewide systems. This adds substantially to all EDP costs.

Decentralized analysis and programming presents many of the above advantages and disadvantages with even greater emphasis. Those advantages relating to user responsiveness are enhanced. However, acceptance testing and cost control of projects may suffer. The disadvantages relating to maintaining standards and system redundancy tend to become more intense.

COMBINATIONS

Combining features of centralization and decentralization is another alternative available once it is realized that the hardware and the systems development function are not necessarily coupled. For example:

1. Centralized hardware with decentralized analysis, or analysis and programming.

2. Centralized analysis and programming of distributed small (or mini) computers.

3. Organization by application, with corporatewide systems centralized and exclusive division systems decentralize either on hardware alone, or with hardware and development.

Reaching a Decision

Change itself is traumatic and the average organization is well advised to avoid it unless it is well justified. For this reason, an EDP manager should look carefully into the question of organization change before acting. In fact one key question should be raised before any detailed analysis is performed.

Why is the centralization versus decentralization issue being raised at all? If the answer is that the issue is politically motivated (and it frequently is), then the manager should attempt to resolve, by means other than organizational change, those factors that created or influenced the political motivation. This can save the time and cost of performing the studies and may avoid the cost of change.

If the issues are in the realm of service, effectiveness and cost, then they must be addressed as "real" issues. It is necessary then to balance the requirements of the divisions against those of the overall corporation in terms of these issues and corporate control of standards, resource utilization and return on investment. To resolve these, the manager must determine all the appropriate questions or considerations for the EDP organization and the company and apply certain weighting factors to a range of positive through negative answers. The resulting matrix will permit an objective evaluation.

It is suggested that initial attention be paid only to developing proposed alternative organizational designs and comparative costs, since the exposure of comparative costs to top management may resolve the question. If, however, the top executive is primarily service-oriented rather than cost-oriented, this may not accomplish the task.

Each EDP manager must determine the organizational and management climate of the individual corporation. The following list developed by Harvey Golub provides an excellent foundation for the list of questions that the EDP manager must answer.[7]

COMPUTER OPERATIONS

1. How many installations are too small or too large to enjoy economies of scale in consolidation?

2. Are some installations growing so rapidly that consolidations may avoid continual equipment conversions?

3. What communications costs may occur as a consequence of geographic dispersion and movement to interactive and on-line systems?

4. How many different kinds and configurations of equipment, languages and operating systems are in use?

5. Is it possible to level workload through consolidation—during a day and over longer periods?

6. Can backup be better provided in consolidated centers?

7. Does centralization allow better control over access to confidential files?

8. Will the organization agree on some degree of commonality?

9. What flexibility now exists in modifying configurations?

10. Can space now used be used by other parts of the organization?

11. Can staff be separated?

12. How many programs must be rewritten?

13. How many programs must be redesigned because of such factors as extensive operator intervention?

14. How dispersed are the users for existing decentralized centers?

15. What business risks would be incurred through consolidation?

16. Should centers be organized by application, organization unit or along geographic lines?

17. How competent are the current managers?

18. What quality of service are users now receiving?

SYSTEMS DEVELOPMENT

1. What opportunities exist for developing common systems?

2. Which functions receive strong central guidance now and therefore offer opportunities for commonality?

3. What variation exists now in levels of sophistication?

4. Do we now have adequate quality and quantity of staff?

5. If more than one business exists, how similar or dissimilar are they?

6. Have we grown by acquisition?

7. Do management people typically transfer among divisions?

8. Do we have a strong central philosophy; are we an operating or a holding company?

9. Do we often add or spin off parts of the business?

10. Are managers used to the systems?

11. Is a great deal of missionary and basic educational work needed?

12. Have we purchased duplicate packages?

13. Is there a strong central thrust to management planning, control and reporting systems?

14. Are users satisfied with their systems?

15. Do systems meet standards of performance in control and efficiency?

16. Is there an opportunity for one division to learn from another?

17. How much travel would be entailed within any option?

18. Are personnel needs in balance over short periods?

19. Can specialists be shared efficiently?

PLANNING AND CONTROL FUNCTIONS AND DECISION AUTHORITIES

1. Do centers do good planning?

2. Are sound equipment acquisition and financing arrangements employed?

3. Do new projects meet basic ROI and other selection criteria?

4. Are programming, documentation and control standards in use?

5. Are purchased packages an important component of costs?

6. Do opportunities exist to share or move hardware?

7. Do line managers require external support?

8. How competent are staffs?

9. Are projects inordinately late or over budget?

10. Are total expenditures well out of line with general industry experience?

11. Does corporate headquarters have a substantial data processing requirement?

Summary

Organization change should not be undertaken without substantial motivation. The organizational mode of EDP must be congruent with the management style, organizational design, corporate objectives and user needs of the corporation. The advantages and disadvantages of each mode must be assessed in light of the above. Both the experience and the research of this writer indicate that the following conclusions are applicable to a large majority of EDP installations:

1. Centralization of computer facilities is usually desirable since it provides greater capacity, permits more sophisticated applications and costs less than other approaches.

2. Centralized programming benefits generally outweigh those of the decentralized approach when considered in the overall corporate context.

3. Systems analysis functions can perform effectively in either the central or user organizations, but if the centralized approach is used, the user group liaison position becomes extremely important.

In conclusion, there is no easy answer or "one best way" to organize the EDP function. Although, as experience is gained, there may emerge common guidelines for certain industries of given size and geographic distribution, at this point each company must determine the proper solution for itself.

References

1. Knight, Kenneth, "Evolving Computer Performance, 1962—1967," *Datamation*, January 1968. Reprinted by permission of *Datamation* magazine, © Technical Publishing Co., a division of Dun-Donnelly Publishing Corp., A Dun & Bradstreet Company, 1968. All rights reserved.

2. Solomon, Martin, "Economics of Scale and Computer Personnel," *Datamation*, March, 1970.

3. Dean, Neal, "The Computer Comes of Age," *Harvard Business Review*, January–February, 1968.

4. Gibson, C. F. and Nolan, R. L., "Managing the Four Stages of EDP Growth," *Harvard Business Review*, January–February, 1974.

5. Reported in *Automatic Data Processing Newsletter*, Volume XIX, December 8, 1975.

SECTION 4 STRUCTURE AND OPERATION OF EDP STEERING COMMITTEES

There *is* something different about data processing. In fact, the EDP function in a company is almost like a company within a company. It is a highly complex, technically-oriented function that has counterparts to all the functions (engineering, production, quality control, etc.) of a manufacturing company. (See Figure 12.) It operates both a job shop and a continuous production shop. It provides services to all segments of the organization within which it resides.

In many ways it is an alien body within the host organization and, if not controlled, can destroy its host. There have been too many instances of runaway EDP costs due to lack of control or executive "computer fever." Because of its unusual character, EDP requires unique

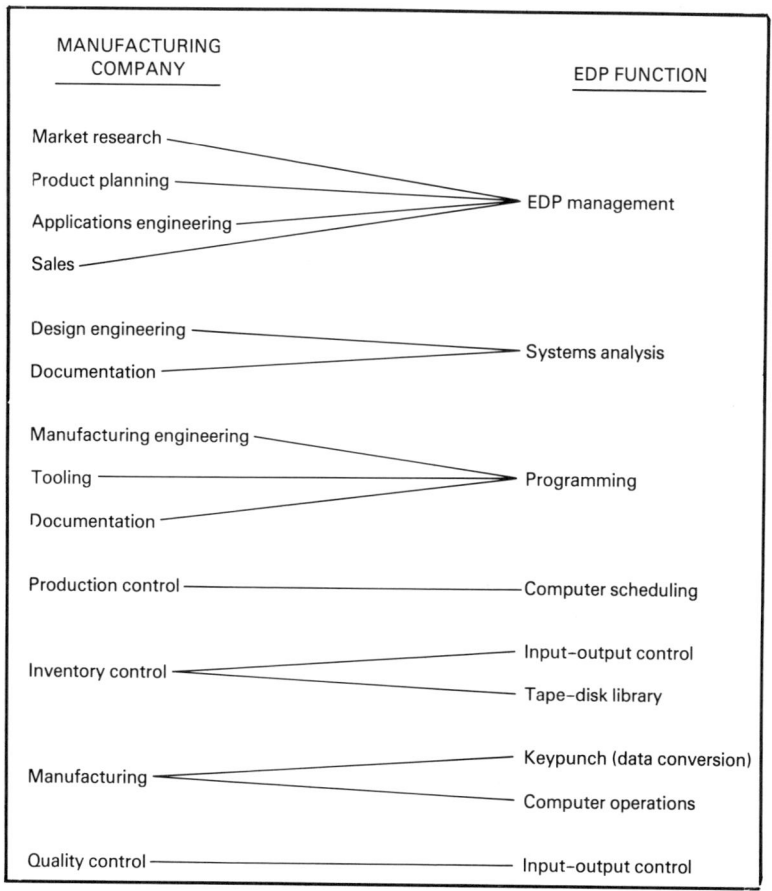

Figure 12. Comparison of EDP functions to those of a manufacturing company.

control methods which would not be applied to any other internal function. This unique control can best be applied through use of a device called a steering committee.

A steering committee is a group acting in an advisory and top level decision-making capacity to a function for which its members are not directly responsible. As a group they are responsible to the top level of the organization, but they are delegated some specific executive powers. As a result, a member of the steering committee becomes partially responsible for the effective and efficient use of the resources controlled by the committee.

The steering committee, in effect, operates as a board of directors. While not normally making detailed operating decisions, the committee acts to control expenses, establish priorities and make economic and policy decisions. The difference between the steering committee and the board of directors is that a board would normally be contributing to the *expansion* of an organization, whereas the steering committee has as its objective the *limiting* and control of EDP costs. Once the decision is made to limit EDP costs, then the committee has created for itself the problem of allocating the distribution of a limited and expensive resource. The steering committee, therefore, also becomes a vehicle for resolving the political problems arising from contention over the limited resources and from the overlapping impact of new systems.

Proper control of the EDP function requires two types of steering committees. The permanent steering committee is responsible for the overall control of the continuing operation of the EDP function. The temporary or project steering committee is responsible for the successful completion of individual projects.

The Permanent Steering Committee

In recognition of the fact that the cost of data processing may run as high as three percent or more of the gross income of many companies, the permanent steering committee should be composed of the president or chief operating officer of the company and those executives reporting directly to him who are users or potential users of the EDP function. Regardless of his reporting relationship, the data processing manager should also be a member of this steering committee. The committee should meet on a regular basis, preferably monthly, with the president acting as chairman. Since most of the reporting will be done by the data processing manager, he should be appointed secretary of the committee.

Duties of the permanent steering committee include the following:

1. Using their knowledge of the company's strategic and tactical plans, determine the level of EDP expenditure and capability desired.

2. Approve specific proposals for acquisition of major data processing equipment.

3. Approve EDP long- and short-range plans.

4. Determine if projects are to be done. This determination is to be made on the basis of payback, lack of alternative methods to the computer, anticipated impact on the organization, business, or personnel and conformity to corporate long-range plans.

5. Determine project priorities.

6. Review and approve cost allocation methods.

7. Review project progress.

8. At specific decision points, determine whether projects should be continued or abandoned.

9. Resolve territorial and political conflicts arising from the impact of new systems.

10. Establish and/or approve corporate information policy.

Experience indicates that permanent steering committees tend to have attendance problems. Executive members of this committee frequently feel that they have other matters of more pressing importance to which they must devote their time. In the view of this author, the magnitude of data processing costs in many companies is such that the attendance of these members should be of prime importance.

Normally, the greatest incentive to continued good attendance is the emphasis placed on the committee by the president himself. Several other techniques may, however, be helpful. Members should not be allowed to name alternates. The anticipated allocation of cost of the data processing function should be included in the budget of each user so that the profitability of its use can be measured. The agenda for meetings should be carefully structured so as to minimize the time consumed. Status reports and proposals for new projects should be distributed in advance. The content of meetings should be limited to questions on the status of existing projects and presentation of proposals that require management decisions.

Historically, many of the decisions relating to EDP cost and the priorities placed on projects have been made by the EDP manager. As a result, many companies have experienced a high turnover of EDP management personnel. The benefits that can be achieved from formation of the steering committee tend to enhance the stability of the EDP function and the security of the EDP manager's job. These benefits include the following:

1. *The gradual education of management in those factors affecting the cost and efficiency of the data processing function.*

While presenting an annual budget for an EDP department, I was once asked by the president of a company, "What is that money allocated to program maintenance? Can't you get these programs written right the first time? I don't see why you should have to touch a program unless a change is requested." I explained the problems of program maintenance to the best of my ability, but I left the meeting feeling that the president still was not convinced. Later, I drew up two charts (see Figures 13 and 14) and used these as an aid in explaining the problems of systems design and programming. I also explained the impact of operating system changes, compiler changes, hardware changes and unanticipated changes in the user environment on program performance and stability. The point of this example is that the permanent steering committee provides a forum for conveying these concepts while discussing specific issues or projects, and that these concepts can best be conveyed in noncomputer language.

2. *The assurance of the continued conformity of the data processing function to the long-range plans of the company.*

Earlier parts of this book have stressed the problems encountered by data processing managers in aligning their goals and plans with those of the organization. The steering committee provides a vehicle for conveying organizational plans to the data processing manager. Even more, it allows top managers to directly apply their knowledge of the organization's plans to the management of the EDP function.

3. *Control of data processing budgets and expenditures.*

Annually, the steering committee should review the EDP budget. The budget should not only show EDP expenditures in detail, but also show how these expenditures will be allocated to the user departments. This will allow committee members to determine how their operations will be affected by EDP costs. This review provides an opportunity for members to explore any alternatives available to the level of cost and to the manner in which funds are spent.

4. *The initial designation and continued review of project priorities.*

This one area has probably accounted for a turnover of data processing managers second only to project failures. Most data processing managers have been making wrong decisions about priorities. "Wrong" not meaning incorrect, but meaning a decision that was not within the province of the data processing manager to make. Only a group constituted in the manner of the steering committee can properly make project priority assignments. As an adjunct to this function, they

MANUFACTURING	SYSTEM IMPLEMENTATION
1. Customer requirement established.	1. Problem recognized.
2. Customer specifications drawn and Request for Quotation released.	2. Problem definition, system survey.
3. Applications Engineering study.	3. System synthesis.
4. Bid or quotation.	4. System proposal.
5. Product Engineering.	5. System specification.
6. Manufacturing Engineering.	6. Program definition.
7. Production.	7. Programming, manual writing, etc.
8. Quality Control.	8. Systems testing.
9. Prototype test or first article qualification.	9. Parallel operation.
10. Delivery.	10. Implementation.

Figure 13. Comparison between systems implementation and manufacturing functions.

MANUFACTURING	SYSTEM IMPLEMENTATION
1. Production standards available.	1. Production standards often not applicable.
2. Performance a factor of group average effort.	2. Performance a factor of individual aptitude, background and speed.
3. Operations clearly defined.	3. Operations require creative skills.
4. Specifications known from customer.	4. Specifications to be developed as part of project.
5. Product to meet limited flexibility requirements.	5. System to provide maximum flexibility.
6. Limited coordination needed.	6. Constant coordination and approval required.

Figure 14. Dissimilarities between systems implementation and manufacturing functions.

can also approve additional resource acquisitions to meet priorities or the cancellation or delay of lower priority projects. It is essential that the steering committee review past priorities to prevent any potential continuation of inappropriate use of the organization's resources.

5. *The approval of new projects and review of projects in progress to determine their continued feasibility and to prevent overcommitment of economic and personnel resources without adequate return.*

A new project proposal should contain most of the elements illustrated by Figure 15. It should *not* be presented to the steering committee by the data processing manager. Past experience with such presentations indicates the greatest success when the member of the

---

NEW SYSTEM PROPOSAL

1. A statement of the request and a description of the system.

2. A statement of the need for the system.

3. Analysis of the financial return on the system.

    a. Discount rate for cash flow (five–year life suggested).

    b. Return on investment.

    c. Payback period.

    d. Gross annual savings (personnel, machine use, etc.).

    e. Annual costs (including depreciation and maintenance).

    f. Net savings.

    g. Annual cash flow.

4. Timing of the installation.

5. Alternative approaches examined.

6. A work plan or PERT chart for implementation and installation of the system.

7. Plans for conversion from existing facilities and methods.

8. Any supporting attachments or exhibits.

9. Management approvals.

Figure 15. Elements of a project proposal.

committee for whom the project will be done presents the proposal. The detailed proposal, however, is usually prepared by the EDP function.

Most steering committees require projects over a minimum dollar cost to be submitted for approval. A figure of $10,000 is used by many. Also, any change to the estimated cost of an approved project that exceeds 30 percent or $10,000 (whichever is least) must be reapproved by the committee. Some projects should be canceled to prevent probable failure to realize a return on investment. The monthly reporting of project status can provide the committee with an early warning system to stop potentially nonproductive projects. The monthly report may be structured in the manner illustrated by Figure 16.

6. *The resolution of conflicting political and economic interests at a top level.*

The committee acts as a forum where such conflicts can be resolved by group pressure or presidential guidance without the data processing manager being the "man in the middle."

7. *The continued education of the data processing manager in regard to the thought processes and methods of operation of the top level executives.*

This feature represents significant benefit to the data processing manager. It also has elements of risk, in that the committee exposes the data processing manager to the evaluation and judgment of top level organization members.

The Project Steering Committee

The project steering committee is structured so that the chairman has direct management responsibility for the success of the project. The chairman would, therefore, normally be the executive in charge of the user group that initiated the request for the data processing service. Members should consist of the executives responsible for other groups in the organization that may be affected by the system, managers of the user functions that will retain operational system responsibility, the EDP manager and the EDP project manager.

Functions of the project steering committee include the following:

1. Coordinate and establish the schedule for project tasks and segments. Segments of the project should be constructed so that decisions as to continuing the project can be clearly determined at several successive checkpoints.

2. Monitor project progress by reviewing periodic reports from the development team.

STATUSREPORT

JANUARY 19--

1. NAME OF PROJECT: Employee Benefit Statements

   Project Leader: Sallie Synergy

2. PROJECT COST: Period Ending January 22, 19--

	LABOR	COMPUTER	TOTAL
Current Month:	4,088	2,035	6,123
Project-to-Date:	7,715	2,132	9,847
3. ESTIMATED COST TO COMPLETE:	7,785	(132)	7,653
4. ESTIMATED COST AT COMPLETION:	15,500	2,000	17,500
5. ORIGINAL ESTIMATED COST:	10,000	3,000	13,000

6. ORIGINAL SCHEDULED COMPLETION DATE:

Installation	Completion
Jan. 31, 19--	Feb. 28, 19--

7. ESTIMATED COMPLETION DATE: Feb. 15, 19--   Feb. 28, 19--

8. PURPOSE:

The system will provide the capability of producing the annual Employee Benefits Statement ready for mailing during the first week of March every year. Also an annual $8,000 reduction in operating cost is anticipated.

9. JANUARY RESULTS

By January 22, all programs were in the final stages of program testing. The various production runs necessary to create the year-end files were proceeding in an orderly manner.

10. FEBRUARY SCHEDULE

Complete testing and verify all programs. If necessary, run special updates to Payroll and Retirement Income files to correct data.

Print Annual Benefits Statement.

Complete documentation of the system and write up all the procedures.

11. PROBLEMS:

None.

Figure 16.   Sample monthly project status report.

3. Assure the proper resources for successful completion of the project.

4. Resolve "territorial" conflicts between various users and between contributing members of the development team.

5. Plan, schedule and obtain resources necessary to conversion to the new system.

6. Make major systems design and economic decisions.

7. Provide management direction to the EDP project manager.

The success of this committee depends largely on the clear understanding that the chairman is directly responsible to corporate management for the success of the project.

The project steering committee provides the EDP manager with a major benefit. By clearly designating the user as having total responsibility for the successful implementation of the system, the pressure on the EDP manager is restricted to its rightful area—that of providing the EDP support functions within the total context of the implementation project.

The user, however, also achieves major benefits. Steering committee reviews assure that the system design specifications meet user requirements, that adequate acceptance testing is performed, that the proper resources are available at the right time and that a feasible schedule for conversion is planned. In addition, the user retains cost control of the project by a clear insight into project expenses as they occur.

Summary

In summary, the permanent and project steering committees provide a clear-cut chain of responsibility that serves to prevent disasters in both project implementation and overall data processing operations and costs.

Discussion Topics

1. What differences would exist between the information policies of a manufacturing company and those of a credit reporting service?
2. Which form of organizing the systems development function provides the maximum support for the end user?
3. Identify the chief issues in the centralization vs. decentralization decision for large multinational companies?
4. How is the centralization vs. decentralization issue influenced by the management style of top corporate officers?
5. Who would the members of an MIS steering committee be in a manufacturing company? In a university?

PROJECT
MANAGEMENT

One of the most worrisome aspects of the life of an MIS manager and/or systems development manager is the demands of on-time, within-budget completion of development projects. This is further complicated by the conflicting demands of many users, each wanting his project to receive the highest priority. Out of this situation there constantly arises a series of questions such as:

- What projects should be conducted?
- When should they be started (and finished)?
- How should they be accomplished (in terms of method and resources)?
- What kinds of factors can influence project success?
- Should we make or buy the system?

These questions involve both project management techniques and development methodology. On the principle of scratching the worse itch first, this chapter discusses some particularly painful aspects of project management. The next chapter will deal with some specific problem areas in methodology.

Chapter 3

The initial section of this chapter deals with assigning priorities and how to avoid being "squeezed" by competing users. The next section discusses one of the key influences on project success: the ability to accurately estimate the time, cost and resources required for a project. Then in answer to the "make or buy" question, there is a section on purchasing and installing software packages.

Finally, one of the major constraints of project development is addressed: project team size. Werner von Braun is alleged to have defined a *crash project* as "one in which you get nine women pregnant to produce a baby in one month." (I quote von Braun not out of any male chauvinist feelings, but to illustrate the potential for failure of crash projects.)

The next chapter will cover questions of methodology. In some cases there is such an interweaving of the subjects of methodology and project management that a clean separation cannot be accomplished. So there is some mixture of material between Chapters 3 and 4.

SECTION 1 ESTIMATING PROJECT COSTS

Probably the most frustrating aspect of the EDP field to both those in the field and to their "customers" is the estimating of systems development and programming time within the environment of the organization.

To those in the EDP field, estimating is a difficult and time-consuming task not generally recognized as a major overhead cost of the systems and programming functions. (In fact, estimating represents a significant drain of available manpower time.) Furthermore, estimates establish a standard against which performance may be measured—often without validity.

The requirement for estimates forces the EDP analyst to consider not only the project itself, but the attitude of management toward that project. If management views the project with favor, they would like an estimate that demonstrates justification for the project and they will excuse or ignore overruns. If they are doubtful or negative about the project, they would like the estimate to be realistic or even high, diminishing the justification for the system and providing an excuse for refusal.

Finally, the EDP analyst is required to provide estimates before sufficient data have been collected to determine the scope of the project. As a result, poor estimates on major projects are the rule, rather than the exception, in industry today.

The reason that the "customer" (the line executive) within the company requires an estimate as early as possible in the investigation of a possible application is obvious. He must make the economic decision as to whether or not the application is worth doing. The line executive also must decide if he can afford the application and establish a budget or plan to pay the implementation cost.

Unfortunately, management often feels that designing and implementing a business system is similar to designing and building a product. There are, of course, some parallels, but there are some notable exceptions. It is difficult for them to understand the size of the estimate, the amount of work necessary to arrive at an estimate, and any overrun of cost by the project. It is almost inconceivable that the complexities of a system frequently exceed those of most products. In fact, there is often little similarity between systems bearing identical names (such as payroll or accounts payable) that exist in different companies. Very few organizations are willing to change to fit a system, *nor should they*. The effective system must be designed to fit the organization. The unique elements of an application constitute one of the major constraints on the predictability of systems and programming cost.

In addition to these elements, changes in the scope or approach to solutions *after* the original estimate is made may invalidate that estimate. Such changes almost inevitably occur since the feasibility study cannot possibly recognize or foresee all the factors involved in the system.

These problems relating to estimating require that several questions be answered:

1. What are the major elements of the systems and programming functions?

2. Are systems analysis and programming equally subject to estimation?

3. What methods of estimating are available?

4. Are the available methods realistic?

5. Is accurate estimating possible?

6. Is there a formula for estimating?

7. How should management view estimates?

General Concepts

The two primary resources of systems development are people and computer time. These must be allocated over elapsed time in order to accomplish the project objective within designated schedules.

The people involved are more than the analysts or programmers assigned to the project. The proper completion of the project requires test case development, documentation, modeling, machine operations, equipment installation and checkout, plans and controls, user review of system design, recruitment and training, support programs, system integration and conversion, managers, secretaries, librarians and others. The estimating process must take cognizance of the cost of these "technical support" functions.

Figure 1 illustrates the curve of manpower requirements over the life of the development project from approval of the preliminary design and feasibility study to the point at which the system becomes operational.[1]

This example of project staffing is fairly typical of commercial applications development. Two dangerous areas for estimating are apparent from this curve. First, technical support functions are frequently not included in estimates. Company management is then unpleasantly surprised to find that the support effort for system implementation puts a major strain on other functions in the company. Experience in major systems development indicates that the cost of technical support functions and user participation in system implementation frequently exceed the cost of analysis and programming.

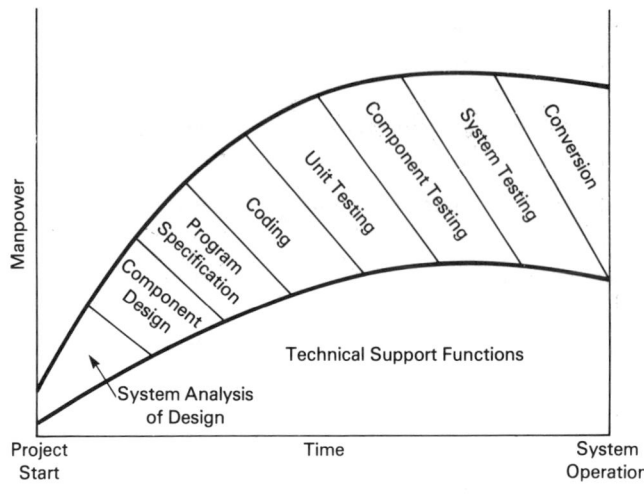

Figure 1.

Second, the time and cost of system testing is often underestimated. Since this phase lies closest to the end of the project, it is too late to reestimate and replan to avoid project schedule slippage.

Computer time must be added to the resources required for system implementation. This cost curve starts later in the project life and builds to a peak during the system test phase. (See Figure 2.)[2]

In major development projects or in a shop with a very high level of computer utilization, the available machine time may influence the

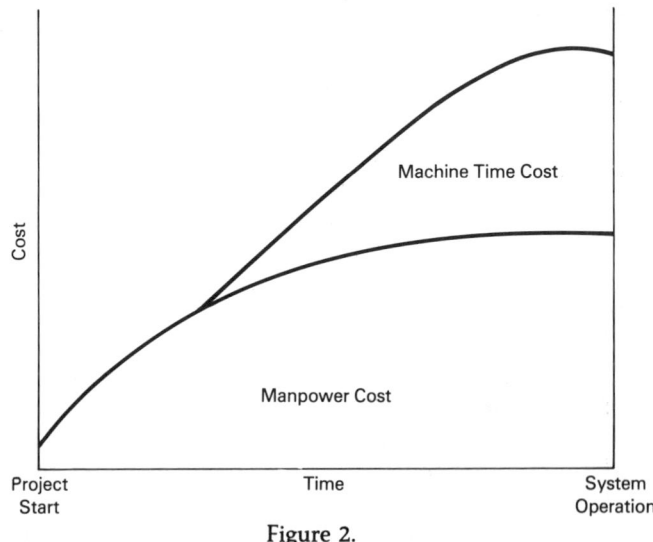

Figure 2.

cost of the project. As more and more machine time is used for com-piling and testing, conflicts for the use of machine resources may delay turn-around time for results. This situation may increase proj-ect costs through the need to purchase compensating outside machine time or through nonproductive periods imposed on programming per-sonnel.

The analyst estimating the schedule for system implementation is faced with a problem in determining the optimal implementation date for the system. Assuming that the application is economically justified, it logically follows that the benefits accruing to the company should start as soon as possible. However, speeding up the project invariably results in increasing the cost of implementation. (This is the well-known cost/time tradeoff dilemma.) Alternative plans may be illus-trated by the curves in Figure 3.[3]

Curve B may increase implementation cost by shortening time to the point that the application is no longer economically feasible. Curve C, on the other hand, may increase costs by requiring dedicated per-sonnel over a longer period of time and delaying the benefits of the new system to the point of economic infeasibility. This illustrates that cost and time are not infinitely exchangeable.

Cost and time are not "tradeable" in a constant manner. In fact, the function is nonlinear.

Figure 4 indicates the cost/time tradeoff function.[4] This function shows that as excessive resources are committed to a project there is a decrease in individual productivity and organizational efficiency.

This decrease in efficiency as group size increases has been noted by Gerald M. Weinberg and by Louis Fried in separate works. Wein-berg's "rough rule" for gauging the impact of increasing staff on a project is that as the size of the staff is tripled, the productive capacity is

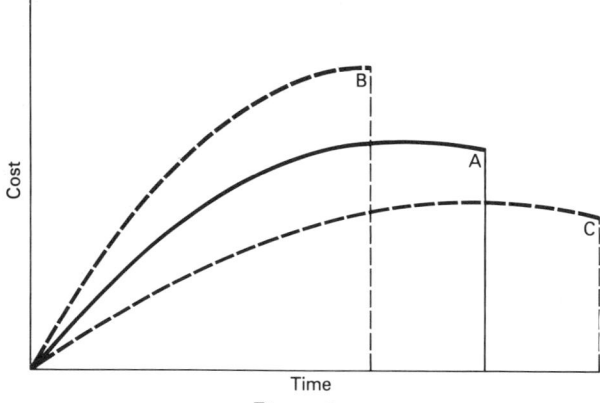

Figure 3.

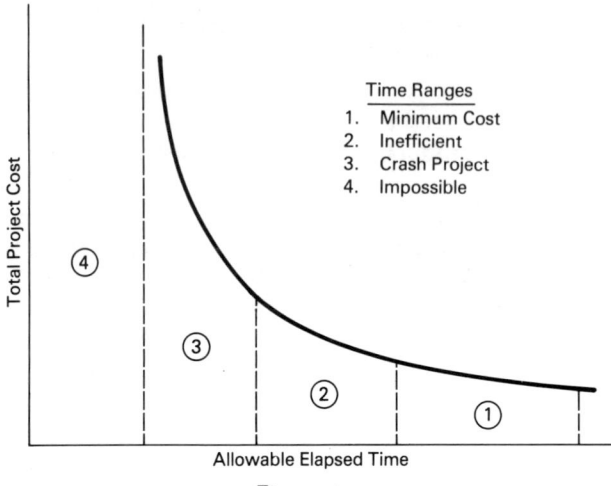

Figure 4.

doubled.[5] Fried's Law is: "There is an inverse relationship between effectiveness (production) and group size in complex technical projects."[6]

The formula supporting Fried's Law (Figure 5) indicates another important source of error in estimating. That is, no employee can be productively occupied for 100 percent of available time. Generally, at least 25 percent of employee time is lost to vacations, sickness, com-

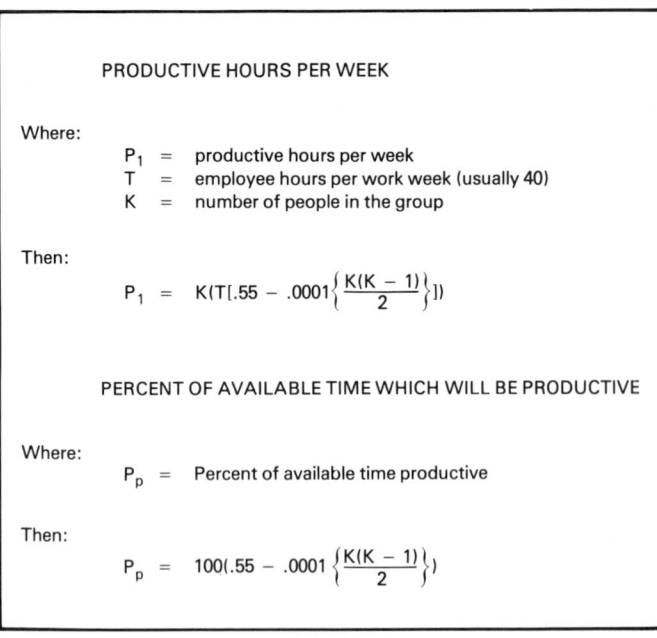

Figure 5.

pany meetings, training, and other benefits or organizationally imposed activities. Furthermore, another 10 percent of employee time is lost to idle time due to project delays, personal conversation and activities. Therefore, while employees must be paid for 100 percent of available time, project costs and schedules must anticipate a productivity rate of no more than 65 percent for extended periods of time. The impact of the combined influences of nonproductive time and group size is shown by the table comparing Weinberg's Rule and Fried's Law. (See Figure 6.)

Note that Weinberg's Rule always assures that *some* productivity will remain. Fried's Law, on the other hand, is consistent with Pietrasanta's graph of a crash project (Figure 4) in that it is possible to enter an area of negative productivity—the "impossible" project.

Defining the Elements of a Project

A precondition to preparing an estimate is defining the content and elements of a project. To some extent, this definition is a function of the size and scope of the project. There is an old auditor's rule that one should not spend more in controlling activities than the potential loss from leaving them uncontrolled. In the same fashion, one should not spend more on estimating a project than the potential loss or risk of damage from a poor estimate. Neither should one use project control tools or system documentation disproportionately to the potential loss that could be incurred by not using them. With this caveat, the following section will explore several approaches to defining the elements of major projects, and thereby cover the elements of minor projects as well.

ELEMENTS OF THE SYSTEMS AND PROGRAMMING FUNCTIONS

Most published studies of estimating have had limited benefit due to the failure to clearly define the elements of work within each major function. It should be recognized that each organization varies in the particular elements that may be assigned to the analyst or the pro-

Programmers Assigned to Project	Productive Capacity Equivalent	Percent of Productivity	
		Weinberg's Rule	Fried's Law
1	1	65%	55%
3	2	44%	55%
9	4	29%	55%
27	8	19%	52%
81	16	13%	23%
243	32	8%	-239%

Figure 6.

grammer, for example, which function is responsible for preparing record layouts, keypunch instructions, or control instructions.

Since a comparative study of estimating is presented later in this section, it is necessary to define the elements on which the study is based. The function of *systems analysis* is divided into eight primary elements, outlined below.

Problem Definition. Investigating the problem or current system in sufficient detail to present alternative suggestions for solution or improvement. The problem definition phase of the systems study should also result in determining the scope and objectives of the solutions.

Systems Survey. Gathering, recording and analyzing the facts relating to current operation of the area being studied. This phase should provide the detailed confirmation of the problem definition.

Synthesis. Creating the methods for meeting the objectives delineated in the problem definition.

Systems Development. Defining the EDP system, programs, controls, forms, and input/output requirements. This includes coordinating all definitions with potential system users for approval and documenting the system.

Analyst/Programmer Consultation. Guiding the programmers working on the project by answering questions related to the definition and resolving any discrepancies in the definition.

Systems Testing. Creating or obtaining test data that can be used to simulate all possible data conditions in the system; observing and approving the final results of a simulated run of the whole system.

Procedure or Manual Preparation. Writing and publishing the manual or procedures necessary to operate the system.

Implementation. Assisting in supervision of pilot or parallel operation, coordinating conversion to the new system and training of personnel in the operation of the new system.

The documentation performed in the systems development phase usually contains the following items:

Systems Abstract. A verbal description of the system.

Systems Flow Chart. A charted representation of the system in its organizational context.

Program Definitions. Verbal descriptions of each computer program—its input, output and necessary processes.

Card and Record Layouts. Illustrations of data fields and their characteristics within each specific record.

Input Document Samples.

Output Report Layouts or Samples.

Keypunch Instructions.

Control Procedures.

Paperwork Flow Charts.

The four primary elements of the *programming* function are:

Program Design. Often referred to as "preparing to code," this function includes study of the program definition, logic flow charting, file organization, etc., which are required before coding can start.

Coding. The actual writing of the program.

Checkout. Assembling, testing and debugging a program until it is proven operational. This function is not concluded until the system is implemented and accepted by the "customer."

Documentation. The completion of those documents necessary to provide a record of the intent and design of the program and to operate the program. This documentation usually consists of:

1. *Program Documentation*

   Logic Flow Chart. A symbolic representation of the program's logic.

   Assembly Listing. A list of the coding and its machine language translation.

   Sample Program Output. A report sample or a printout of a file created by the program.

   Static Test Data. Test data prepared by the programmer to meet the specified conditions of the program definition.

   Source Program. The program deck or tape as written in the coding language.

2. *Operating Documentation*

   Object Program. The machine language program ready for operation.

   Parameter Cards. Control cards for the program that may be required by the operating system.

   Operating Instructions. Describing how the computer is set up to run the program. These instructions also define any unusual conditions for which the program may halt.

   Offline Processing Procedures. Describing operations not performed on the computer.

   System Operating Flow Chart. Symbolically representing the relationships between all programs in the system.

ACTIVITIES AND PRODUCTS

There has been a long history of viewing projects from the standpoint of activities and events. This approach was the foundation for PERT (Project Evaluation and Review Technique) and CPM (Critical Path Method) in their use as project planning and control tools.

Dick Brandon has presented a list of the activities associated with project development in his book, *Project Control Standards.*[7] This list of activities (Figure 7) introduces the concept of transfer points and management presentations during the course of the project. These "checkpoints" are the completion of activities in which tangible products are produced. They are used to validate the work performed to date, to confirm the estimates for the remainder of the project, and to reaffirm the design and commitment to the project on the part of management. The gradual recognition of the relationship of tangible *products* to the process of project control has enhanced the approach to the estimating task by more clearly defining the results to be expected of any activity.

An example of this relationship of products to activities is provided by Figure 8 which illustrates the project development cycle.[8] The products (lettered) in the following list are related to the numbered activity codes by the chart.

PRODUCT	PRODUCT NAME	ACTIVITY CODE
A	Request evaluation report	1
B	Survey plan	2
C	Result of survey	2
D	General business requirements and system design	2
E	Detailed business system requirements	3
F	Detailed system design	3
G	Program specifications	4
H	Procedure specifications	5
I	Developmental testing plan	5
J	Acceptance test plan	5
K	Programming	7
L	Procedure writing	6
M	Acceptance testing	9
N	System installation	10
O	Operations documentation	7
P	Post implementation evaluation	11,12
Q	Manual writing and training	6,8

General	Study Phase	Analysis Phase	Design Phase	Programming Phase	Implementation
Indentify present problem.	Develop study plan.	Forms analysis.	Design reports.	Review of specifications.	Organize system test.
State objectives and anticipated benefits from new system.	Interview user management.	Reports analysis. File analysis.	Design files. Design input documents.	Logic decision and block diagramming. Desk checking.	Conduct system test. Review system test with user.
Define project scope.	Collect existing documentation.	Analyze information requirements.	Design clerical procedures.	Coding.	
General survey of user operations.	Collect operating statistics and cost data.	Procedure analysis. Develop alternatives.	Write programming specifications.	Program test data creation. Testing.	System and operating documentation.
Preliminary general design.	Collect sample documents. Observe present process.	Cost analysis. Management presentation.	Test material collection. Management presentation.	Program documentation.	Monitor system performance.
Preliminary cost estimate.	Summarize present system.				
Assign resources to project.	Present study results to management.				
Develop project schedule.					
Develop project budget.					

Figure 7. Sample list of activities.

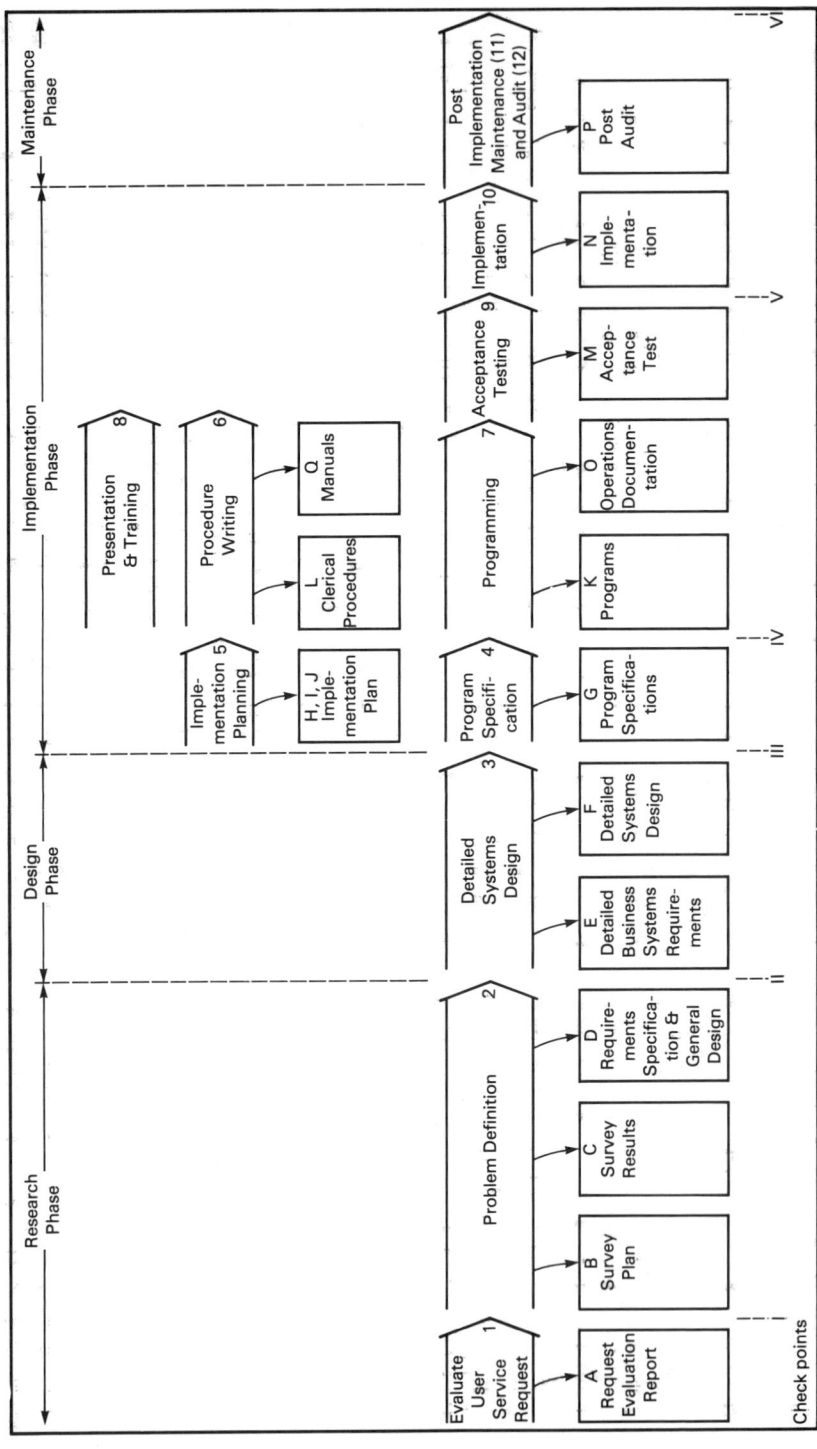

Figure 8. Project development cycle.

In its evolution from the activity-oriented approach, the product-oriented approach to project planning has retained its division into phases and retained the checkpoint system.

With this background in general estimating problems and with a common ground of project content established, we may now more thoroughly investigate the estimating process.

Estimating Systems Analysis

Parallels have been drawn in a previous section between systems implementation and the production process. The inference made is that, as many line managers insist, the cost of systems implementation can be estimated in a manner as reliable as the cost of a product. This inference is correct *insofar as the parallels drawn are true.* For example, if a standard number of labor hours per unit is used to estimate product cost and no comparable standard exists for systems and programming units, then no direct comparison is valid.

It is important to note that parallels between the production process and the systems elements of problem definition, systems survey, and synthesis (the systems specification phase) do not exist. These elements are the ones that establish the parameters, specifications and scope of the application. The closest parallel that can be drawn to this phase of systems development is that work done by the customer in establishing specifications for the product he is ordering. It may also include some elements of the product specification work done by the "applications engineer."

In any event, that effort necessary to define the product sufficiently for the prospective producer to prepare a fixed-price bid for its manufacture is generally *not included in the direct cost of the product itself.* The Department of Defense has recognized this fact and established the so-called product definition phase as a cost-plus development phase preceding the actual fixed price contract for production. When applied to the systems and programming activity, this concept is so important that Charles P. Lecht says:

> One of the most catastrophic mistakes which a computer programming manager can make in estimating is to assume the existence of a project upon receipt of the external functional specifications ... Performance of the analysis phase must occur before any accurate estimating can even begin to be achieved.[9]

Lecht identifies the analysis phase as occurring between receipt of the external functional specification (developed by the "customer") and the programming functional specification from which programs will be written.

Dick H. Brandon calls for a problem analysis phase to determine the detailed specifications of a solution. He suggests that the "problem analyst" be a systems analyst expert in the particular application and possibly a member of the using department.[10]

John Dearden maintains that the entire task of "systems specification" should be done by analysts in the user departments with the functions of data processing implementation (EDP system design only) and programming performed by a centralized group in the same organization as the EDP equipment.[11]

The experience of these authors and of many systems and EDP executives illustrates the fact that the cost of that portion of the systems function concerned with problem definition, systems survey and synthesis *cannot be estimated with any degree of accuracy.* Any estimate prepared for these elements will generally be based on the previous experience of those doing the estimating. It cannot, however, be related to any consistent set of standards.

The cost of these elements varies with the:

1. Nature, scope and complexity of the system.

2. Experience of the analyst in that application.

3. Level of the user organization from which the effort is being directed (higher level reduces cost).

4. Exposure of user personnel to EDP systems and methods.

5. Coordination required to establish specifications (higher level decision-making can reduce the cost of coordination).

One of the chief reasons for management dissatisfaction with the EDP organization is cost overruns and schedule slippage. These conditions often arise from the inclusion of the systems specification phase in the systems estimate.

To help solve this problem, several firms today have established independent system requirements groups in the "customer" organization. These groups define the general system and its inputs and outputs, i.e., complete the systems specification phase. Estimates for the balance of the systems and programming work are then prepared by the EDP group. Generally, however, the EDP organization has failed to communicate to line management the fact that the systems specification phase cannot be estimated and must be considered a part of the organization's overhead in the same manner as a feasibility study.

The remaining elements of the systems function comprise two phases:

1. The systems definition phase includes the elements of systems development, analyst/programmer consultation and procedure or manual preparation.

2. The systems implementation phase includes the elements of systems testing and implementation.

Reasonably accurate estimates may be prepared for the systems definition phase based on the number of programs to be defined, the complexity of the programs and the number of interfaces with other systems. Statistical bases for estimating the system development element can be established in much the same manner as for programming (described later). The analyst/programmer consultation element is constrained to a duration equivalent to that of programming and debugging the system. It can be reasonably estimated after the project schedule is developed.

The procedure or manual preparation elements can also be estimated based on statistical evidence for time per page. There is some element of risk in this estimate arising from the need to coordinate procedures. Any element of the systems task that requires coordination with user personnel is subject to variations as described above in the systems specification phase. If, however, the specifications have been clearly stated and coordinated, this risk in the systems definition phase is sharply reduced.

The need to coordinate design proposals and obtain management approvals can act as a major inflationary factor to both elapsed and actual time used in the systems specification phase. Ideally, the system design is independent of the individuals within the user organization, the individual being, within realistic limits, a replaceable component of the system. In practice, however, the system reflects the characteristics of the analyst who designed it and the management who approved each segment of the design. The completed design is invested with the concepts and prejudices of the line manager participating. If this management changes during the development of the system, the entire design may have to be redeveloped and recoordinated.

Similar excessive development costs can arise from changed management thinking due to altering business needs. Inflated coordination costs can also result from the need to coordinate with too many line personnel when centralized project direction is not assigned by management.

Despite these difficulties, management still wants, and has a need for, estimates upon which to base their decisions to proceed with or abandon the proposed project.

Brandon and Gray have developed the System Development Estimating Guide illustrated by Figure 9. An excerpt from their book, *Project Control Standards* explains the Guide as follows:

The Guide is divided into five sections:

1. Interviews
2. Document Analysis
3. Conclusions and Recommended Approach
4. Presentation and Preparation
5. Final Design and Documentation

In each section, a certain number of man-days are allowed for each of the functions. For example, 0.5 man-days is allowed for each management interview, 1.0 man-days for each supervisory interview, and so forth. In Section B, 0.5 man-days is allowed for each input to be analyzed, 0.5 man-days for each report. Sections C and D are similar, where the man-days estimates for preparing design alternatives and presenting them to management are a function of the anticipated number of each of the items listed. Section E, Final Design and Documentation, depends for its values on the total man-day estimates developed in sections A, B, and C. A total man-day estimate can thus be computed for all system development functions through system design.

Following is a detailed description of the steps in completing the form.

Section A. In the column headed "Number," on line 1, insert the anticipated number of interviews to be held with management personnel. In the same column, on line 2, insert the anticipated number of interviews to be held with supervisory personnel. On lines 3 and 4, insert the anticipated number of interviews with technical and clerical personnel, respectively. Then, multiply each inserted number by the number next to it in the column headed "Factor," and write the result in the column headed "Base Days." (For example, if four management interviews were anticipated, four would be multiplied by the factor 0.5, and the result, 2.0, would be written in the column "Base Days" on line 1.) Then, multiply each number in the column headed "Base Days" by the number next to it in the column headed "Referral Allowance," and write the result in the column headed "Total" (Continuing with the example, if 2 appears in "Base Days" on line 1, it would be multiplied by the referral allowance of 1.20, giving a result of 2.4, which would be written on line 1 in the column headed "Total.") Add the values on lines 1, 2, 3, and 4 of the column "Subtotal," multiply the sum by 1.25, and write the product on line 5 of section A, and on line 1 of section E, in the column headed "Total."

Section B. In the column headed "Number," on line 1, insert the anticipated number of input forms that must be analyzed. On line 2 of the same column, insert the anticipated number of reports that must be analyzed. Similarly, on lines 3 and 4 insert the number of files, documents, and card input/output forms to be ana-

Date _____

Project No _____ Project Name _____ Estimated by _____

_____

A. INTERVIEWS _____

Type	Number	Factor	Base Days	Referral Allowance	Sub Total	Interrupt	Total
1. Management		0.5		x 1.20			
2. Supervisory		1.0		x 1.20			
3. Technical		1.5		x 1.50			
4. Clerical		0.5		x 1.50			
5. Total Man Days—Interviews							

B. DOCUMENT ANALYSIS

Item	Number	Factor	Total
1. Input Form		x 0.5	
2. Report		x 0.5	
3. File Layout		x 2.0	
4. Machine Readable Input/Output		x 0.5	
5. Total Man Days—Document Analysis		x 1.5	

C. CONCLUSIONS AND RECOMMENDED APPROACH

Item	Number	Factor	Total
1. Interviews		x 0.5	
2. Documents		x 0.5	
3. Functions in New System		x 1.0	
4. Variations Provided		x 1.5	
5. Subtotal			
6. Alternatives Presented		x 0.25	
7. Man Days to Formulate Conclusions			

D. PRESENTATION AND PREPARATION

Item	Number	Factor	Total
1. Attendees		x 0.25	
2. Locations		x 0.5	
3. Approvals Required		x 1.0	
4. Charts Needed		x 1.0	
5. Man Days—Presentation			

E. FINAL DESIGN AND DOCUMENTATION

Man-Days	Number	Factor	Total
1. Interviews (A5)		x 0.25	
2. Document Analysis (B5)		x 0.5	
3. Formulate Conclusions (C7)		x 0.5	
4. Total Final Design Man Days			

Figure 9. Systems development estimate guide.

lyzed. Multiply each inserted number by the number next to it in the column headed "Factor," and write the result in the column headed "Total." (For example, if it is anticipated that twenty reports will have to be analyzed, 20 would be multiplied by 0.5 and the result, 10, would be written on line 2 in the column headed "Total.") Then add the numbers in the "Total" column and write the result on line 5 of section B and on line 2 of Section E, in the column headed "Total."

Section C. In the column headed "Number," insert the anticipated number of interviews, documents, old functions in system, new functions in system and variations provided, on lines 1, 2, 3, and 4, respectively. Add the numbers in the column headed "Number" and write the sum on line 5 in the same column. Multiply the number on line 5 by 0.25, and then multiply the result by the number of alternatives to be presented, and write the result in the column headed "Total" on line 6. Multiply each of the numbers in the column "Number" on lines 1, 2, 3, and 4 by the number next to it in the column headed "Factor," and write the result in the column headed "Total." Add all the numbers in the column headed "Total" and write the sum on line 7 section C and on line 3, section E, in the column headed "Total."

Section D. This section computes the number of man-days needed for presentation to management of the proposed system or systems. Insert in the column headed "Number" the anticipated number of attendees, the number of locations at which the presentation is to be given, the number of approvals which must be obtained and the number of charts needed for the presentation. Multiply each entry by the number next to it in the column headed "Factor" and write the result in the column headed "Total." Add the numbers in the column headed "Total" and write the sum on line 5, section D. This is the number of man-days required for presentations.

Section E. Multiply each number entered in section F by the number next to it in the column headed "Factor" and write the result in the column headed "Total." Add the results of the multiplications and write the sum on line 4, section E.

To find the total number of man-days to be allowed for all system development functions through final system design and documentation, add the results found on line 5, section A; line 5, section B; line 7, section C; line 5, section D; and line 4, section E."[12]

SYSTEMS ESTIMATING HINTS

Whatever tool is used for estimating, there are several precautionary measures that should be taken. These guard against introduction of bias, missing major elements of consideration, estimating based on insufficient study and failure to recognize schedule constraints. These measures are especially important in the systems design phases of the project since estimates for the total project are required at an early stage of project life.

It is often the procedure for senior analysts and project managers to prepare project estimates. Senior analysts and project managers arrive at these positions because of their experience and exceptionally good performance. Frequently they tend to create estimates based on their personal experience and capability. Such estimates may be very optimistic if the estimator will be depending on other, less experienced, personnel to do the job. For this reason, estimates should always be reviewed with the person who will be doing the work (or with a person of similar experience).

On major projects this concept should be extended as a part of the *technical review*. The purpose of the technical review is to look for potential problems in the proposed design and project structure and to offer creative solutions to any such problems identified. Technical reviews should be conducted at the completion of requirements specification and general design, at the completion of the detailed system design, and at the completion of programming specifications. (These are checkpoints II, III and IV in Figure 10.)

Technical reviews should be called by the project manager after the above named products have been distributed to members of the review team and they have had a suitable opportunity to digest the content. Review teams should include systems supervisors not involved in the project, the data base manager, the systems programming manager, the operations manager and any technical specialists who may offer unique reactions to special design considerations. Questions or suggestions arising from the technical review meeting should be answered and incorporated into the completed product and estimates before presentation to user management.

A scheduling tool such as PERT should be used on major projects and carefully reviewed during technical review meetings to assure appropriate resource commitment and evaluate the critical path and dependencies. Activities within a PERT network (see example, Figure 11) can be estimated using a format such as that illustrated by Figure 10. (Smaller projects can be estimated in total using this format.)

As previously stated, many estimates are failures because they are prepared with insufficient knowledge of the task to be done. One way to avoid this problem and still provide a guideline for management decision-making is through "renewing" estimates as more knowledge of the project is gained. Again referring to Figure 8, checkpoints I through IV are points at which new estimates should be provided to the user. Estimates should be presented according to the following rules:

PROJECT ESTIMATING WORKSHEET

PROJECT NAME ______________________ CODE NUMBER ______________________ PAGE ______ OF ______

IF APPLICABLE (PHASE ______________________ SUB-CODE NUMBER ______________________ NAME ______________________)

ESTIMATED BY ______________________ DATE ______________________ USER ______________________

ESTIMATING DATES START ______________ TARGET ______________

ESTIMATION SCHEDULE ☐ MONTHLY ☐ WEEKLY

TOTAL COST $ ______________

LABOR COSTS

JOB CLASSIFICATION	1	2	3	4	5	6	7	8	9	10	11	12	13	14	15	TOTAL HOURS	RATE	LABOR $
TOTAL $																	TOTAL CHARGE →	

COMPUTER COSTS

COMPUTER HOURS																	TOTAL COST →	

PURCHASES AND OTHER COSTS

ITEM (EQUIPMENT, PRINTING, TYPING, KEYPUNCHING, ETC.)	COST
(TOTAL COMPUTER AND OTHER COSTS) PURCHASE $ →	

COMMENTS ______________________

UC-4128

Figure 10.

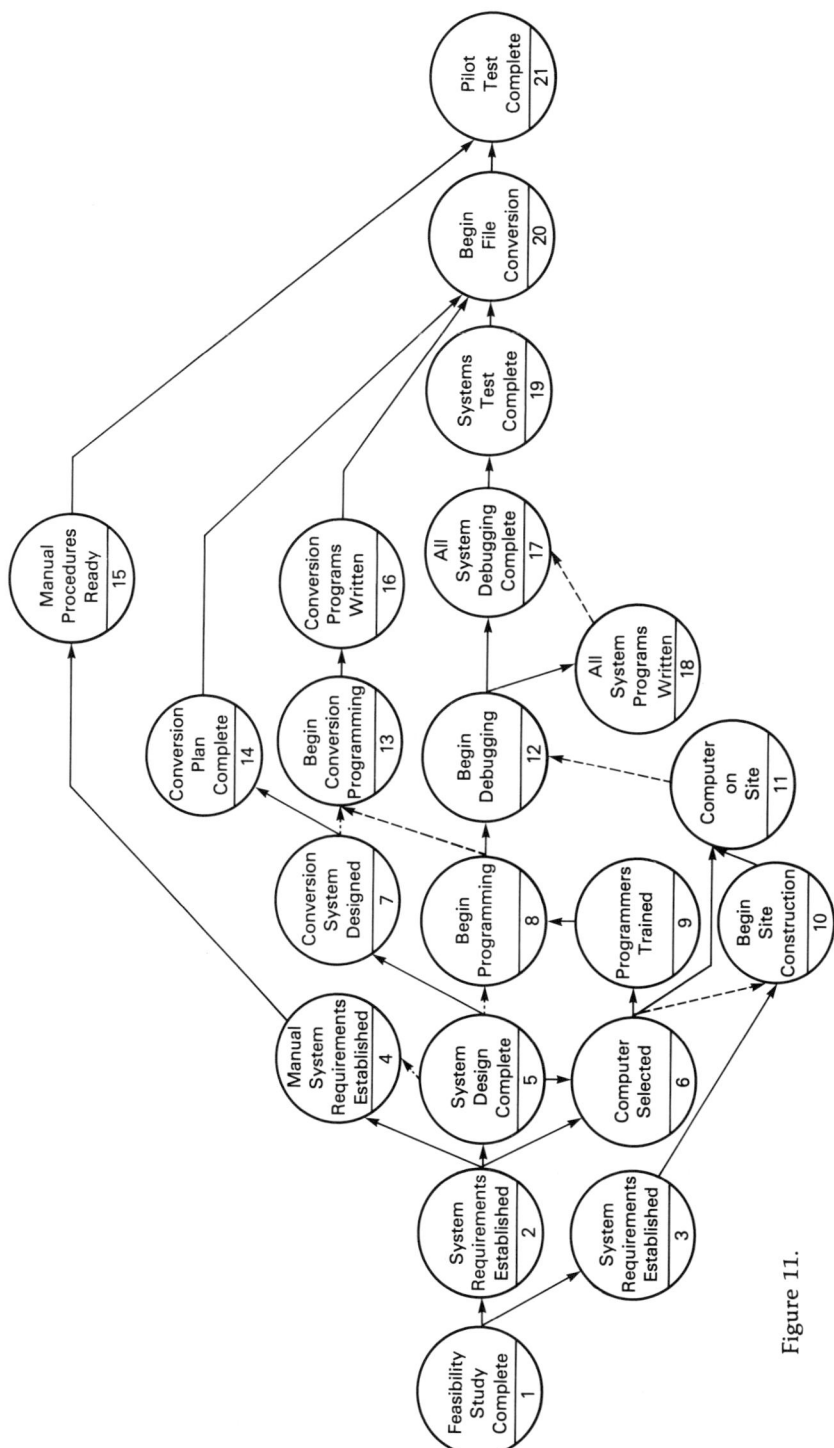

Figure 11.

91

CHECKPOINT	NEXT PHASE (ACCURACY)	TOTAL PROJECT REMAINING (ACCURACY)
I	Research phase (± 10%)	(± 50%)
II	Detailed design (± 10%)	(± 25%)
III	Programming specifications (± 5%)	(± 15%)
IV	Balance of project (± 5%)	

Checkpoint IV should be considered a "design freeze" point. Changes requested to system design beyond this point should be either held until after project completion or estimated as to schedule and cost impact and approved by user management before inclusion in the project.

ESTIMATING STANDARDS

There are three major factors that influence standards in systems analysis. These are analyst competence, prior experience with similar systems and the complexity of the application.

The sample factors provided in Figure 9 may not be appropriate to individual analysts or the complexity of the project. The best such factors can only be developed by maintaining a history of performance in a given installation. However, what with normal personnel turnover and the fact that most organizations rarely design and implement the same system twice, some general standards are useful.

Assuming that a senior analyst-project manager with a high level of competence would take .70 man-days to perform a given task, then a factoring method such as the following would be appropriate:

| | COMPETENCE LEVEL | |
	Low	High
Senior Analyst	1.0	.7
Intermediate Analyst	1.8	1.1
Junior Analyst	2.8	1.9

A similar scale of factors for job knowledge should be utilized:

| | KNOWLEDGE REQUIRED | | |
Knowledge Available	Little	Average	Much
Much	0.0	0.1	0.3
Average	0.0	0.2	0.7
Little	0.1	0.5	1.0

Finally, in the area of system complexity, Ralph A. Szweda[13] has developed some guidelines which may be summarized as follows:

MAN DAYS

Task	Simple	Complex	Very Complex
Collection of Documents	1	2	3–5
Interviews	.50–.75	1–1.50	2–2.50*
File Analysis (per file)	.25	.35	.50
Flowcharts (old system)	.50	1.50–2	3.50–4**
Other Graphics	1.50–3	2.50–4	3.50–6
Evaluation of Present System	2.50–4	5–7.50	7.50–10
New Flowcharts	.50–1	1.50–2.50	3–5***
File Specifications (per file)	.25	.30	.35
Design of New Documents	.50–1.50	1–3	1.50–3.50****
Preparation of Specifications	2.50–5	5–8	8–15
Conversion Procedures	2.50–4	3.50–6	5–10
Conversion of Data & Files	2.50–7.50	5–15	7.50–30
Training	5–15	10–25	15–30
Systems Test	5–7.50	10–30	20–45
Final Documentation	.50–1.50	1–2	2–3

* Basic interview only. Add .5 hours for each additional interview conducted.
** Plus .5 hours per function flowcharted.
*** Plus .5 hours for each logic function flowcharted.
**** Plus 2–4 hours per document.

The three factors; analyst competence, analyst knowledge of the application, and system complexity may be combined in the following manner.

Where an overall activity is being estimated (such as "evaluation of present system" or "training") and:

C = analyst competence factor
K = analyst knowledge/knowledge required factor
S = system complexity standards

Then:

$$(C + K)\ S = \text{Estimate for activity.}$$

For example:

An intermediate analyst with high competence and average knowledge of the application, assigned to a complex evaluation of an existing system requiring much experience would generate the following estimate:

$$(C + K)\ S = \text{Estimate}$$
$$(1.1 + .7)\ 5 = 9\text{ man days}$$
$$(1.1 + .7)\ 7.50 = 13.5\text{ man days} \left.\right\} \text{ Range for estimate}$$

Where the guidelines for system complexity are based on a number of analyses within an activity (such as "file analysis" or "file specification") then the number of these analyses must be incorporated into the formula (such as the number n of files):

$$(C + K)\ Sn = \text{Estimate}$$

It is immediately apparent that the above factors and standards can vary from one organizatior to another. Therefore the organizatior should adjust the indicated standards in terms of its own experience. Ir addition, the elapsed time required for coordination and approvals varies substantially by company and has not been included in the above estimating techniques. What is presented above is a methodology based upon the experience of various authors in the field and this must be tempered by the experiential evidence of each organization. Finally, it should be reiterated that extensive estimating procedures are appropriate to *major* projects and should not be used for lesser projects.

Estimating Programming

While it appears that accurate estimating of many elements of the systems function is not practical, the estimating of programming based on a clearly defined programming specification from the systems analyst is definitely feasible. There is, however, a wide range of methods from the extremely simple (with little cost) to the highly complex, very costly estimating process. Each of these may be valid for use depending upon the:

1. Size of the project being estimated.
2. Need for accuracy in the estimate.
3. Size of the programming group.

Obviously, a great deal of cost should not be incurred in preparing an estimate for a relatively small project. Also, if only an approximation is required by management, an extensive study is wasteful.

It is not quite so obvious that the size of the programming group can be a factor in the choice of the estimating method. Statistical data related to average programmer performance can be reliably applied to major projects spread over a large group of programmers. Average performance data can be misleading, however, when applied to either a

small project assigned to a single programmer or a large project assigned to a small group of programmers. In these cases the previous
performance of the *individuals* is far more pertinent than averages. For
this reason, while some generalized guidelines can be established for
large project estimating in large programming organizations, these
guidelines cannot be applied in the majority of smaller organizations.
As a result, a primary constraint in estimating programming cost is that
generalized methods for estimating programming can be defined, but
generalized average guidelines or "prefabricated" estimates do not
exist.

All estimates are based, in some way, on experience. This can be
in the form of personal experience of the estimator, historical data collected relating to similar projects, data collected relating to previous
work by the same group or individual or data acquired from reference
sources. The most reliable experience upon which estimates can be
based is that most closely paralleling the project to be estimated.
Therefore, the ideal estimate would be based on having previously
completed the same project with the same staff under the same conditions (language, hardware, definition, etc.). This ideal is obviously not
practical, so experience must be developed to reflect data on those elements which are common from one project to the next.

In developing an estimating method applicable to extremely large
projects, E. A. Nelson identifies 97 possible variables that can affect the
cost of programming.[14] Such an analysis is not often economically feasible so that most variables must usually be assumed to be constants.
Estimates can then consider a few major variable factors within the
areas of hardware, software, personnel, procedures and the complexity
of the specific project.

Hardware Variables. Is there sufficient memory and peripheral devices to easily accommodate the program? Reducing program size
to fit the machine is time-consuming work.

Software Variables.

1. Is the program able to utilize available macroinstructions,
subroutines, or utility programs? "Canned" sort, merge or other
utility programs can be used to save work.

2. The programming language used can influence the cost.
Some studies have indicated that on average business applications
a problem-oriented language (such as COBOL) saves time over a
machine-oriented language (such as Assembler Language). For
problems requiring complex processing or maximum efficiency a
machine-oriented language will probably be best.[15]

3. Is the assembler or compiler reliable? New software issued by most computer manufacturers can be expected to have "bugs." Some extra effort will be required to debug both the program and the vendor software if a recently released compiler is to be used.

4. Diagnostic aids vary among compilers and among manufacturers. The better versions can considerably reduce program debugging time.

5. Program development tools may be used to support portions of the programmer's work.

Personnel Variables.

1. Is the programmer experienced with the organization and the application? This type of experience can save time in communication and reduce errors in interpretation of commonly used terminology for the organization or application.

2. Is the programmer experienced with the programming language and the equipment being used?

3. Is the programmer experienced with the standards, conventions and documentation requirements of the organization?

4. Is the programmer fast, average or slow? Is he a senior or junior man?

Program Complexity Variables.

1. If the program stands alone and does not have to relate to other programs, less effort is required for implementation.

2. Is creative logic planning required? Innovative thinking requires more time than routine program development.

3. Programming complexity can be judged by estimating the number of source instructions that must be coded, by the number of files processed by the program and by the number of record layouts processed in the program. Increases in all these variables require increases in programming time.

The key to more accurate estimating is in perfection of the historical information to establish a base for estimates and to eliminate variables. For example, if statistical data has been collected for some time on a group using COBOL, then estimates for future programming in COBOL can eliminate those variables having to do with the language used, the compiler used and the diagnostic aids. These elements have become constant for the group.

The history of one group cannot easily be transferred for use by another group. This condition exists due not only to the above variables, but also to the differences in the definitions of the programming function. This can be illustrated by the results of a one year study of a programming group compared to available external information in Figure 12.

The table indicates that variances exist not only between groups but between the same group using different languages, operating systems and computers. But meaningful historical information can be developed for the group.

			BRANDON[3]			TEST GROUP[4]	
	Delaney[1]	RCA[2]	Simple	Avg.	Complex	Autocoder	Assembler
Program Design	25%	30%	11%	27.5%	30%	11.9%	7.3%
Coding	31%	20%	11%	24.0%	27%	30.0%	29.4%
Checkout	31%	45%	50%	34.5%	33%	39.9%	46.9%
Documentation	13%	5%	28%	14.0%	10%	18.2%	16.4%

[1] William A. Delaney, *Predicting the Costs of Computer Programs.* (Data Processing Magazine, October, 1966). The percentages presented by Mr. Delaney included 20 percent analysis, which was removed for purposes of this comparison.

[2] RCA, *Manpower Management Techniques.* (RCA internal publication, 1967). RCA assigns much of the documentation to systems or clerical personnel.

[3] Dick H. Brandon, "Management Standards for Data Processing." (D. VanNostrand Company, New Jersey, 1963), pp. 249-298.

[4] Stanley Jeffries (Bourns, Inc. internal reports). The analysis of group activity using Autocoder was performed in September, 1967. The analysis using RCA Assembler language for the Spectra 70 was performed in July 1968 after six months of using the new language. Personnel remained relatively constant during this period as did documentation requirements.

Figure 12.

There have been several attempts to design estimating methods that are independent of those variables related to one or more of the major variable factors. The personnel variable is most generally discarded in an attempt to generalize the method for application in many installations.

Dick Brandon has presented several formulae for estimating based on assigning a fixed number of man-days for levels of complexity, program size and the major elements of the programming function (logic, coding, documentation, etc.). These formulae are presented as being valid for specific equipment, memory size, programming language, average program size and a specified documentation standard.[16] Brandon also indicates the value of building performance history to provide a base for future estimating.

RCA, at one time, established a guideline for estimating programming manpower requirements.[17] This method considers the variables of program size, program type (edit, update, etc.), programmer experience, language and elements of the programming function. Their working formula for computing elapsed time estimates is:

$$T = \frac{I}{22PR}$$

where:

I T = time in months
I I = total number of instructions to be coded
I P = number of programmers
I R = number of instructions per day per man
I   22= constant (work days per month)

The R factor is determined on the basis of a table of production rates for language and programmer experience. A table of average program sizes (number of machine instructions) is provided for the different program types.

The danger in estimating by expected lines of coding is that individual programs vary considerably in complexity. For example, an update program can vary in complexity by a factor of five or more depending on the nature of the system and files. Not only do instructions vary from program to program, but also from *programmer* to *programmer*. An experienced programmer may save as many as 50 percent of the number of coded instructions necessary.

The number of instructions is also affected by the standards (for editing, label checking, etc.) of the installation, and by the macroinstructions available for use in the program.

Probably the most popular method of estimating is the SOP method (*seat of the pants method*). This method consists of the estimator using his past experience and his knowledge of the program requirements to estimate the man-hours and elapsed time required. Considering that the estimator is generally familiar with the installation, its standards, its personnel, its language, and often with the system requirements, the SOP method can be relatively accurate. The SOP method suffers from a personal bias as in estimating systems analysis. Because often those in charge of estimating have superior talents and capabilities in programming, their SOP estimates may be far short of the actual effort since the work may be done by average, rather than superior, programmers.

It is fairly obvious that no panacea to the programming estimating problem is available in the form of a single formula, method, scale or standard. Instead, several methods must be used in a manner appropriate to the situation. The extensive and costly method delineated in E. A.

for preparing estimates. From these reports a range of time can be constructed for each type. For example, a study performed with a group utilizing a third generation, tape/disk computer, assembler language and a disk operating system showed the following ranges:

PROJECT HOURS[19]

Type A	4 to 6
Type B	35 to 55
Type C	85 to 115
Type D	120 and up

The complexity of the program determines which part of the range is applicable. It may be completely outside the range or types indicated. If this is the case, the program may be a combination of two types or may have to be estimated by the SOP method supported by the available statistics.

ESTIMATING LARGE PROJECTS

Large or critical programming projects deserve commensurately sophisticated estimating. Such detailed estimating can only be performed properly on the basis of a complete written systems and programming specification. One approach to accomplishing this is to develop the user manual before any other part of the system. From this, a complete system design and specification is generated and estimates can be made for system development. This approach to estimating has been developed by William S. Donelson as follows:

The preliminary user manual provides the focal point for project estimation. The quantifiable components for estimating are the numbers of each functional type of module or program which will be required to construct the system, and by this time we should have an accurate forecast of the number of each type due to the preliminary system flowchart in the manual. A typical commercial system has at least twelve categories of functional components:

1. *Data definition books.* File, record and transaction layouts which are stored in a library and copied into programs as required.

2. *One-time utilities.* Programs to create files, generate test data, simulate processing and test called subroutines.

3. *Conversion utilities.* Programs to convert or reformat data files and transactions from existing systems to the new system format.

4. *General purpose utilities.* Modules to perform repeated functions which are used by different control modules (date conversions, table lookups, calculations, etc.).

5. *Data base interface utility.* Here I am advocating the use of a "bridge" between application programs and most data base management systems to provide a higher degree of data independence, to assure physical integrity of the data base (by auditing adds, deletes and updates), and to provide file content and utilization statistics. This bridge relates functional entry points (open, close, read, write, explode, implode, etc.) for application modules to technique-oriented entry points and commands supplied by data base management packages (MRAN, CDIR, ADD-M, DELVD, GET UNIQUE, etc.).

6. *Edit modules.* Programs which assure the logical integrity of data entered into the system and which provide error listings or alerts. (One module per transaction type or family of transactions is assumed.)

7. *Update modules.* Programs which update the data base. This function may be performed within the same module as the editing function, but is, nevertheless, a separate function which produces audit trails or activity reports.

8. *Processing modules.* Programs which do extensive calculations, analyses and manipulations of data, resulting in possible additional file maintenance.

9. *Major data base extracts.* Programs which select data from the data base for subsequent (or simultaneous) analysis and reporting.

10. *Minor data base extracts.* Same as Item 9, but less complex.

11. *Major reports.* Programs which report the results of major extracts and processing and which are complex in nature (multiple levels of control breaks and totals, sophisticated row and column formatting and possibly further access to the data base.)

12. *Minor reports.* Same as Item 11, but simple in structure. (Note that the project manager who tightly controls the data definition books and data base interface utility will produce a well-constructed system in terms of architecture and adaptability to change. Also, if the file maintenance function is strictly confined to file maintenance modules, there will be less latitude for the occurrence of difficult-to-locate system bugs.)[20]

For typical commercial application systems, each class or type of module has a mean number of statements per module (and standard deviation), and also has a measurable programming rate in terms of mean and standard deviation of numbers of statements per hour. Computer test requirements are also quantifiable by module type. (For system modifications, as opposed to new systems development, other languages, on-line processing, or other hardware, different statistics will have to be compiled. These statistics will no doubt vary somewhat by installation due to differences in methods, standards, and personnel experience levels, and each installation should adjust these statistics to account for these differences.)

Systems analysis and design hours are approximately 110 percent of programming hours for an entire project, assuming that this function has responsibility for project management, analysis, design, user manual preparation, program specification writing, program quality control, test results analysis, user training, system implementation (as opposed to program implementation and operations support, which is typically done by lead programmers) and post implementation review. COBOL programs may be keyed and verified at the rate of 125 statements per hour, assuming an average of 32 characters per statement (if more characters per statement are coded, the number of statements per module should decrease, and the total keystrokes per module class should remain fairly constant).

By determining the number of modules in each class, it becomes feasible to forecast systems analysis and design hours, programming hours, keyentry hours and computer test hours. Knowing the cost per hour of these resources, it is possible to estimate project costs as follows:

Total cost =

$$\sum_{i=1}^{12} Mi \left[\left(\frac{(Si + \alpha i + \sigma Si)(1.1 \, Rs + Rp)}{(Pi + \beta i \, \sigma Pi)} \right) \right.$$
$$\left. + \left(\frac{(Si + \alpha i \, \sigma Si) \, Rk}{125} \right) + Ti \, Rc \right]$$

Where i = module class or type
  M = number of modules per class (from planner's estimate)
  S = mean number of statements per module per class
  σS = standard deviation of S
  α = selected multiple of σs (from planner's estimate)
  P = programming statements per hour
  σP = standard deviation of P
  β = selected multiple of σp (from planner's estimate)
  T = mean number of computer test hours per module per class
  Rs = hourly charge for systems analysis and design
  Rp = hourly charge for programming
  Rk = hourly charge for keypunch
  Rc = hourly charge for computer test time

This cost algorithm and set of statistics address the costs of project development through implementation and post implementation review which accrue within the MIS/EDP department. (Note that this estimation technique is very much akin to building construction cost estimating, a primary tool of which is cost per square foot.)

Ralph Szweda has documented what he refers to as the "IBM method."[21] This method consists of estimating the man-days required for completing a *single* program through the use of several factors and calculations. These factors include input/output characteristics, major processing functions, programming know-how and job knowledge. The total weighting points for each factor are used to compute the estimate. Weighting points for input/output characteristics are:

CHARACTERISTIC

Input	Weighting Points*
Card—single format	1
—multiple formats	2
Each tape per file	1
Each disk per file	1
Output:	
Print per record format (headings plus data)	1
Each tape per file	1
(Note: when tape is completely formatted for slave printing by a lesser machine, assign weightings as though output were print.)	
Card—single format	1
—multiple formats	2
Each disk per file	1

* Included under i/o weightings are such program requirements as DTF entries, DIOCS entries, establishing work areas and data movement commands.

Weighting points for processing functions are assigned according to processing function complexity and the programming language used.

These terms from the table at the top of page 105 need clarification:

Restructure Data. Includes such functions as combining, condensing, deleting, or rearranging data. Output formatting is excluded from consideration here because it is considered to be an i/o characteristic.

Data Retrieval and Presentation. Includes such functions as table look-ups, file search, record access techniques, and related index construction.

Calculate. This grouping is concerned with arithmetic computations.

Condition Checking. This is primarily concerned with the error-checking functions built into the program to ensure accuracy.

Linkage. Includes such programming activities as checkpoint and restart, overlays, and interfaces with other programming systems, programs, and/or modules.

Programming System	Major Processing Function	Weighting Points			Range*	
		Simple	Complex	Very Complex	Min.	Max.
S/360 with COBOL	Restructure data	1	3	4		
	Condition checking	1	4	7		
	Data retrieval & presentation	2	5	8		
	Calculate	1	3	5		
	Linkage	1	2	3		
	Total	6	17	27	4	27
S/360 with BAL	Restructure data	4	5	6		
	Condition checking	4	7	9		
	Data retrieval & presentation	4	7	9		
	Calculate	3	5	8		
	Linkage	2	3	5		
	Total	17	27	37	12	37
Utility or package programs (i.e., OPCON, Sort 90, S/360 multi-utility programs)	Control card changes only	1	n/a	n/a		
	Own coding required	2	3	4		
RPG (S/360)		2	8	13		

* Range represents the minimum weighting points that can be developed from the proper use of these tables as applied to a single program. n/a—not applicable

The factor for programmer know-how or competence is selected from the following table on the basis of evaluating the programmer assigned to the program being estimated.

Overall Programming Experience	Man-Days Per Program Weighting Point
Senior Programmer	0.50 to 0.75
Programmer	1.00 to 1.50
Junior Programmer	2.00 to 3.00
Trainee	3.50 to 4.00

Finally, the job knowledge factor is selected from the following table based upon evaluation of the task to be performed and the knowledge of the programmer in that particular task or application.

JOB KNOWLEDGE AVAILABLE	JOB KNOWLEDGE REQUIRED		
	Much	*Some*	*None*
Detailed knowledge of this job	0.75	0.25	0.00
Good general knowledge of this job, with fragmentary detailed knowledge	1.25	0.50	0.00
Fair general knowledge of this job, but little or no detailed knowledge	1.50	0.75	0.00
No job knowledge, but general knowledge of related subjects	1.75	1.00	0.25
No job knowledge, no general knowledge of related subjects	2.00	1.25	0.25

It is obvious that this approach requires a detailed specification of the program being estimated as well as prior selection of the programmer to be used on the project. The selected factors are drawn together in the following example:

Input/Output Characteristics	WEIGHTING POINTS
Input Characteristics:	
Tape Files (3)	3
Output Characteristics:	
Tape File (1)	1
Print Format (1)	1
Single Card Format (1)	1
Total I/O Characteristics	6
Major Processing Functions	
Functions:	
Restructure Data (Complex)	3
Calculate (Simple)	1
Condition Checking (Complex)	4
Data Retrieval & Presentation (Complex)	5
Linkage (Simple)	1
Total Processing Function	14
Total Complexity Points	20
	Man-days Weighting
Programming Know-how	1.00
Job Knowledge	1.25
Total Man-days Weighting	2.25

Est. Programming Time = Complexity X Man-days Weighting
= 20 X 2.25
= 45 Man-days

Since this is actual *work* time it must be recognized that *scheduled* time will be expanded by factors for loss and nonproject activity, just as indicated in the section on systems analysis.

Szweda uses a loss factor of 10 percent and a nonproject factor of 25 percent to determine schedule time as follows:

Estimated Programming Time   45 Man-days
Loss Factor Calculation
   Loss Factor Time = Est. Programming Time × Est. Loss Factor
              = 45 Man-days × 10 percent
              = 4.50 Man-days
Nonproject Factor Time Calculation
   Nonproject Factor Time
              = Est. Programming Time × Est. Nonproject Factor
              = 45 × 25 percent
              = 11.25 Man-days
Optimal Project Time (Man-days)
   Est. Programming Time   45.00 Man-days
   Loss Factor Time   4.50
   Nonproject Factor Time   + 11.25
   Total Optimal Project Time   60.75 Man-days

A simplified form of this approach is illustrated by Figure 13. This format is used by several large companies for estimating applications programming.

Schedule time estimates developed by any of these methods should then be plotted using either a format similar to Figure 10 or with the use of a PERT network to determine the estimated elapsed time to completion.

Other Resources

Several resources other than analyst and programmer personnel should be considered in the estimating process. One of the most significant of these is computer time. Unfortunately, no universal standard is applicable to estimating computer time since the experience of one installation is rarely, if ever, transferable to another.

PROGRAMMING ESTIMATING WORKSHEET

Project _____ Sub-Code Number _____ Name _____

Program _____ Estimated By _____ Date_____

A. Input and Output Files

Single Format Files   (Number of Files)_____ X 1 = _____

Multiple Format Files   (Number of Files)_____ X 1.5 = _____

Reports   (Number of Files) _____ X 1.5 = _____

A Total _____

B. Processing Complexity

	Simple	Average	Complex	
Data Restructuring	1	3	6	_____
Condition Checking	1	4	8	_____
Data Retrieval and Presentation	2	5	9	_____
Calculation	1	3	6	_____
Linkage & Checkpoint	1	3	6	_____

B Total _____

C. Programmer Competance

	High	Low
Applications Programmer	0.75	1.00
Senior Applications Programmer	1.00	1.25
Lead Applications Programmer	1.35	1.60

C Total _____

D. Programmer Knowledge

Knowledge Available	Knowledge Required		
	Much	Average	Little
Much	0.45	0.20	0.00
Average	0.65	0.35	0.00
Little	0.85	0.50	0.20

D Total _____

A_____ + B_____ = _____
C_____ + D_____ = _____   } AB _____ X CD _____ = _____ Total Man Days

Programming Task Requirements

Program Logic	20%		= _____
Coding	30%	X _____Total Man Days	= _____
Testing	40%		= _____
Documentation	10%		= _____

Figure 13

Factors which influence compile time for programs include the:

computer hardware

operating system

compiler

use of diagnostic aids and program development tools

use of linked library routines

job mix running during a compilation

In addition to these, testing of programs is influenced by factors that include the number of files used and channel contention. (An overall influence on the programming effort is also found in the turnaround time for compiles and tests or use of on-line programming.) As a result of these influences, each organization must develop standards for estimating based upon its own experience.

Standards for compiling programs can be developed with relative ease by timing a significant sample of compilations during normal working hours and computing the computer time per instruction compiled. Standards for testing are more difficult, but may be developed by recording experience with operational programs having similar input/output and operational characteristics. Run time for these programs may be factored by the number of records processed to develop standards which may be projected for estimating test time on new programs.

Additional factors which should be included in estimates are:

- the design and printing of new forms
- new equipment or computer peripherals required
- outside purchases of computer time or consulting services
- user time for clerical work, test data preparation, and training
- use of a DBMS

The Twelve Cardinal Sins of Estimating

The following list of guidelines for the estimating process is provided as a reminder to aid in avoiding potential estimating failures.

1. Do not provide "firm" estimates for systems analysis. Always quote ranges of estimates or a single estimate *plus or minus* an appropriate percentage.

2. Do not provide estimates with insufficient information. As information on the problem becomes more complete, estimates can be refined.

3. Do not ignore risk factors. If the project indicates any organization or technical risks of successful completion, inform management as soon as they are known.

4. Never base estimates on your ability alone. Estimates should be reviewed for reasonableness by other members of the systems group, by programmers, and by supervisory personnel.

5. Do not assume that performance of individuals will remain constant if the size of the project team is increased.

6. Do not estimate more than 65 percent productive time for extended periods of time when scheduling a project.

7. Do not spend more effort on estimating than the potential loss that could be incurred from a bad estimate.

8. Never assume that the project is complete when the system becomes operational. Include time for further debugging and user consultation after implementation in the original estimates.

9. Never assume that approvals will be obtained in a short time. Schedules should include at least one week for all major approval points.

10. Don't assume that Murphy's Law applies to everyone else. Constraints on resources, personnel, internal knowledge and capability, computer time, and management considerations should be attached to estimates. The assumptions used in creating the estimates should appear in detail.

11. Don't assume that small changes requested during the project will not affect the estimate. The cumulative impact of small changes may be disastrous. Establish a "design freeze" point after which all requested changes must be reviewed for impact on the estimated cost and schedule.

12. Don't assume that experience in one environment is directly transferable to another. Review standards for estimating periodically as the environment, personnel, and software change.

Summary

Management must know the estimated cost of systems development and implementation in order to make proper economic decisions. Experience and evidence, however, indicate that the specification phase of system development cannot be reliably estimated. The cost of the balance of the system definition can be estimated with some reliability and the programming can be estimated upon completion of the program specifications.

To achieve maximum management satisfaction with system implementation efforts, the following procedure is recommended.

1. Establish system and reporting requirements and specifications through the use of an activity phase completely independent of the system definition phase. This can be done by establishing a system specification group within the "customer" organization or by devoting systems analyst personnel from the EDP systems group to such an effort *before an estimate is required.*

2. Once a system specification has been completed *in writing,* a reliable estimate of the systems work required for implementation can be prepared. This can be accompanied by a tentative estimate of programming effort, but since the programs have not yet been designed, no reliable estimate can be made.

3. Upon completion of program specifications, a reliable estimate of the programming cost can be prepared based on methods outlined in this article.

Two rules are basic to successful measurement of performance against estimates. First, reliable estimates cannot be prepared without written specifications of the work to be performed. Second, changes in the scope or specifications must be adequately reflected by changes to the original estimate.

Finally, recognize that the best worked-out estimate is still a "guess." The single most important ingredient in any estimating process is the experience of the estimator.

Footnotes

1. Pietrasanta, Alfred M., "Resource Analysis of Computer Program System Development," from *On the Management of Computer Programming* edited by G. F. Weinwurm, © 1970 Litton Educational Publishing, Inc. Reprinted by permission of Van Nostrand Reinhold Co., p. 74.
2. *Ibid.*, p. 80.
3. *Ibid.*, p. 81.
4. *Ibid.*, p. 83.
5. Weinberg, Gerald M., *The Psychology of Computer Programming*, Van Nostrand Reinhold, 1971. p. 69.
6. Fried, Louis, "Don't Smother Your Project in People," *Management Advisor*, March–April, 1972, pp. 46–49.
7. Brandon, Dick H. and Gray, Max, *Project Control Standards*, New York: Brandon/Systems Press, 1970, p. 86.
8. Fried, Louis, *Ampex Project Guidelines Manual*, 1975, p. 101.4.1.
9. Lecht, Charles P., "Management of Computer Programming Projects," New York: American Management Association, 1967, p. 50.
10. Brandon, Dick H., "Management Standards for Data Processing," New Jersey: Van Nostrand Co., 1963, pp. 34–36
11. Dearden, John, "Computers in Business Management," Illinois: Dow-Jones Irwin, Inc., 1966, pp. 164–166.
12. Brandon, pp. 139–143.
13. Szweda, Ralph A., *Information Processing Management*, New York: Van Nostrand Reinhold Co., 1972. pp. 359–372.
14. Nelson, E. A., *Management Handbook for the Estimation of Computer Programming Costs*, Santa Monica, Cal.: SDC, (Commerce Clearinghouse No. AD648 750) 1967, pp. 119–131.
15. Software Sciences Corporation, *Dimensions in Data Processing*, New York: SSC, 1968. p. 6.
16. Brandon, Dick H., *Management Standards for Data Processing*, New Jersey: Van Nostrand Co., 1963, pp. 249–298.
17. RCA, *Manpower Management Techniques*, RCA internal publication, 1966.
18. Nelson, E. A., pp. 119–131.
19. Jeffries, S., *Internal Report*, Bourns, Inc., August 1968.
20. Donelson, William S., "Project Planning and Control," *Datamation*, June, 1976, pp. 72–80. Reprinted by permission of *Datamation* magazine, © Technical Publishing Co., a division of Dun-Donnelly Publishing Corp., A Dun & Bradstreet Company, 1976. All rights reserved.
21. Szweda, pp. 349–359.

SECTION 2   SETTING APPLICATION PRIORITIES

In the area of systems development two major concerns occupy the applications development manager. The first of these is obvious: getting the projects completed on time and within the estimated cost. The second, not equally obvious but perhaps even more important, is getting the *right* project done at the right time. Failure to assign the proper priority to projects may be the greatest cause of EDP management turnover.

There is no quicker way to arouse the ire of a user than to tell him that the task he considers "essential" cannot be done within a reasonable time because higher priorities have been assigned to another user's work. Of course, someone else's project is always "trivial."

With this constant contest for the allocation of scarce resources in mind, this section will describe the process of setting application priorities within the context of organizational and business constraints.

The Purpose of Business Systems

Priorities must be established in a manner that satisfies the perceived needs of management. For this reason it is necessary to explore the way that management views the need for (and purpose of) business systems.

There are two main functions of business systems. These are: (1) to inform or direct someone to do something, and (2) to inform someone of the fact that something has (or has not) been done.[1]

The information provided by a business system (which, in the language of EDP has come to be called a *management information system*) is used to satisfy an essential and basic requirement of good management: the requirement that each organizational unit and each person be held accountable for the satisfactory performance of his or her duties.

This implies that business systems provide the information that is the "raw material" for planning, organizing, staffing, directing, controlling, and the other classical management functions.

Logically, then, it can be seen that the business system is management's tool for applying and auditing conformity to organization policy as it has been established to accomplish the organization's objectives.

In most business organizations this objective is to provide a suitable return on the investment of the owners—an objective that can be measured objectively as profit. The purpose of a business is to provide service or a product of sufficient quality, on schedule, and within competitive price ranges so as to provide for the firm's survival and growth by making a suitable profit.

Any investment undertaken by the firm must be justified in terms of its eventual contribution to profit. (This includes charitable contributions when viewed in the overall perspective of the firm's place in the community.)

Therefore, management must properly view an investment in a business system in the same context as it would view an investment in a new plant, trading in a drill press for a newer model, or purchasing any tool which might contribute to profit.

Potential Applications

The priority-setting process operates on a broad spectrum of potential applications for an array of users. While many of the applications are proposed by users on their own initiative, the systems analyst must be prepared to examine these proposals for feasibility, extend the concepts of these proposals to enhance their profitability to the firm, propose alternative approaches, or suggest potential applications to the user. For these functions, the following guidelines are reviewed.

John Dearden, Professor of Business Administration at Harvard University, has analyzed and classified different kinds of business information in order to aid in the understanding of information systems.[2] These classifications appear as dichotomies of information function.

On the basis of these classifications, Dearden makes the following generalizations about business information.

1. Action, recurring, documentary, internal, historical information is the prime candidate for automation.

2. The timing and accuracy of action information is usually important.

3. Precise timing is not important to nonaction information.

4. Nonaction information is a prime candidate for elimination.

5. Nondocumentary information is just about impossible to control.

6. The higher the management decision, the more important becomes external information and future projection.

At the time Dearden wrote this he felt that nonrecurring information was usually not subject to automation. Since that time (1966) nonrecurring information has become increasingly susceptible to automation. However, the other generalizations he developed remain valid and provide a guide to system selection.

A brief overview of potential applications to which these classifications apply follows.

Marketing Systems
  Customer analysis
  Product analysis (and product by customer)
  Sales analysis and projections from orders
  Geographical sales analysis
Engineering Systems
  Configuration control
  Drawing control
  Engineering change order control
  Text editing for product manuals
  On-line designing aids
  Curve plotting for mathematical analysis
Manufacturing or Logistics Systems
  Shop order status reporting
  Procurement system
  Material requirements planning
  Shop loading (queuing analysis)
  Inventory control
Personnel Information Systems
  Personnel information
  Automated review systems
  EEOC reports
  Benefits reports to employees
  Skills inventory
Research Systems
  "Key word in context" files
  Library systems
Financial Systems
  Cash flow analysis
  Accounts payable
  Accounts receivable
  Cost accounting
  Budgeting
  General ledger
  Fixed assets control and depreciation
  Stockholder records, proxy voting
  Physical inventory
  Customs reporting
  Check reconciliation
Strategic Planning
  Business simulations
  Return on investment analysis
  Present value analysis

The above list is necessarily brief and incomplete. There are a host of applications relating to specialized industries (menu planning, demand deposit accounting, trust management, stock portfolio analysis, cattle feed formulation, etc.). The analyst is cautioned to look for relationships between the applications in order to eliminate data redundancy and its associated cost.

The decision as to which system to automate may be crucial to the success of the data processing department. A simple application may have little payback and may delay the implementation of a more important system. On the other hand, a very large, complex application may result in management dissatisfaction because of the length of time it takes to implement and because users may not have had the skills necessary to absorb the changes to operations required by the new system.

Some things to remember when selecting projects are:

1. User sponsorship of the system is essential to successful implementation. Users must be "sold" on the system.

2. The probabilities are high that product-related systems will contribute more to profit than administrative systems.[3]

3. The projects selected should be technically feasible and not beyond the capability of the MIS staff.

4. Proposed systems should pass some test of economic feasibility.

Criteria for Project Selection

Selecting projects is a matter of choices—managerial choices and decisions. This implies a selection between available alternatives. The best decisions are made when these alternatives are presented in two senses:

• Alternative projects for differing purposes (e.g., accounts payable compared to shop floor control or order entry).

• Alternative approaches to the same system (e.g., batch processing, on-line processing, manual).

In this context it should always be noted that choosing to retain the present methods or *not* selecting a new project also constitutes a managerial decision. Therefore these are very real alternatives and must be presented as such.

The decisions involved in project selection are based on managerial criteria that may be clearly documented, may have been implied from previous selection processes, or may only be known to the decision makers themselves.

The analyst must attempt to satisfy these criteria. However, if they are unknown to the analyst, the task of selection is much more difficult. Identification of the criteria that will be used for project selection becomes the analyst's first task.

This should be approached by requesting concerned management to define their criteria for project selection in three areas: qualitative, institutional, and quantitative. The definitions received may not be complete or may be ambiguous at first. Several iterations may be necessary to obtain a workable set of selection criteria. It may even be necessary for the analyst to develop a draft of proposed criteria and circulate it for management approval. In any case, a final statement should include most of the following elements.

QUALITATIVE CRITERIA

As data processing applications have become increasingly sophisticated there has been a tendency to explore areas beyond the simple use of a computer as a high-speed adding machine or clerk. Justification of these new applications cannot be stated in the straightforward economic terms of the older systems. For example, it is doubtful that an on-line airline reservation system could be justified in terms of clerical savings alone. However, if customer satisfaction, government regulations on flight booking, profitable plane loading factors, and competition are considered, *there may have been no other way to continue the operation of the business without the system.* The so-called intangibles are crucial to the business.

Qualitative factors for systems used in the operation of the firm (production control, inventory control, etc.) are readily apparent. Successful applications in these areas are dependent on the speed, quality and accuracy of transaction input and subsequent processing and reporting. A production control report containing a high error rate can severely damage the productive capacity of the firm. The same report, if completely correct, but issued too late for use by production planners or line foremen, is useless.

In data processing, as in automobiles, however, one must remember that speed costs money. The solution cannot be inappropriate to the problem. For example, on-line processing of a general ledger system used to produce monthly reports probably represents some degree of "overkill."

Another area in which qualitative factors may have a major influence on project selection is the impact of competition. Some hotel chains have attempted to justify the use of on-line reservation systems on competitive, rather than economic grounds. For some, the cost of operating these systems has been so disproportionately high that they have been forced to abandon the system. Nevertheless, the selection of the project was made on the basis of competitive factors. Using the factor of competition as the *major* criteria may be dangerous, but it is certainly a valid criteria. Other examples have been more successful when supported by economic benefits.

Where this is a factor, management must weigh the potential benefits and may find a preference for a project with a lower quantifiable dollar benefit that provides a competitive edge in their industry.

In some ways the competitive factor is closely associated with another intangible, that of prestige. The public relations effect on the image of the firm is often considered to be related to the modern appearance projected. A highly visible application, such as computerized billing, may gain points in the selection process because of its expected impact on the firm's image. Again, this criteria should be handled with care. Using the same example, automated billing systems have damaged the image of the firm as frequently as they have helped.

Systems that have high public visibility should also consider another criteria, that of service. Those systems that provide a service to the ultimate user as well as to the firm have a better chance of contributing to the image and competitive stance of the firm. One example of this is shown by a California bank that provides customers with a statement listing the checks by the customers' check numbers as an aid to balancing their checkbooks. Another banking example is immediate on-line verification of account balances provided by the Bank of America system in California. This system not only helps the tellers, but allows a customer to cash a check in any branch in the state without waiting.

The last area of qualitative criteria to be explored is that of management decision-making. This area may be approached in two ways. First, systems that automate the decision-making process may show both tangible and intangible benefits. The classic example of this is the use in inventory systems of economic order quantity analysis or min-max routines. Second, improving the quality of information and the manner in which it is presented to management may serve to improve the quality of decision-making. One significant area in which this approach has been used is in cash management. By-products of the accounts receivable and accounts payable systems have been used to maximize the ability to make short-term investments, thus adding to the earning power of the firm.

While complex simulation systems and extremely flexible financial analysis systems have been developed, it is not necessary to go that far to aid in decision-making. Such a relatively simple idea as producing summary reports in graphic form can aid management by reducing the time needed for the user to analyze the content of the report and assimilate it for decision-making purposes.

INSTITUTIONAL CRITERIA

Where the systems development group operates within the environment of the firm, the firm operates within the broader environment of society. Both these environments impose constraints on the selection of applications.

Within the firm there is a need to maintain an equity—a balance—among users. An overemphasis on product-oriented applications to the virtual exclusion of financial or administrative applications will tend to create a body of unhappy managers. One consideration then is to avoid committing all system development resources to application for a single set of users. Even if some users are not disturbed by a lack of attention, a significant potential for improvement or savings may be missed by ignoring the need for balance.

Also within the firm there is a requirement to develop systems that are congruent with the policies and objectives of the organization. No proposed application that violates these can be successful. However, the analyst and the MIS manager must be careful to avoid a rigid interpretation of corporate policy and objectives. For example, during the fuel shortage of 1973 several firms developed car-pooling systems and made them available to the communities in which the firms operated. While the selection of these projects may have had no relationship to the profitability of the firm, they were apparently seen as being within the objectives of the firm in terms of meeting its social responsibility.

The lesson from this is that the policies and objectives of the firm *are what top management says they are,* and that their interpretation may change with time, circumstance, and personality. Reasonable projects must be proposed to managmement in conceptual form to test the boundaries of policy and corporate objectives when changes in the environment indicate changes in interpretation.

Consideration of the above institutional factors raises one other that many would prefer not to mention. The internal political environment of an organization may dictate certain constraints on application selection. For example, in one situation alternative means for solving the same application problem were presented. One approach proposed an on-line system to a centralized data base. The other proposed the use of minicomputers and a distributed data base. Both systems appeared to be economically feasible but the on-line approach would have cost significantly more. A top corporate official insisted that he wanted "centralized" data processing and therefore refused to consider the less expensive proposal. The users, who preferred the less expensive, minicomputer proposal were forced to accept the other system. Political feasibility has a powerful impact on the selection process.

One factor that might not normally be considered under institutional criteria is hardware. However, when a firm purchases a computer with the intent of achieving a certain payback, an exceptional justification would be required for replacement before the return on investment is gained. In this sense the commitment to the hardware places a constraint upon implementation of applications that might exceed its capacity.

Finally, one must consider the human element as it applies to constraints on available resources. Some questions that apply to application selection in this regard are:

Do the skills exist on the staff to properly implement the project?

If consultants are to be used, do the skills exist to monitor their work, implement the product, and maintain the system thereafter?

Is the user staff capable of adapting to and operating the system after implementation?[4]

QUANTITATIVE CRITERIA

A detailed examination of cost-benefit analysis is presented in another section, but a brief overview is appropriate in a discussion of project selection. Quantitative criteria simply means criteria that have been stated in terms of the explicit cost/earning relationship for a project. What we are really interested in is the effect on the firm's profit and loss statement. So quantitative factors are presented in terms of dollars which have been estimated with a reasonable degree of confidence.

Any analysis of this type depends upon a baseline for comparison. This baseline is provided by the costs of the existing method. A detailed feasibility study will start with a determination of present costs. However, in performing a preliminary comparison for project selection, it is usual to concentrate on potential savings without such a detailed study.

The comparison of the present method with one or more alternative approaches should consider the:

Estimated cost of project development and implementation.

Before tax earnings or savings expected.

Monthly cash flow of the above factors.

Payback period.

Return on investment.

Management may establish criteria in terms of payback period, return on investment, and P & L impact. Individual firms vary in their treatment of project development costs. Some may expense these costs while others capitalize them. The impact on the P & L will vary. The accounting department of the firm should be consulted on the best manner in which to present this analysis.

Some firms prefer to use a comparison that discounts the cash flow to present value. Others are more concerned with the immediate impact on cash flow. Again, the accounting department should be consulted for the manner in which to present this information.

Many firms allocate the cost of data processing development and operation. This can result in a confusion of allocated cost vs. "real" dollars. Project selection should always be based on a comparison of out-of-pocket costs and real savings rather than on internally allocated costs or savings derived from a few minutes time of many individuals.

For this reason the sponsorship and *commitment* of the user are necessary. Ultimately the user will be held responsible for producing the savings envisioned by the proposal.

Opportunity cost is another concept frequently used by management in examining alternative investments. Opportunity cost (or *loss*) may be defined as that profit foregone as a result of selecting a course of action other than that in which a maximum profit could be realized. Many firms use the interest income that their money could earn as a minimum guide to the earnings expected from any other investment. So, for example, if money could be invested in securities at a before-tax return of ten percent, then management would require a projected return of greater than ten percent for any proposed investment in the business. Considering a decision to implement a new system in the same light as any other investment would lead to viewing this decision from the standpoint of opportunity cost.

Setting Application Priorities

The reason for the foregoing examination of system purposes and selection criteria becomes apparent from one continuous theme, that of decision-making. The decision-making action culminates in the act of setting priorities. However, it can be seen that setting priorities for applications is not merely the final act of decision-making, but is an extensive process which requires many individuals in the firm to participate. This portion deals with the responsibilities of the individuals involved in the process.

PLANNING FOR PRIORITY SETTING

Whether the concern is with selecting an alternative for the implementation of a single application or choosing from among a list of competing applications, the process of amassing and coordinating the documentation and information necessary for final decision-making takes time and effort. The first responsibility is that of the director of MIS (or whoever is the top data processing executive) to allocate the necessary personnel and budget to the planning and application selection process. We will first examine the broader case of selection among applications, dealing with selection between alternative approaches to a single system later in the portfolio.

Initially, the director, with a committee of his managers and key application analysts should perform a brief survey of potential applications. This survey should simply identify all potential projects for new or replacement systems. This survey can be aided by informal discussions with users and/or potential users. At this point no application idea should be discarded as unfeasible.

This same committee should then establish a budget and a proposed plan for accomplishing the steps in the selection process that will be described in the following paragraphs. This budget and plan should be presented to top management for approval. Timing here is important. An ideal time to present this proposal is when annual budgets are being constructed.

A FEW WORDS ABOUT TOP MANAGEMENT

Even in a highly centralized company where final budgetary decisions are made only by the president, the support and understanding of users is both desirable and necessary.

Forming an MIS steering committee composed of the key executives from user groups can aid in obtaining this support. This steering committee usually has the following duties:

• Using its collective knowledge of the firm's strategic and tactical plans, it determines the appropriate level of EDP expenditure and capability that it desires.

• It approves specific proposals for acquisition of major items of DP equipment.

• It approves long- and short-range DP plans.

- It selects the application projects to be done.

- It determines project priorities.

- It reviews project progress and determines whether or not projects should continue or be abandoned.

- It resolves territorial and political conflicts arising from the impact of new systems.[5]

The support and weight of opinion expressed by this committee usually has considerable impact on final budget approval. This group expresses a consensus on what they feel is the level of EDP support necessary for the members to adequately perform their functions.

DOCUMENTING ALTERNATIVE PROJECTS

Once the necessary effort has been approved, the project selection process may actually begin. Analysts are assigned to each potential application on the list initially established.

Background investigation is performed through user interviews, examination of existing documents and reports, examination of accounting records and any other sources deemed necessary to *briefly* describe the current method of operation and the current costs of each application. The objectives of a new system are identified and a proposed method of achieving these objectives (through system development, purchase of a package, etc.) is documented. The estimated costs of implementation and future operation of the proposed method are constructed, and the benefits to be derived from the project are identified and documented. Finally, a rough plan for project implementation is developed to indicate the expected time and cost for the project.

The result of this process should be a summary for presentation to management that will include:

1. A description of project objectives.

2. An analysis of expected costs and benefits.

3. Qualitative and institutional factors.

4. A rough plan for the use of resources to perform the project.

At this stage of project selection we are dealing with rough estimates and approximations. It should be made clear that these do not constitute firm commitments and that detailed feasibility studies will be performed prior to final project approval. Nevertheless, certain key points should be covered in each section of documentation for a proposed application.

The section on objectives should state (in narrative form) the purposes to be served by the project, the nature of the new system, the technical feasibility of the project, the estimated overall economic impact, and the place of the project in relation to corporate goals and objectives.

The section on costs and benefits should include not only the financial impact (which may be presented in both a tabular and narrative form, but some description of the qualitative and institutional benefits to be gained by implementation of the system.

Finally, a rough approximation should be made in both narrative and graphic form of a plan for project development and implementation. This should include a development plan, a conversion plan, and an operating plan with some comment on the nature and extent of user participation required.

It is good for purposes of presentation to summarize the essence of these sections into a short statement of conclusions to be placed at the beginning of the presentation.

ESTABLISHING SELECTION CRITERIA

Concurrently with the investigation of potential applications, it is the responsibility of the director of MIS, or his designated representative, to document the selection criteria that will be used by management for evaluating applications. This process has been described previously, but if a steering committee has been formed, the members of this committee should be consulted on selection criteria.

PRE-SCREENING POTENTIAL APPLICATIONS

Having established and documented the selection criteria, the potential applications should be screened for conformity and the manner in which they satisfy these criteria. This screening should be done by the director of MIS with a committee of his managers and key analysts. The pre-screening has two purposes. First, any proposed application that cannot pass the test of the criteria should be abandoned. (Note that upon examination of the proposed applications the criteria may indicate futher avenues of study which should be performed before a final decision to eliminate the application is made.)

The second objective is to assure that the proposals are satisfactory for presentation to management and that the survey does not result in too many proposals.

At this stage, no more than six applications should remain for consideration by management in the priority setting process. This does not mean that the balance of applications are not to be considered at some time in the future. However, those which offer the greatest benefit and return on investment should be emphasized.

USER REVIEWS

If users were involved in the original survey, they should be informed of the results of the pre-screening. The remaining high payback application proposals should be reviewed with the users in such a manner as to cover all detail available at this point. The intent of this review is to gain any user comments that might substantially affect the content of the proposal, familiarize the user with the proposed application approach, verify the anticipated benefits, and obtain the user's commitment to support the proposal to top management.

The user should understand that at this point the commitment extends only to obtaining top management approval for considering the project as a high priority and authorization of an appropriate feasibility study. No commitment is being made by either party as to resources, schedule, or benefits until completion of the feasibility study.

On the basis of the user review, the analyst should refine the documentation and prepare final documentation for presentation.

PREPARING THE PRESENTATION

A presentation to top management and/or the MIS steering committee is the next step. This presentation should contain the following elements.

1. The documented proposals for the application projects selected. These should be prepared with a one-page cover summary of the costs and major benefits for each project.

2. A proposed implementation plan. Preferably in graphic form, the implementation plan should suggest the sequence in which the high priority projects should be approached, the EDP manpower and equipment resources anticipated, and a tentative schedule for project development and implementation. On the basis of this planning material a budget indicating headcount and dollars should be drawn up covering the period of the tentative schedule.

The implementation plan is constructed by the MIS director with the support of the EDP managers and analysts after review of the application proposals which have been prepared by the analysts. Note: It is essential that the EDP operations manager be included in this planning process to assure that operations resources will be adequate for support of the selected projects.

MANAGEMENT REVIEW

The complete proposal is now presented to the MIS steering committee and/or top management. Some suggestions for this presentation are:

1. Wherever possible use visual aids (flip charts, slides, etc.) so as to center the attention of the attendees.

2. Rehearse the presentation beforehand and check the timing. Try to keep the presentation brief.

3. Set aside enough time for the meeting to cover the presentation and expected discussion.

4. Designate someone from the EDP staff to act as a secretary for the meeting. The secretary's task is to record any decisions made and to note any questions raised that cannot be answered during the course of the meeting.

5. If possible, get the user representative to the meeting to make the presentation for his application. A convinced user will be able to "sell" a project to management more easily than someone from the MIS group.

At the conclusion of the meeting review the decisions briefly with the attendees. If another meeting is necessary to reach final conclusions, try to schedule it before this meeting concludes.

After the meeting document and publish the results, distributing this information to all concerned parties.

Documentation of meeting results should include the priorities established for each application, responses to any unanswered questions (if a second meeting has not been called for this), a copy of the agreed-upon schedule for projects, and a list of the attendees at the meeting.

SELECTING ALTERNATIVE APPROACHES TO A SINGLE SYSTEM

Initially it might appear that the process of setting priorities applies only to contention between different applications. Upon closer examination of single applications, however, we find that these may be segmented and priorities established within a project. It is the task of the analyst or project manager to determine for each proposed application two things: 1) can the application be segmented either by partial implementation or by installing successively more sophisticated versions and 2) do circumstances exist that would make such segmentation desirable?

Several circumstances could warrant segmentation of a project. There may be insufficient budget to accomplish all objectives within the planned period. There may be a greater payback on some aspects of the application than on others. The user may have an emotional preference for specific functions. Some functions may require faster implementation if *any* benefit is to be obtained. The user may not be able to adapt to a highly sophisticated system in one jump, but may feel it necessary to install simpler functions first. Finally, the budget or capability of the resources of the EDP group may prevent implementation of a complete system in the course of the initial project.

If any of these considerations exist, they should be reviewed with the user(s) to determine the best course of action. The best approach is to establish a project steering committee consisting of representatives from the user groups and from EDP. A presentation of the alternatives and the cost and benefit of each alternative should be made to the committee by the analyst/project manager. The project steering committee would then establish the priorities and select the course of action in the same manner as the MIS steering committee operated.

SOMETIMES THERE ARE NO CHOICES

Some years ago the state of California passed legislation to provide for withholding state income tax from employee paychecks. Throughout the state there was a sudden flurry of activity as firms that did not have this type of capability built into their payroll systems started projects to modify or replace their existing systems.

In another case, the Insurance Commissioner of the state of Ohio required all companies in one segment of the insurance business to initiate and maintain certain record keeping functions. Again, the affected firms had to find a way to comply.

In another case, a firm involved in a lawsuit had to find a way to collate and cross reference voluminous records for presentation to the court. This could only be approached through an EDP system.

These examples are provided to indicate that the priority setting process can be drastically influenced by external factors. When such conditions arise the only course of action is to inform all affected users of the impact on existing project priorities and comply with the demands of the emergency. Sometimes there are no choices.

Summary

The single, most important fact in setting priorities is to remember that the final decision on application priorities is the responsibility (and right) of the top management of the organization. The responsibil-

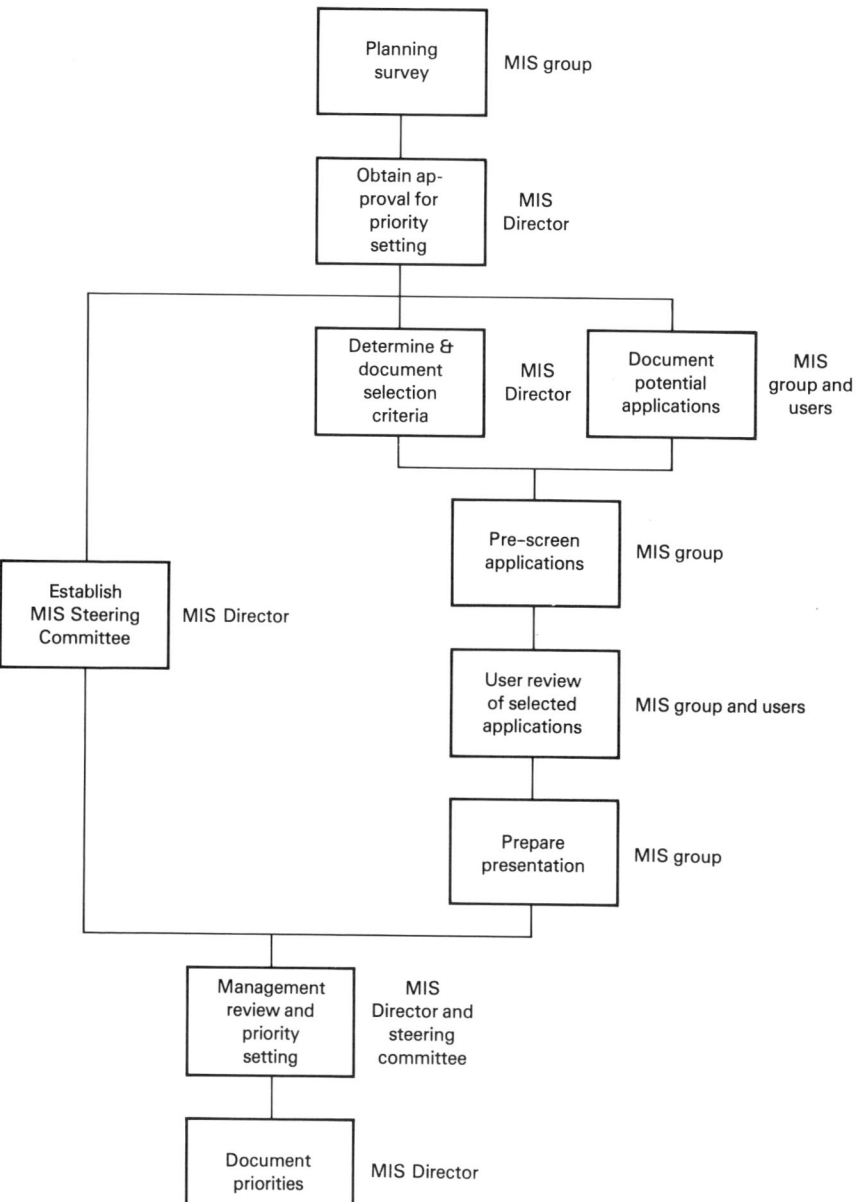

Figure 14. The application priority setting process.

ity of the EDP group is to provide all the necessary information (and their recommendations) to assure that the management decision is the optimal one for the organization as a whole.

Some key concepts to remember in the process of selecting and establishing priorities for applications are the following:

- Criteria for project selection must be clearly defined and documented. These criteria should include qualitative, institutional, and quantitative considerations.

- Applications must conform to the objectives of the firm. These objectives do not remain constant.

- The process of application selection and setting priorities takes time and money. Management must approve the cost of this process.

- The use of steering committees can expedite priority setting and improve the chances for project success.

- Formal documentation throughout the priority setting process not only simplifies the process but provides initial groundwork for subsequent feasibility studies and a file of future applications in those that are weeded out in the pre-screening.

- Presenting too many alternatives to management may result in a suboptimal decision or no decision.

- User understanding and sponsorship of the proposed applications is essential to success.

Finally, it should be noted that priority setting is not a one-time task. It should be repeated at each time that the resources become available to start a new project. The process is simpler after priorities have been established the first time since most of the documentation already exists. Only proposed implementation schedules and budgets must be redrawn.

In each subsequent review of priorities, existing projects in process should be reviewed along with proposed new projects. Management criteria, objectives and priorities may change in the interval between reviews.

Footnotes

1. Smith, Paul T., *Computers, Systems, and Profits*, New York: American Management Association, 1969. p. 78.

2. Dearden, John, *Computers in Business Management*, Dow Jones–Irwin, 1966. pp. 115–117.

3. Couger, Daniel J., "The Benefit Side of Cost/Benefit Analysis," *Data Processing Management Series*, Auerbach Publishers, 1975. No. 1-01-07, p. 10.

4. Several concepts in this section have been derived from M. H. Schwartz, "Computer Project Selection in the Business Enterprise," *Design and Management of Information Systems*, David H. Li, ed., Chicago: Science Research Assoc., 1972, pp. 122–135.

5. Fried, Louis, "EDP Steering Committees," *Data Processing Management Series*, Auerbach Publishers, 1975. No. 1-04-06, p. 2.

SECTION 3   PURCHASING AND INSTALLING SOFTWARE PACKAGES

Purchasing

Commercial software packages have become a major market factor in the data processing industry. Most packages are well designed, well documented, and usually debugged. They permit the installation of new systems for as little as one-fifth of the cost of in-house development. They allow relatively small installations to get maximum benefit from a limited programming staff and good data throughput from a well-designed system. And they permit management to obtain a reasonably reliable estimate of cost for systems and to establish dependable schedules for implementation.

To the buyer the package generally represents benefits in cost and reliability. To the systems analyst and programmer, the package represents an opportunity to avoid the waste associated with reinventing systems that have been done over and over again. For instance, any in-house programmer who develops a new payroll system is probably dissipating his company's money and his own time. Such professional talent can more suitably be expended on development of systems unique to the organization.

In addition to these benefits, the purchaser who deals with a reliable vendor insures himself against the risks associated with maintaining the package. If he loses or fails to develop the ability to maintain the package in house, he can usually rely on vendor personnel to maintain or modify the system for him.

With all these benefits, there is no question about the worth of buying appropriate program packages to fulfill system needs. The real questions are how to select the appropriate package and how to establish the criteria by which alternative packages can be evaluated.

ORGANIZATION

Once the need for system improvement has been determined, an evaluation of alternative methods for this improvement is required to prepare a proposal for management's approval. The process of evaluating and selecting a software package, presented in flowchart form on page 131, is a distinct segment of the task of preparing that proposal. The experience of several firms indicates that a project-team approach to the preparation of the proposal is usually most successful. This project team is usually composed of members of the department requiring the system and members of the company's systems staff. The project manager may come from either group as long as his responsibility is clearly defined. In organizations with no systems staff, the system user may have to perform all functions in the project team.

Systems evaluation requires knowledge of the intended applications, general systems design, and programming. If all of these capabilities are not available in house, it is advisable to hire an independent consultant—one other than the package vendor—to provide the missing capabilities.

EVALUATION

The first step in the evaluation process is to indicate such general system requirements as:

• *Scope of the system.* What functions will the system perform and which areas of the organization will it service?

• *System characteristics.* List as many required system characteristics as possible. Be specific in the system requirements.

• *Resources needed for system operation.* Specify the resources in manpower and money that the company can afford for both implementation and operation of the system.

• *Anticipated system benefits.*

At this point it is feasible to find and start investigating the commercial program packages available for any given application. Reference works, which may save a great deal of costly search time, can help locate these packages. New software packages are described in most trade magazines. In addition, consultants and programming contractors can frequently help locate appropriate packages.

Software vendors should then be contacted and requested to provide descriptive material on their systems. While most vendors' sales personnel would prefer direct personal contact at this point, it is generally more practical to perform some preliminary screening based on the system documentation alone. This preliminary screening, based on the established general system requirements, should be performed by the project team—the intention being to reduce the number of packages being considered to those that appear most likely to meet the needs of the organization.

The next phase of evaluation is a detailed examination of the capabilities and features of each package. As the packages are examined, the general list of characteristics can be refined to include more detailed features.

System Interaction Corporation, publishers of *Software Packages: An Encyclopedic Guide,* suggest that weighting factors and points be assigned to these characteristics to facilitate the comparison of the program packages. An arbitrary value or weight factor should be assigned to each selection criterion. For example, cost may be assigned a value of

25 QUESTIONS TO ASK ABOUT SOFTWARE PACKAGES

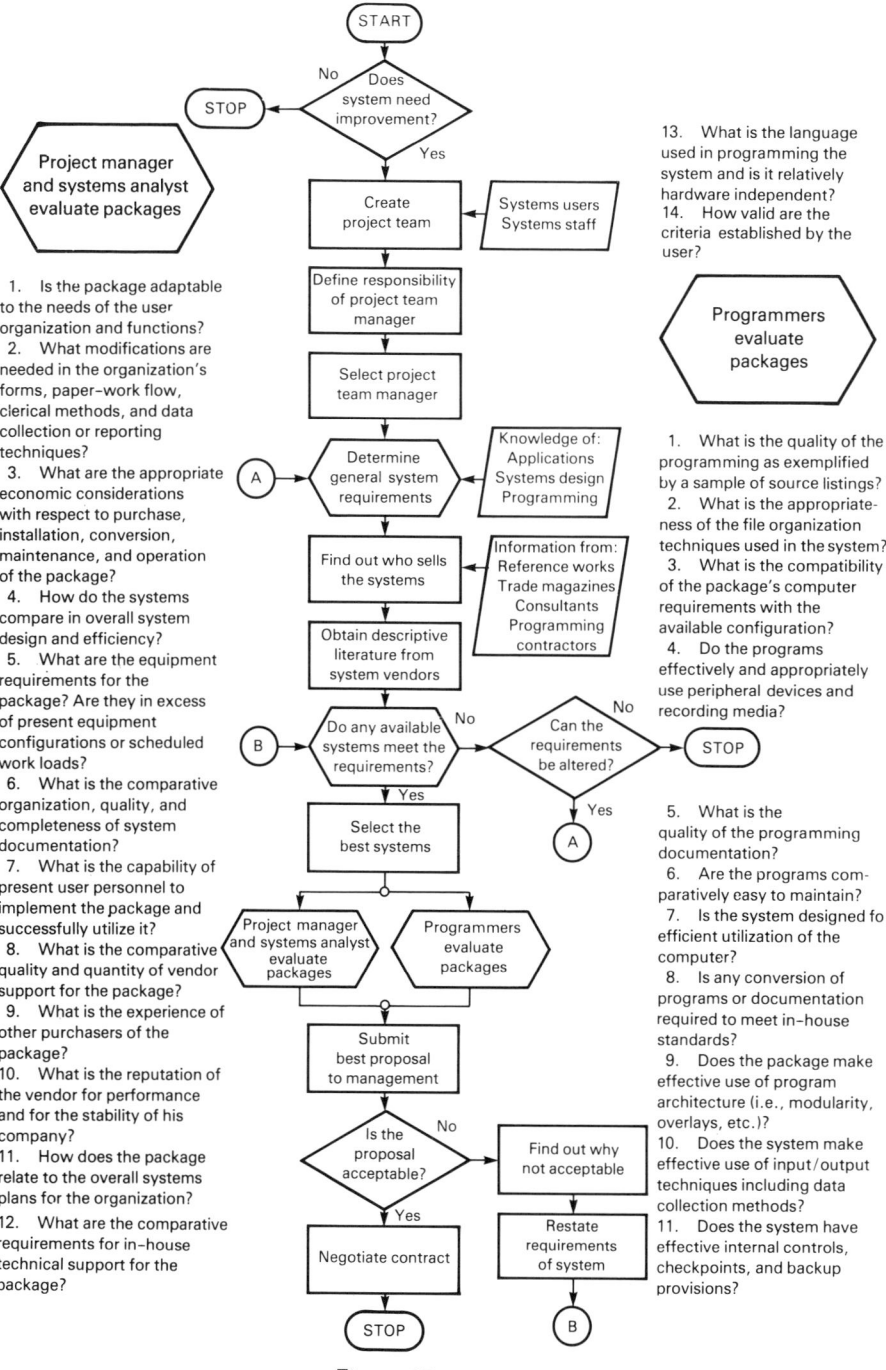

Project manager and systems analyst evaluate packages

1. Is the package adaptable to the needs of the user organization and functions?
2. What modifications are needed in the organization's forms, paper-work flow, clerical methods, and data collection or reporting techniques?
3. What are the appropriate economic considerations with respect to purchase, installation, conversion, maintenance, and operation of the package?
4. How do the systems compare in overall system design and efficiency?
5. What are the equipment requirements for the package? Are they in excess of present equipment configurations or scheduled work loads?
6. What is the comparative organization, quality, and completeness of system documentation?
7. What is the capability of present user personnel to implement the package and successfully utilize it?
8. What is the comparative quality and quantity of vendor support for the package?
9. What is the experience of other purchasers of the package?
10. What is the reputation of the vendor for performance and for the stability of his company?
11. How does the package relate to the overall systems plans for the organization?
12. What are the comparative requirements for in-house technical support for the package?

13. What is the language used in programming the system and is it relatively hardware independent?
14. How valid are the criteria established by the user?

Programmers evaluate packages

1. What is the quality of the programming as exemplified by a sample of source listings?
2. What is the appropriateness of the file organization techniques used in the system?
3. What is the compatibility of the package's computer requirements with the available configuration?
4. Do the programs effectively and appropriately use peripheral devices and recording media?
5. What is the quality of the programming documentation?
6. Are the programs comparatively easy to maintain?
7. Is the system designed fo efficient utilization of the computer?
8. Is any conversion of programs or documentation required to meet in-house standards?
9. Does the package make effective use of program architecture (i.e., modularity, overlays, etc.)?
10. Does the system make effective use of input/output techniques including data collection methods?
11. Does the system have effective internal controls, checkpoints, and backup provisions?

Figure 15.

131

fifteen, while the use of COBOL may receive a value of three, and machine configuration a value of 90. Thus the package most closely meeting the overall requirements receives the maximum total number of points and the other packages are scaled down from there. More complex methods may be used, but in any method, weights or points should be assigned in advance of the comparative evaluation to insure objectivity.

Whether this weight analysis or a more subjective method is used, the project manager or a systems analyst must first independently, then comparatively, evaluate each package which passes the initial screening. Each system should also be rigorously evaluated by programming personnel.

To get complete answers to questions posed by the project manager, systems analyst, and programmers, it is usually necessary to work with vendors' sales and technical personnel. A detailed examination of the system by the in-house programming group or by a consultant requires samples of programs and programming documentation. It may even be necessary to prepare a sample of the organization's problem data and arrange for a test of the system. Most package vendors anticipate these requests and will accommodate the customer.

SELECTION

Comparative selection criteria should deal with the financial status of the buyer, the design and limitations of the system, and the system support capabilities of the vendors. The project team's preliminary screening should eliminate from consideration those packages which cost more than the purchasing organization has available. It is then necessary to compare packages on additional economic criteria. Besides determining the cost of each package, the buyer must calculate the cost of training user and maintenance personnel and the cost of maintaining the entire system. Cash flow and payback analyses should be conducted. Impact on the operating cost of the user organization and impact of the conversion from the existing system are additional economic parameters to be considered. The following questions should be raised to evaluate the vendors:

- How long has the company been in business?
- How many employees does it have?
- Did the company design the system or is it only marketing the system?
- What is the business, technical, and applications background of the members of the firm?

- Is the company profitable?
- Will the vendor support the installation of the package?
- Does the vendor include training of user and technical personnel in the package price?
- Is the user documentation well written and easy to understand?
- Will the vendor later support the system?

The comparative evaluation can be made by preparing a chart that lists criteria on one axis and competitive packages on another, weighting all criteria for each package, and comparing totals for all criteria for each package. Following program package selection, proposals are made to obtain management approval.

CONTRACTING

Package selection involves contract negotiation, except for relatively trivial software. Software package contracts should deal with the rights and obligations of both parties. It should treat areas of package ownership, warranties, and financial terms and conditions.

Many packages were originally developed as applications by individual computer users and not intended for the package market. These packages have subsequently been generalized to meet the needs of a broader market. In some instances, the program originator and the vendor are not the same. The agreement between the marketer of the program and the originator of the program may vary from direct sales to a commission. Furthermore, the agreement does not necessarily include a warranty by the originator of the software.

The right of the vendor to sell the package should be clearly stated in the contract and the customer should be relieved of any liability resulting from claims against the vendor by the program originator.

The vendor must warrant the performance of the system to meet the specifications of his system description and sales literature. While some vendors may seek to limit their liability by establishing a time limit on such warranties, many customers are successful in negotiating a warranty for the life of the product. If this cannot be done, the customer should at least assure himself of a warranty period which is long enough to adequately test every feature of the system.

The contract should cover improvements to the system for a given period of time. It should also assure that errors discovered and corrected at another user's site will be corrected at the customer's site. In addition, if major improvements or modifications are made to the system, a customer should be granted some favorable rate or option for upgrading his system.

Packages may be bought or leased, but either agreement generally requires limiting the use of the package to a single data processing facility. If a lease and purchase plan are available, the method suggested by a cash flow analysis should be selected. For a leased package, payment should begin with the first month of successful implementation. For a purchased system, final payment should be deferred until all features of the system have been successfully tested.

Installing

The average data processing user installing a software package for the first time will probably be extremely optimistic about the potential savings to be derived from this approach. If he has done an adequate job of research he has assured himself that the system is the best available match for his needs. He has determined that the firm he is dealing with is reputable and he has checked with other customers about their satisfaction with the package. He has reviewed the documentation and it appears to be better than that which is usually done in house. Finally, he has assured himself that the contract is equitable and that suitable guarantees exist.

The potential savings from installing a package, as contrasted to original in-house design and implementation, is considerable. The system design and documentation are already completed, the programming is done, and the system is often actually operating in other installations. The vendor provides training in the use of the system and has a competent staff of experienced professionals available for assisting in installation.

After careful consideration the data processing manager prepares an estimate of the installation cost and it is approved by management. The bad news will come later when it is discovered that the actual costs may be double or even triple the estimate before installation is completed. What happened?

A CASE HISTORY

An actual case involved the purchase of a system consisting of over 40 programs. The intent was to install it in four months from the original delivery date of the program tapes. The first problem encountered was that inadequate test and assembly time was available during regular working hours. Large blocks of time needed were only available on weekends.

An OS version of the system had been purchased and two tapes were delivered. One tape contained the JCL and test data, the second tape contained the source listings. After considerable difficulty trying to read these tapes under an OS system, it was determined from tape dumps that, while the proper OS programs and JCL were on the tape, the tapes had been created under a DOS operating system and therefore had DOS labels. Four weekend sessions were lost in trying to determine the problem and circumvent it before the vendor was notified.

Upon notification the vendor delivered the latest version of the OS system on tapes having OS labels. The tapes contained a program designed by the vendor for use in maintaining and updating source programs in the system. Documentation for this program was not delivered with the package and further delay was encountered in learning to use it.

Several more weekend sessions were used before the system source library was finally built. Upon completion of the source library, program compilation was started. The system used a modular approach which is normally advantageous. However, a module commonly used throughout the system indicated an error in compilation and prevented the subsequent compilation of a substantial number of programs. The vendor responded to notification with an immediate correction and compiling was resumed.

Two months after the starting date, the test data files supplied by the vendor were successfully created on disk. This effort was hampered by an almost complete lack of documentation on the test data itself. In an attempt to test the programs some of the following problems were encountered. A module was missing from one of the programs (this module was used elsewhere but the documentation did not indicate where it could be located). The JCL was not present for one program. The forms alignment feature did not work on several reports. The JCL provided did not allocate enough room for the test data files provided by the vendor. Testing had to be halted intermittently to provide space parameters for files. Control cards prepared according to the specifications were not accepted by the programs. One sort procedure defined a format that was not present. One sort did not have the output data set defined. One sort used twice in the system created duplicate data set numbers on the same volume. Punctuation was missing from JCL cards intermittently throughout the system. At several points the documentation did not match the programs as compiled.

It later developed that the system had been operating in several installations under DOS but that this was the first OS installation and the OS JCL had not been tested by the vendor before delivery. In addition, the vendor delivered Version V of the programs and documentation initially. A month later, when the vendor was requested to provide a new tape of the programs, he provided Version VI of the programs JCL, and test data, but he did not update the documentation.

By this time two and one-half months of the intended four-month schedule had elapsed. The manpower and machine time initially intended for use on conversion and program modification had been used on the initial compilation and test effort.

As if these problems were not enough, the project had yet to encounter some even more formidable obstacles. It was found that a basic difference between installing a software package and implementing an in-house system was in the degree of familiarity that systems personnel had with the elements of the system. When a system is designed and programmed in house, the analyst has a complete understanding of the system that he has designed and one or more programmers are familiar with the structure and logic of each program in the system. The analyst might have to work years to develop an equivalent understanding of the internal structure of the software package. As a result, the definition and programming of modifications to the package take considerably longer than what is customary for systems and programs designed in house. Under these conditions system specifications required three to ten times the number of hours originally estimated and programming required twice the hours estimated.

In repeated conferences, the system user gradually became more familiar with the characteristics of the system. As a result, additional changes were requested, exceeding in scope those that were anticipated when the package was originally selected.

The documentation of the software package was excellent. However, it was organized to provide maximum support in maintaining or modifying the system. Due to this type of organization the documentation was unsatisfactory as a training tool. If an analyst or programmer knew where to look, the documentation contained the answers he might be seeking. But he had to learn the system first to know where to look for answers.

The task of conversion was underestimated because the original data set contained errors, specific fields of the original data set had to be converted to fit field requirements in the new system, and some data elements required by the new system were not present in the original data set at all.

During conversion one key programmer left the firm. By this time the project had long past its original installation date and the analyst in charge of the project received his third notification to report for thirty days of jury duty.

As a result of the delays in installation, work on the new system was affected by year-end requirements. Annual reports required major amounts of computer time, limiting the test time available for the project. In addition, the old system required maintenance due to changes in business conditions and corporate requirements. The personnel working on the new system had to be diverted to the maintenance of the old system.

It was finally determined that the documentation delivered with the software package was not adequate for user training and operation. An operating manual for the system had to be written and published before system installation.

PLANNING FOR INSTALLATION

If the above case history sounds like a nightmare, it's only because it was. Every aspect of the installation task was grossly overrun. Although many of the problems may have been attributable to the vendor, it must be remembered that the buyer has the ultimate responsibility for successful installation. It may seem trite, but it is true to say that most of the problems could have been avoided with proper planning.

Other articles have dealt extensively with the problems of software package selection. They usually deal with the need for comparing the candidate package to other packages, checking with other users, investigating the reliability of the vendor, and developing mutually satisfactory contractual agreements. But it is likely that no caveat covered in these articles is as important as the need to develop a clear set of requirements for the package based on the company's own requirements. In theory, this dictum is almost absurdly obvious; in actuality, it is rarely acted upon.

Repeated experiences indicate that the potential for installation problems is directly related to the number of changes made to the software package. Therefore, the package selected should conform to the requirements of the organization or the organization should consider changing its operation to conform to the package. In addition, since all planned changes increase the possibility of error and delay, estimates for conversion and installation should include some evaluation of the risk factors.

One other item concerning package evaluation should be emphasized. This is a review of user documentation by the *actual user*. For example, if an accounting system is being selected the operating documentation for the accountant should be reviewed by an accountant. Most software packages are significantly deficient in this area of documentation and allowance must be included in the installation estimates to remedy this deficiency.

INSTALLATION SUGGESTIONS

At the Applied Data Research Users Conference in Princeton, N.J., December, 1971, several hundred software package users from across the United States voiced their observations on the pitfalls of installing software packages. Following is a compilation of their suggestions for avoiding installation problems divided into categories having to do with applications software packages, systems software packages, and general areas common to both.

Applications Software. As previously mentioned, user documentation is one of the weakest aspects of commercial software packages. It is generally necessary to create a user manual or handbook for the system. It is also normally necessary to recreate the computer operating documentation completely in order to conform to the installation's standards.

Installing a new system frequently provides the opportunity for changing input methods. If any such change involves a heavy contribution from user personnel (such as changing from forms-input-to-key-punch to user-input through on-line terminals) consideration should be given to changing the input technique only after the user has become accustomed to all the other aspects of the new system.

The testing and debugging of a package is significantly different from that of a system developed in house. The in-house system is normally tested program by program through a gradual development schedule before the whole system is available to test. On the other hand, because the package has all programs immediately available for testing, the entire system testing procedure is compressed and all programs are in a highly active test mode concurrently. General experience indicates that it is desirable to keep all package programs on a separate program library during the test phase and move them to the common library only after the parallel phase has begun.

The size of all data sets in tests or in actual operation should be carefully defined since many operating systems do not permit the overflow of stated data set areas. Overflows will abort the run creating delays in testing for production.

Specific personnel should be designated to act as liaison with the vendor. At least one of these people should be from the *actual* user organization.

Systems Software. Some systems software packages improve on capabilities that exist in the software normally supplied by the computer vendor. For this reason they provide an alternate method of accomplishing a given function. This is particularly true for high-level programming languages, program library methods, debugging aids, and other such software. Assuming that management desires to make the selected software package a standard, an all-out effort should be made to sell the product within the organization rather than simply demand that it be used. This "selling" approach must begin with thorough training of all personnel who will use the system.

A test run of the system should be made on a special project and all bugs found should be reported to the vendor. If they cannot be fixed before the system is used, they should be reported to the technical personnel using the system to avoid (or at least reduce) the frustration they might experience from encountering the bugs without any warning.

All users should be thoroughly informed about product capabilities and limitations so that no one expects more than the product can offer. Users should be urged to report any difficulties or suggestions.

Once management is satisfied that the product performs as intended, a standard requiring its use may be published. If practical, it should be made physically impossible *not* to use the new system by removing from the active library any previously used programs. If this is not possible then the authority to reject nonstandard input should be granted to the computer operations area.

Training of all technical personnel who will use the package is mandatory. Internal training documentation should be developed in a manner suited to the installation's needs and based on the vendor's reference material. A lesson plan for internal training sessions should be created and capable training personnel selected. It is frequently a good idea to conduct training sessions at a site other than the normal working environment. It is especially important that technicians have the opportunity immediately after initial training to use the package. This immediate direct experience serves to reinforce all previous orientation and education and to improve user acceptance.

Where possible, a book of examples covering a wide range of specific situations and environments should be created. This "cook book" approach can be an effective way to outline possible errors programmers might make and techniques for avoiding or solving those errors.

Technicians and programmers frequently feel that some software packages, e.g., high-level languages, pose a threat to their role and to their marketable skills. Management must approach this problem openly and discuss it with their personnel. In most cases it can be demonstrated that the newly acquired techniques permit programmers to operate at a higher level of creativity, relieving them of much "housekeeping" or minor detail. Occasionally it is possible to enrich a programmer's job responsibilities by assigning additional lower-level analysis tasks to keep him occupied and productive.

General Software Areas. Since most program packages are delivered on magnetic tape, it is vital to know the operating system and the version of the operating system used to create the tape. The differences between releases of operating systems and releases of compilers may create problems. If only object programs are delivered they may not function at all under different operating system versions.

It is invariably necessary to modify the job control language of the software package to match it to the machine and software configuration of the user installation. At this time, the system should also be reviewed for maximum job stream efficiency.

Almost all packages are periodically enhanced by their vendors. Care should be taken to assure that the version of the documentation delivered is coordinated with the version of the programs delivered.

Summary

A good motto for the software buyer should be *"semper caveat emptor."* In the eyes of top management, the installing group always bears full responsibility for the success—or the failure—of the installation. With this in mind, the key steps of purchasing and installing software packages are summarized below:

1. Determine the need for system improvement.

2. Organize an evaluation project team composed of members of both the systems group and the *user organization.*

3. *Define the user's requirements.* This is probably the most critical point in the process.

4. Explore alternative solutions, determining whether or not appropriate software packages exist.

5. Match the features of available software packages to the defined requirements.

6. Evaluate the software package vendors.

7. Select the most appropriate package requiring the least modification (preferably none) and having the best vendor support.

8. Negotiate a contract with appropriate safeguards.

9. Plan the installation.

10. Select and organize the installation project team, again including user personnel.

11. Compile and catalog all programs. Modify the job control language to meet the requirements of the installation's hardware and operating system configuration.

12. Assuming that the requirements definition has clearly stated the necessary modifications, prepare detailed program modification definitions.

13. Before making any changes test the original programs delivered by the vendor with the vendor's test data set.

14. Review the results of the above test with the vendor and make any necessary corrections.

15. Based on the results of the above test and the known modification requirements, prepare *actual* user documentation.

16. Construct a user test data set including all anticipated data conditions including those arising from multiple iterations of the system.

17. Modify the packaged programs according to the requirements definition.

18. Prepare computer operating documentation for the system to conform to the standards of the installation.

19. Test the modified system with the user test data set.

20. Review the results of the above test and make necessary corrections.

21. Begin the initial pilot or parallel operation with provision for a review of the operating results and correction of any errors detected.

22. Train user personnel.

23. Install the full system.

SECTION 4 PROJECT PERFORMANCE VS. TEAM SIZE

Since the early days of World War II our rapid advances in science and technology have created an environment in which it is necessary to undertake increasingly complex technical projects. These projects have increased not only in complexity, but in size and in the apparent required number of people to accomplish the tasks within a given period of time.

Among those areas in which this phenomenon has been most noticeable is the effort involved in large computer programming projects. For example, the SABRE Airlines Reservations System was reputed to have over 400 programmers working on it at one point.

Managers, especially those paying for these large technical efforts, have become increasingly concerned with the rapid expansion of the groups involved. It has been noticeable that production does not increase at the same rate as the size of the group.

In 1959, C. Northcote Parkinson humorously elucidated one aspect of the case in his third law, "Expansion means complexity and complexity, decay." While the third law remains a good generalized observation, Parkinson failed to establish a sound scientific basis of support.

In the special case of complex technical projects, group size is increased in an honest effort to accomplish the task. The rationale for group expansion is as follows:

1. The task must be completed before such time as its completion would become meaningless due to technological or economic obsolescense.

2. The above target cannot be met if the task is performed in a linear fashion by one person.

3. Dividing the work into successively smaller segments will allow many people to work on the project concurrently, thus reducing the time to completion.

By reiterative use of the above logic, groups can be expanded at an exponential rate.

Considerable field research in data processing management has led to proposing Fried's Law:

> There is an inverse relationship between effectiveness (production) and group size in complex technical projects (programming, electronic design engineering, etc.)

In itself, the above law is a reasonable generalization. However, an analysis of the data gathered through observation has led to development of the formulae for computing the productive time and the percentage of productive time of groups. The following premises support these formulae.

People in formally organized groups cannot be productive 100 percent of their time for extended periods of time. In the average organization at least 25 percent of employees' time is required for vacations, sick-leave, personal time off, training, coffee breaks, and administrative and organizational meetings.

In addition, a conservative average of 10 percent of employee time is spent in nonproductive status due to late completion of activities on which the employee is dependent, poor work scheduling, nonwork-oriented conversation, and other forms of "idle" time.

Each new member entering a group must communicate with others about the task and ongoing task-oriented communication must take place. In small groups (five or less) this can take from 10 percent to 30 percent of his time. As the group size increases beyond five, members must spend more and more of their time communicating until they reach an upper limit of approximately 90 percent.

The frequency of communication is dependent on the number of interactions available to each member of the group. Assuming that there may be a two-way interaction between each member of the group and every other member, the formula for computing the possible number of interactions (I) is:

$$I = \frac{K(K-1)}{2}$$

where K = the number of people in the group.

As Figure 16 indicates, the number of possible interactions increases very rapidly with small increases in group size.

In order to be as conservative as possible, let us assume that until the group reaches ten members in size, the individual spends a maximum of 10 percent of his time in communicating with others. However, when the group size exceeds ten each individual will spend .01 percent more of his time communicating for each member of the group over ten. (This amounts to an average of less than two seconds per day per interaction.)

On the basis of the above, the nonproductive time expected is 25 percent for vacation, etc.; 10 percent for idle time; and 10 percent for time spent in communicating. We may therefore estimate that 55 percent of each employee's time can be considered productive time up to a group size of ten.

We may compute the percent of productive time by the following formula where:

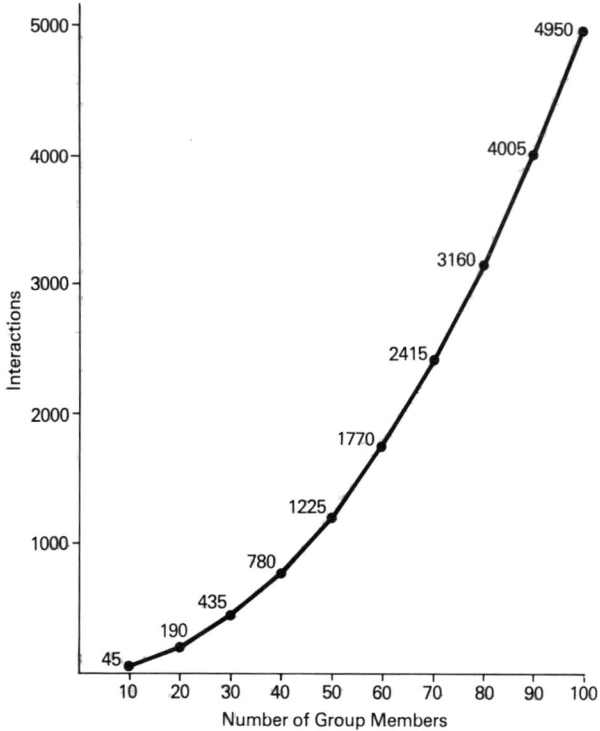

Figure 16. Number of interactions by group size.

P_t = productive time
T = individual employee hours per work period
K = the number of people in the group
    then:

$$P_t = K\left(T\left[.55 - .0001\left\{\frac{K(K-1)}{2}\right\}\right]\right)$$

Solved for a group of 90 people working a standard 40-hour week (a total of 3,600 available hours), the result is as follows:

$$P_t = 90\left(40\left[.55 - .0001\left\{\frac{90 \times 89}{2}\right\}\right]\right)$$

$P_t = 90(40[.55 - .0001\{4005\}])$
$P_t = 90(40[.1495])$
$P_t = 90 \times 5.98$
$P_t = 538.2$ hours

Also, we may compute the percentage of productive time available from any specific group using the following formula, where:

P_p = percent of productive time
K = the number of people in the group
   then:

$$P_p = 100\left(.55 - .0001\left[\frac{K(K-1)}{2}\right]\right)$$

There is a limited span of control in the management of complex technical projects. Therefore, large groups engaged in these enterprises are generally organized into many small groups structured in several layers of management. It may be argued that organization into such subgroups limits the number of possible interactions between members. There are, however, several factors inherent in such organizations that offset any potential reduction in interactions. Some of these are:

1. The new organization increases the time spent on each interaction (and may actually *increase* the number of interactions).

2. As organizations acquire size, depth, and formality, all communications tend to be in writing with multiple copies. Not only is communication time increased but the resulting memos must be filed for future reference.

3. A hierarchy of managers is created who do absolutely *nothing* productive.

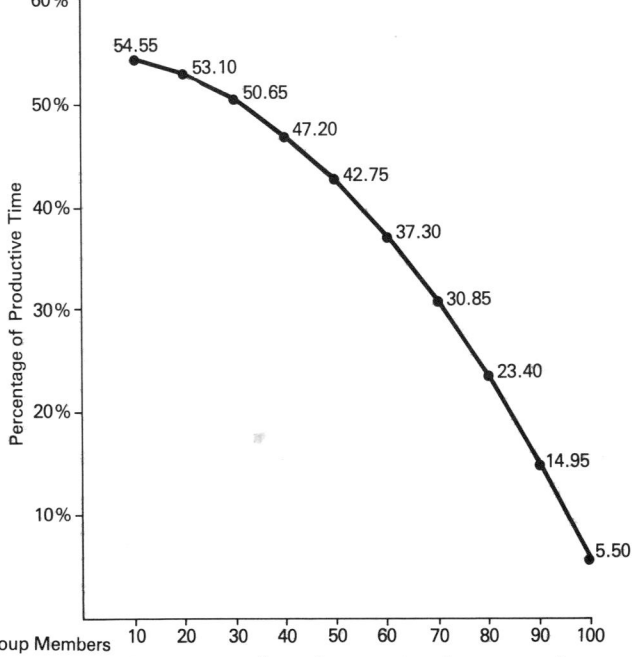

Figure 17. Percentage of productive time by group size.

It is almost unnecessary to emphasize the conservative nature of the premises used to create the formula. However, the formula does assume that all employees are honest, hard working, competent, and present for work except for authorized absences. Factoring in dishonesty, laziness, and incompetence results in negative production over most of the scale.

Figure 17 illustrates the application of the formula for computing percentage of productive time over group sizes from ten to 100. As indicated, a group of 95 people could be expected to spend 10.4 percent of their time on productive effort.

Furthermore, it is apparent that a group of twenty people will generate more productive time than a group of 95.

GROUP SIZE	PRODUCTIVE HOURS (40-HOUR WEEK)
95	395.2
20	424.8

Beyond 100 group members the formula becomes less reliable, but some large groups have been known to enter the range of negative productive output.

SYSTEMS DEVELOPMENT METHODS

This chapter addresses some areas of the methodology of system justification and development that observation indicates are particularly weak points in many MIS organizations. As previously indicated, some of these are closely related to the area of project management.

For example, the first two sections deal with the question of whether or not a proposed project for application development should be undertaken.

The first section presents the basic methodology for conducting a feasibility study. The second is an in-depth look at performing cost/benefit analyses. In this section consideration is given to tangible and intangible benefits and to political consid-

Chapter 4

erations as well. It should be read keeping in mind the prior section on estimating project costs.

The third section also concerns feasibility studies and is written from a user's perspective. It points out some of the fallacies in traditional feasibility studies and reports.

Fourth, as an adjunct to the prior section on estimating and to provide the ability to improve programming estimates, there appears a section that reviews the requirements for a complete system specification.

The last section in this chapter is an analysis of top-down and structured design methodologies. This section also has implications for the project management team.

SECTION 1 OBJECTIVES AND REQUIREMENTS OF A FEASIBILITY STUDY

With increasing frequency, organizations that used to plunge directly into systems design and programming at the drop of a user request are now conducting feasibility studies prior to any development-oriented work. Whether this is the product of the growing maturity of the EDP industry or the result of having been burned too often, it represents a healthy trend.

The feasibility study is not new. It has been used for years in engineering and in general business for capital investment consideration.

This section addresses the objectives for a feasibility study, the requirements for conducting the study, and the content of the feasibility study report.

Objectives

In response to the question, "Why conduct a feasibility study?" one corporate president answered succinctly, "I don't step into a hot bath without testing the water with my toes first!"

From a top-level corporate position, this response is a fairly good overview. However, from the viewpoint of the MIS manager or the project leader, the answer is more complex.

Since the result of a feasibility study is usually reported to corporate management for a decision on whether or not to proceed with the project, a central objective of the feasibility study is to determine whether or not the proposed project is justified. Such justification may be demonstrated on the basis of one or more of the following considerations:

• *Payback.* There should be adequate return on the investment of development and implementation cost to warrant proceeding with the system as an alternative to other potential investments of the company's money.

• *Mandatory.* Some development or modification efforts are imposed by external authority and become a requisite of remaining in the business. These demands may come from government regulatory agencies, external auditors, supporting banks, or insurance companies.

• *No reasonable alternative to the computer exists.* Typically, these types of projects may involve heavy computational loads. For example, analysis of weather data or statistical analyses of large data samples. A second consideration may be response time. While the task could be done by other means, only a computer solution can provide the results in time to be useful. Some high-technology process control applications fit this model, but it can also apply to some clerical operations.

• *Corporate directive.* Realistically, all computer applications may not be justified in the objective sense. Some are the result of corporate policy changes or the directives of management. Despite the apparent mandatory nature of these "requests," the feasibility study has substantial value. Policy has been changed or directives rescinded when the promulgators became aware of the total cost and other impacts of their original decisions.

Based on the above, one might say that the objectives of a feasibility study are to assure that the project solves a *real* problem (as contrasted to a management whim) and to assure that the problem is worth solving by use of a computer (that there is sufficient return on investment).

A closer look at frequent results of feasibility studies and some entire projects would lead us to add a few other objectives as well. The feasibility study should provide management with a basis for allocating corporate investment and EDP resources among competing demands. Therefore, one objective should be to provide information for setting a priority on the project. Next, the feasibility study should assure that the proposed project is consistent with corporate objectives and goals and with corporate and EDP long-range plans. If inconsistencies do exist, they should be pointed out to management for resolution.

Another objective of the study is to acquaint management with any potential risks in the project. These risks may involve unknown elements in the conceptual design of the system, estimates of cost and duration of the project, introduction of new software, acquisition of appropriate development personnel, and the capacity of existing or proposed hardware to support the application.

The feasibility study should, when possible, provide more than one reasonable alternative to the present methods used in the application area in order to enhance management's range of choices.

Finally, it should be an objective of the feasibility study to establish the credibility of the MIS organization to develop and implement the application successfully. This may be demonstrated through showing a thorough knowledge of the application area, a good grasp of the hardware and software considerations, the informed participation and consent of the user in the study, a tentative plan for providing the appropriate expertise to the project team, and the overall quality of the feasibility study report.

In summary, the objectives of the feasibility study are to:

• Determine whether or not a proposed project is justified.
• Provide a basis for determining priorities and allocating resources.
• Assure consistency with corporate and MIS goals and plans.

- Evaluate project risks for management.

- Provide alternative solutions for management consideration.

- Establish or confirm the credibility of the MIS organization to successfully implement the project.

Requirements

Before a feasibility study can begin, there should be several management conditions met within the organization. Both MIS and user management should agree that a problem amenable to computer solution exists and that it appears to be worthwhile to solve. Projects proposed by MIS alone, without user consent and support, rarely succeed. Since feasibility studies themselves cost money, there should be a company policy supporting feasibility studies for given levels of project work.

The usual progression of events leading to a feasibility study is:

1. *Recognition of the problem.*

2. *Request for MIS service.*

3. *Brief evaluation of the request.* This process is generally less than one week of effort. It is designed to screen requests for general feasibility and roughly approximate the size of effort required to meet the request.

4. *Response to requester.* This short report to the requester contains four possible answers: (a) the request is not practical or is denied for other reasons, (b) the request is small, feasible, and will be scheduled if the attached estimate is approved, (c) the proposed project is mandatory and a cost estimate and schedule is being developed, (d) the request appears to be of a size or complexity that requires a feasibility study. If the response is (d), a schedule for providing a proposal for a feasibility study should be established.

A feasibility study is, in itself, a project. The proposal for a feasibility study should contain the following elements.

- *Objectives.* List and briefly explain the objectives of the feasibility study, the subjects to be covered, major questions to be answered, and why they are important to the design of the system.

- *Methods.* Describe how major questions will be answered in terms of the procedures to be used, observations, and units of measure (if the data are objective/quantifiable). If the data are subjective/qualitative, indicate who will be interviewed (level, title, function) and what processes will be observed.

- *Schedule.* Indicate where and when the survey will take place.

- *Personnel Requirements.* Show the number of people required for the feasibility study, their work classifications or titles, and from where they will be provided (MIS, user department, consultant, other).

- *Skills and Training.* For the above personnel, indicate what skills or knowledge each requires and/or what training will be needed to make up any deficiencies. If possible, a training schedule should be included showing any outside costs and who would do the training.

- *Estimated Time and Cost of the Study.* Schedules and cost estimates should cover direct labor, travel expenses, any data reduction (processing and analysis), and report preparation.

- *User Participation.* Define the user's role in consultation and familiarization of the MIS analysts with the business operation. List offices, files, and information to which the study team must have access. Indicate any other support that will be expected of the user and show a tentative schedule of user personnel time requirements. If special data gathering efforts will be required of the user, a sample of the reporting format(s) should be included.

Upon approval of the feasibility study proposal by the user, it may go to top management or a steering committee before work can begin. After final approval, the feasibility study may begin.

As with any other project, consideration must be given to project team organization, project planning, and control. Bringing the study to conclusion on time and within estimated cost helps to meet the objectives of establishing credibility for the potential subsequent development project.

Related materials in this chapter address specific details of conducting the feasibility study and performing cost/benefit analysis. In addition to these, the reader should refer to the sections on Setting Application Priorities and Estimating Project Costs.

A brief summary of the activities involved in conducting the feasibility study is presented below.

1. Training and orientation of project personnel including setting up project team and project control mechanisms.

2. Refine the objectives of the study by projecting the objectives of the proposed system. Spell out exactly what we seek to accomplish by solving the problem or completing the project.

- Are we looking for a faster process? (Earlier reports, bills, or refunds? Improved delivery dates? Quicker turnover of inventory? Reduced inventory? Lower working capital?)

- Are we looking for a smoother operation—to give our supervisors more effective time for supervising—requiring less of their time to be spent correcting defects?

- Are we looking for a better end-product—the same quality at less cost, or better quality at the same cost, or better quality at less cost?

3. Collect present system documentation, if any.

4. Observe and document present system flow, job steps, decision elements, inputs and outputs.

5. Identify the cost of the present operation, the effects of business volume on costs, the effects of inflation on costs.

6. Project the costs of continued operation of the present system including any costs of adverse impact on the business from its continued operation. Present and projected cost of the existing system should include the following elements:

- Operating personnel
- Overhead
- Computer costs (if any)
- Maintenance costs
- Supplies
- Amortization
- Business costs

7. Determine the information requirements by establishing the requirements for processing, decision-making, and reporting.

8. Determine any constraints on the system design (legal requirements, response time requirements, data inquiry needs, etc.)

9. Define file content requirements (data elements, tentative file organization and access methods, etc.).

10. Develop one *or more* alternative general system concepts to the level of a narrative synopsis of the proposed alternative and an overall flow chart. Note: From this point on, each remaining reasonable alternative should be treated in the same manner.

11. Identify and define preliminary hardware and software requirements for the alternatives.

12. Estimate the costs and indicate possible schedules for alternatives. The following major areas of implementation cost must be considered:

- Systems design and programming effort through final systems test. Note that it may be desirable to include in this cost the maintenance effort required for the first few months of operation, since this is the "debugging" phase of the project.

- System modifications are treated as a separate item for those instances where the alternative is to purchase a software package.

- Preparation for conversion, which includes review and cleanup of existing files (manual and automated). This may also include planning for organizational change or acquisition of temporary help for the conversion period.

- Development and publication of new and revised policies, job descriptions, and operations manuals for user personnel.

- Conversion of manual files to machine-readable form or conversion and reformatting of existing computerized files.

- Training of the personnel who will utilize the system. Special training of analysis of programmers may be included with design and development cost.

- Pilot operation of the new system or parallel operation of the new system concurrently with the old.

- Miscellaneous project tasks.

- Capital expenditures for equipment, software, or specialized forms for conversion, etc.

13. Estimate the operating costs of the proposed alternatives including the same elements as in Item 6, above. In addition, consider any business benefits that may accrue as a result of implementing the new system.

14. Document any intangible benefits of the alternatives and the risks of each approach.

15. Prepare the feasibility report.

16. Review the report with the user and make any necessary adjustments.

17. Present the feasibility report for management approval.

Documenting the Feasibility Report

All of the data gathered during the course of the feasibility study would be overwhelming if presented in the final report. However, it does have considerable value if the proposed project is approved. All project documentation should therefore be well organized and filed by the conclusion of the study.

The feasibility report itself should consist of three major sections.

1. A brief management summary of the conclusions of the study. This section should be as short as possible and still convey the major objectives of the proposed system, the conclusions reached by the study, and the key reasons for reaching those conclusions. Ideally this section will be between one and five pages long and will be preceded by an approval page for appropriate signatures.

2. The body of the report.

3. Any appendices to the report.

The body of the report contains the supporting documentation for the management summary. It, too, should be as concise as possible but the length will be a function of the scope and complexity of the system and the number of alternatives examined.

The report should use a consistent format throughout for easier reading. Alternatives should be presented in sections identically organized so that they may be readily compared. Charts or graphs describing similar data or events should use the same formats for ease of comparability. The body of the report should contain the sections described below.

Introduction. This section should briefly outline the genesis of the study, identify the requester(s), and delineate the initial objectives of the study.

Problem statement. This section should briefly outline the problem that the proposed system is intended to solve.

Constraints. This section describes any constraints on the company or on MIS that influence the system design alternatives. These constraints may be of a legal, technical, corporate policy, or business nature. For example, constraints may include limitations on capital investment, limits on manpower budgets, tax considerations, present hardware or software capabilities.

Scope of the system. What functional areas does the system address? Is this a new application or a modification? What departments will be affected and in what manner? Does the implementation of the system require changes in corporate policy or procedures? What levels of approval are required to proceed with the project?

Desired results. In general terms, describe the results desired by the user. This section should cover such considerations as response time, service levels, size of user staff, net change in user operating cost, and increased information visibility. Note that this describes the user *desires* only, not the final results of each alternative, as these may represent some compromise with desired results.

Alternatives. The following sections should be repeated for each alternative presented. They should be arranged so that each alternative is presented as a complete picture from concept to tentative schedule.

Solution concept. This is a brief (one to three page) description of the major features of this alternative solution. It should identify both manual and automated processes and the general flow of the system. If necessary for understanding, a top level flowchart may accompany this section.

Cost/benefit analysis. For a complete view of the contents of this section, refer to the section on Performing Cost/Benefit Analysis. In short, this section should contain the supporting detail for:

- Implementation cost of this alternative
- Conversion costs
- Operating cost projection
- Any earnings projected
- Savings projected
- Intangible benefits

Hardware and software impact. What is the effect on the present configuration of hardware and software in use? Will additional equipment be needed? Will additions or modifications to systems software be required? In general, how would the above be provided?

Conformity with corporate/MIS plans. Indicate whether or not the proposed alternative conforms to corporate and MIS goals and long-range plans. If not, what short- and long-term effects may be expected?

Schedules and staffing. Using a bar chart or similar illustration, show a tentative implementation schedule for the alternative and how it would be staffed. Schedule is important because it affects cost and the point at which benefits may begin to be realized.

Risk. Describe any risks involved in this alternative including those pertaining to schedule, estimated cost, systems software modification, hardware reliability or limitations.

User participation. Describe the extent, approximate schedule, and type of personnel that the user will have to contribute to assure the success of the project. This is the concluding section for each alternative.

Summary and recommendation. This section should summarize, for all alternatives presented and for the continuation of the present system:

- A cash flow analysis.
- Computation of the payback period.
- Return on investment.
- Intangible benefits.
- Risks.

A concluding paragraph should indicate the project leader's recommendation as to the appropriate course of action.

Appendix. This section should contain any supporting technical or financial detail that may be of interest to management or that may support critical decision-making.

Summary

The feasibility study is a tool for management decision making. Its primary purpose is to eliminate unwanted "surprises" for company management. In this context it may be viewed as an insurance policy. However, it must be used with discretion and in such a manner that the *premiums* (the cost of the feasibility study) do not exceed the *potential loss*.

If a feasibility study seems appropriate, there are a few things in addition to the above that should be remembered:

- Be as accurate as possible but clearly identify any figures that may lack accuracy.
- Give credit to all sources of information used in the study.
- Neatness counts! It's your professional image that is being presented in the final report.

Discussion Topics

1. At what stage in the system development life cycle can costs be estimated most accurately?
2. What is the most important ingredient in the estimating process?
3. Should the MIS Director assign project priorities?
4. What activity will provide the greatest reduction in risk in purchasing and installing a software package?
5. If a project is behind schedule, can it benefit from the addition of more members to the project team?
6. What is the impact on the likelihood of project success when top management establishes a deadline for project completion?

SECTION 2 PERFORMING COST/BENEFIT ANALYSES

In performing the feasibility study for a potential application, there is probably no more influential segment of the study than the cost/benefit analysis. Indeed, in most instances, the future of the proposed project will be decided by the results of this analysis. For once the technical feasibility has been assured, management's decision to abort or proceed with the project will usually be made on the same basis as with any other investment, that is, the adequacy of the return on the investment as contrasted to competing demands for the organization's funds.

This section will examine cost/benefit analysis by describing the preparation of such an analysis, but this description really illustrates the final step. Three topics must first be explored to provide a background. They are: the value of information, the analysis of costs, and the analysis of benefits.

Before proceeding, a word of caution is necessary.

Cost/benefit analyses cost money and time. Obviously, the more money that is spent, the more refined will be the analysis, and (hopefully) the more accurate will be the conclusions. An extensive study can reduce the uncertainty of the conclusions. As in considering any other investment, one would not want to spend money out of proportion to the expected return. On a small project, or where the payoff from a project is fairly obvious, it would be wasteful to perform a comprehensive analysis.

The cost/benefit analysis must be viewed as a tool for reducing risk in an investment decision. Where the proposed project is large, the potential impact of the project is substantial, the net benefit questionable, and/or the proposed project is competing for available funds, then time and money should be spent on the study in a manner proportionate to the scope of the decision.

This section will address the subject from the standpoint of comprehensive analysis, recognizing that smaller studies are subsets.

The Value of Information

In addressing the value of information, Gregory and Van Horn have considered such elements as accuracy, quantity, timeliness, relevance, and the consequences of information.[1] All of these might be summarized in the term "quality," which can be used as a conceptual device for examining the balance between value and cost.

One might initially assume that the value of information goes up in direct proportion to the quality. But a few moments of thought will bring to mind examples in which this is not true. For example, if the quality is improved by speed, does it pay to implement an on-line fixed assets depreciation system with inquiry capability when depreciation is reported monthly? This extreme example shows that beyond a certain point the value of information becomes less responsive to increases in quality. (See Figure 1.)

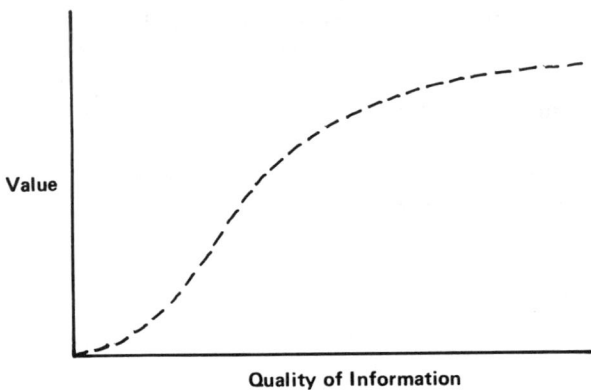

Quality of Information

Figure 1. Value as a function of information quality. The value of information goes up as its quality increases. At high levels of quality, further improvements yield relatively small incremental benefits.

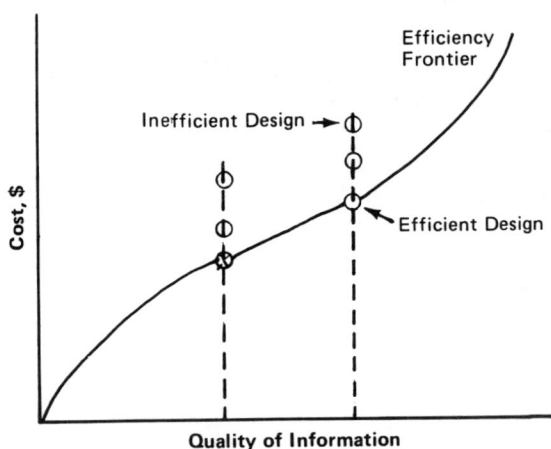

Quality of Information

Figure 2. Cost as a function of information quality. Information is obtained from a specific system. Alternative systems vary in their efficiency, and so the cost of a given quality of information depends on the efficiency of the design used. The *efficiency frontier* represents the set of systems that provide each level of quality at the lowest cost. For a given level of efficiency, cost rises with increased quality.

Similarly, the relationship of quality and cost is not constant. At the lower level, relatively small investments can gain substantial improvements in information quality. In complex, highly sophisticated systems, on the other hand, large sums spent on further improvement may result in relatively small increments of quality gained.

Each level of quality represents a different set of specifications. Given an available technology, the most efficient set of specifications would produce a curve such as that shown in Figure 2.

These curves are, of course, generalizations. It would be difficult to assure the validity of such curves based on estimates for a proposed application. However, they do serve to illustrate the concepts.

These curves comparing value to quality and cost to quality are superimposed to find the range of optimal quality. The point where incremental value matches incremental cost in Figure 3 is also the point identifying the design configuration for a system that maximizes net benefits.

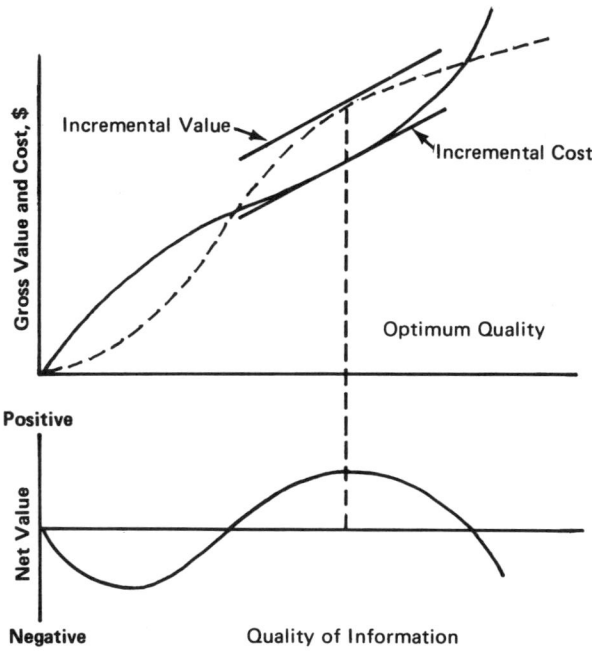

Figure 3. Determination of the optimum system. The optimum level of quality occurs at the point at which net value (i.e., gross value minus cost) is maximum. This can also be viewed as the point at which incremental value equals incremental cost. Obviously, the optimum system does not provide all useful information; there will always remain unfulfilled information "requirements" that cost more to satisfy than they contribute in benefits.

Systems design specifications must consider both the cost and value of information because some information costs more than it is worth, as Figure 3 illustrates.

One other key point should be considered in this concept. That is, costs are responsive to advances in technology. Experience over the last twenty years of data processing shows that the cost per element of data processed has been repeatedly reduced by each generation of computers. Both hardware and software advances have not only lowered the cost of processing information but have provided new levels of capability and capacity.

Responses to the advances of technology can take several forms. In the simplest approach some organizations may take advantage of new technology to lower the cost of processing only. This could be done by a straightforward conversion of the present system to the new technology. In terms of our cost/value concept, this would shift the cost curve to the right leaving the value curve in place (assuming that since no changes are made to the system, the value of the information remains constant).

On the other hand, the system could be redesigned to take advantage of new capabilities provided by the new technology. This might enhance the information value as well as reduce the cost of processing. The resulting optimal system design (the point at which net benefits are maximized) would be at a higher level of quality.

Conversion techniques such as emulation or simulation have frequently permitted achievement of both objectives by simple conversion for the short range and redesign for the longer range.[2]

Techniques for Increasing Value or Reducing Cost

Those characteristics which have been discussed as composing "quality" have each separate implications for the value and cost of systems. One major benefit to be derived from a cost/benefit analysis is that it should lead to examination of alternative ways to solve a given application problem. Although functional specifications have already been prepared by the time the cost/benefit analysis is begun, these cannot remain unaffected by obvious inefficiencies discovered during the analysis. The functional specifications should be considered as a *working document* concerned primarily with the objectives to be attained by the application and being mutable in regard to the detailed methods for achieving these objectives.

The goal of optimizing quality in terms of value and cost of information should be kept in mind throughout the cost/benefit analysis. As each characteristic is examined a close coordination between the system designer and the user should be maintained. Some considerations that may result in increased value or reduced costs are the following.

ACCURACY OF INFORMATION

One usual justification of EDP systems has been accuracy of information. Accuracy cannot be viewed as a binary function; it has various degrees. In addition, increasing accuracy implies increasing the cost of operating a system. These increased costs appear in such areas as:

• Error detection routines in programs.

• Collection and maintenance of redundant information for error detection and correction.

• Externally maintained controls.

• Hardware devices for increasing input accuracy.

• Internal program-to-program run controls.

• Redundant processing.

• Extensive program testing and validation.

• Rigid and extensive program change control procedures.

The amount spent on each of these activities should be consistent with the level of accuracy demanded by the system. And accuracy has different values for different purposes.

Establishing a program for computing results to three decimal places is futile if the input data is reliable only to one decimal place. It is not only futile, it could be dangerously misleading if the user assumes the apparent level of accuracy to be valid. Available input reliability should dictate the level of accuracy designed into the processing functions. In no case should reports imply an accuracy that does not exist.

Accuracy therefore consists of presenting the closest possible picture of reality (ideally). Decisions based upon information presented to a user may be more or less optimal, based on how closely that information conforms to reality.

Organizationally, the operating activities generally require higher levels of accuracy than administrative activities. One need only consider the difference between a few dollars in the wrong account on a month-end closing statement and that same amount of error on a paycheck. High levels of accuracy are demanded by such applications as payroll, check reconciliation, purchasing, and invoicing.

A certain tolerance for error is expected in some other systems such as inventory, shop floor control, and those others for which periodic verification, such as physical inventory or replanning of the work flow, are a part of the ongoing system and result in regular replacement or validation of the files.

Another level of accuracy is permitted in monthly reports to top management which are often summarized and rounded to the nearest thousand dollars. Still another level should be anticipated for demographic studies such as market surveys, opinion polls, and censuses. The fact that the last United States census has been demonstrated to be in error by several millions of persons has not materially affected the governmental decisions made on the basis of the census reports.

The rule for accuracy then, is that the cost of operating a system will be unnecessarily increased by specifying levels of accuracy beyond those actually valid or usable.

QUANTITY OF INFORMATION

It seems obvious that the cost of processing data correlates to the volume of data processed. But a closer look at the causes for levels of quantity can provide avenues for reducing volume and cost.

Again, let us consider the value of information. This value is directly proportional to its "surprise" content. That is, information that you already have is redundant and worthless, information that confirms expectations has increasing value, but information that illuminates the unexpected or previously unknown has the highest possible value. Of course, the underlying assumption is that the information is relevant to the operation and decision-making needs of the firm.

On this basis we may look at the potential information as containing the following subsets:

1. Collected, relevant, and displayed.
2. Collected, irrelevant, and displayed.
3. Collected, relevant, and not displayed.
4. Collected, irrelevant, and not displayed.
5. Not collected and relevant.
6. Not collected and irrelevant.

Item 1 is the ideal. All information gathered, processed, stored, and displayed serves a useful purpose. Item 6 can be ignored. Items 2 and 4 increase the cost of processing while not adding to the value of information. Item 4 is otherwise benign, but Item 2 can have further costs associated with user confusion resulting from the display of excessive and irrelevant information.

Item 3 represents a failure in system design that incurs the cost of collecting and processing data while cheating the user of the information he should be receiving for decision-making.

Item 5 is the most difficult to deal with. The possibility of missing potentially relevant information has frequently led to adding data fields that are *currently* irrelevant in the hope that they will be relevant "some day." Yet the system designer is plagued by the fear of failing to include some critical data element.

The optimal decision on the collection and display of information can best be guided by the relative penalties attached to the two extremes of design. If failing to display relevant or critical information carries a greater penalty than the cost of displaying irrelevant information, then it is to the designer's advantage to display too much.

The design process for the system must be concerned with quantity of information collected and displayed in its impact on the content of the data base, the summarization of detail, the design of reports and display methods, and the use of the exception principle.

Data base content and the cost of operation increase with the level of detail and length of retention. Conversely, the incremental value of information decreases with the increase in detail and age of the information. For example, if sales information is collected by model number alone the files will be far smaller than if sales information were collected by model number and salesman code. Sales information retained in detailed form for more than a year has increasingly lower value for decision-making. In addition, the cost of retrieving the information increases as file sizes increase.

The data base content can be improved in terms of cost/value by minimizing the degree of detail and length of retention, by retaining summarized (rather than detailed) information, and by seeking update and retrieval methods that avoid accessing all master file records.

Summarization of displayed information is useful in reducing print time as well as in making reports easier for some management levels to utilize. While the ease of use of the report is a primary concern, there is always some risk of reducing visibility into some essential data. As a result, requests for changes to systems after implementation frequently consist of new sequences for summarization and reporting. In this area the more money spent on requirements definition and system design, the less risk of high cost in post-implementation work.

This concern with design extends to emphasizing the human factors elements of presenting the information in order to maximize the ease of use (and enhance the value) of the information. Some general rules for good display of information are:

1. Use standard report formats, headings, and definitions to avoid confusion. (We have all witnessed columns labelled "dollars" on one report and "amount" on another, or "quantity" on one report and "amount" on another.)

2. Each item should be labelled or have a clear meaning.

3. Don't indicate calculations to four decimal places when the information is only reliable to whole numbers.

4. Use comparative information when it is available (such as prior month and same month last year compared to current month). This enhances the value of the report by reducing the work of the user to analyze and interpret the results.

5. In a hierarchic series of reports which are increasingly less detailed summarizations of data, provide some method of tracing back to the most detailed report.

One should also consider using graphic displays wherever possible in reports intended for top management.

From the standpoint of management we must also determine if the exception principle can be applied to the reports designed for the application. A well-designed exception reporting structure can add greatly to the value of the information. However, it may mean collecting and carrying more detailed data. The exception principle requires reporting information when it deviates from an established standard, threshold value, or range of values.

The exception principle should be used when the value of this approach in terms of user effort, speed of detection, or ease of use in decision-making exceeds the cost of maintaining the necessary standards or parameters for determining the exception.

Other approaches closely allied to the concept of exception reporting are those of on-line inquiry and the use of parameter-driven report generators. On-line inquiry costs may be quite high in terms of special equipment needed, communications lines, and the need to retain the data base availability during potential inquiry hours. Report generators can be quite inexpensive, especially if they are so constructed as to run concurrently with regular file update activities.

TIMELINESS OF INFORMATION

The element of speed in data processing has two aspects. The first is the speed or frequency of updating the information and the second is the speed of response to user needs or the frequency of reporting. It would be costly to assume that these two are automatically linked. Applications may require quick update and retrieval, quick retrieval only, or neither quick update nor retrieval. In some applications the need for on-line update and response is readily justifiable. Examples include airline reservation systems, and process control systems.

Some inventory and production control applications dealing with very high volumes may justify this approach in terms of avoiding stockouts while minimizing the size of the inventory carried. In many such applications it is sufficient to provide overnight updating with on-line inquiry or overnight updating and reporting. Speed of response dictates the processing method to be used and the methods used vary in cost. Tape-oriented batch processing may be least costly, but when the demand for faster response time occurs and the frequency of processing must be increased, then this method can become burdensome and costly. The next step would be to disk-oriented indexed sequential processing. Finally, if response time is reduced to the minimum (immediate, or on-line inquiry) then a random processing approach becomes most economical. The comparison of the costs of these methods is illustrated by Figure 4.[3]

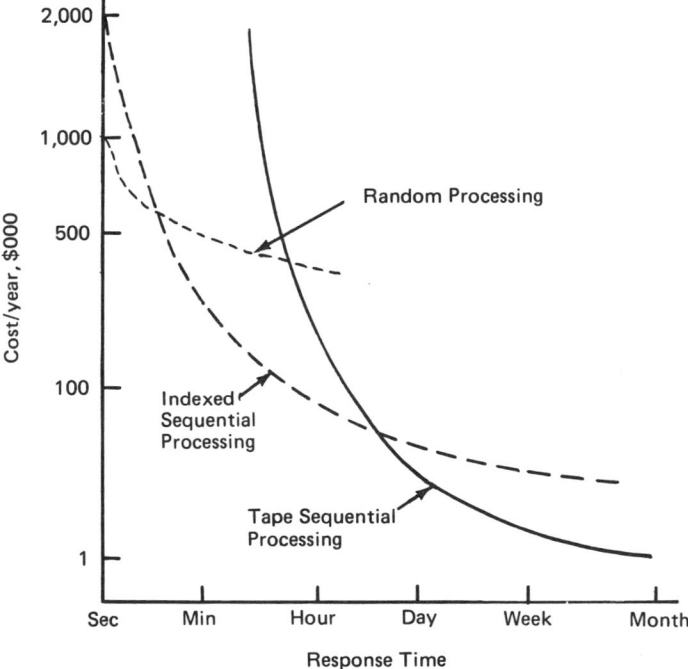

Figure 4. Cost as a function of response time. Economical batch processing with magnetic tape can be used when response time is not critical. As response time is reduced—and hence run frequency is increased—total input/output time grows rapidly. Eventually batch processing with an indexed sequential file becomes less expensive, since it allows skipping over inactive portions of the file and thus reduces input/output time. If response times are reduced still further, eventually random processing of a randomly organized file becomes the least expensive approach.

EXTENT OF AUTOMATING DATA PROCESSING

A final consideration in the cost/value tradeoff is how much of an application should be automated. There is an old marketing observation that 80 percent of the business is done with 20 percent of the clientele. This "80/20" rule (Pareto's Law) has been found to be applicable to many other areas. In application design we may find that 80 percent of the benefit can be gained from spending 20 percent of the cost, while the remaining 20 percent of benefit will require 80 percent of the project cost to obtain. The proportions, in practice, may be different, but the rule carries the sense that automation should stop at a point within the real areas of payoff.

Generally, simple decision-making that follows clearly defined parameters that remain fairly constant can be automated. (Complex decision-making in an area of flexible and ill-defined goals is the forte of humans.) The computer's advantage also lies in processing large amounts of data, speed, accuracy, and the ability to produce results from lengthy, complex, *well-structured* processes.

Each process in the proposed application should be examined for allocation to either machine or human processing. The only reason for inclusion of a task that could be done more efficiently by a human into the automated portion of a system is that the results of that task are integral to the further processing of information by the total application.

Analysis of Costs

Analysis of costs contains three major elements:

1. Present operating cost and its projection.
2. Operating costs of proposed alternatives.
3. Implementation cost of alternative system.

The analysis of each of these elements will be examined in the following section. There are two overall considerations regarding cost/benefit analysis that should first be noted. Since there is a one-time investment involved in the decision to develop and implement a new system, the analysis of costs and benefits must be projected over sufficient time into the future to amortize the initial investment. Corporate investment guidelines may usually be obtained from the accounting department. These guidelines may indicate that corporate management expects a payback on investments in one, two, three, or five years (in some cases even longer). With this guideline, the projection should not be carried much further than the payback objective stated since any proposal not meeting the criteria within that period would be economically unfeasible. One other guide should limit projections: the anticipated life of the system.

If the anticipated life of the new system is estimated at three years (for example) after which replacement or major modification will be required, then this period should limit the projection regardless of payback criteria. Anticipated minor modifications within the life of the system may simply appear as costs within the projection.

The second overall consideration is the type of cost to be used, fixed and/or variable. Generally, fixed costs may be defined as those which do not vary with volume, whereas variable costs are those which change as volume changes. Fixed costs may include such items as building rent, property taxes, and business licenses. If other areas also remain fairly constant despite volume changes, they are often included. These may be power supply, telephone and even such functional areas as purchasing, inventory control, payroll operating expense, and management.

Variable costs would include raw materials, labor, supplies, and tools. If a fixed level of personnel is required regardless of volume, then only that portion that would change with a change in volume of work would be correctly considered to be variable.

Performing an analysis using both fixed and variable cost leads to an unnecessary amount of work on the part of the analyst. Therefore, unless the organization's management requires the analysis to contain both, the analyst is well advised to simplify the task.

Since the objective of a new application is often to affect the level of fixed cost, the usual definitions used by the firm cannot be used in the analysis. Instead, the analyst must carefully identify those cost elements that will be impacted by the new application, defining all others as fixed cost. A statement of fixed cost elements should be contained in the analysis, specifically excluding them from consideration.

COST OF THE PRESENT SYSTEM

The cost elements described in the following are treated as variable cost unless otherwise identified. Restricting fixed cost elements to those which are positively identified provides the widest latitude for exploring cost/benefit.

Operating Personnel. These costs frequently represent the major portion of the cost of the existing system. Using the documented analysis of the existing system which has been completed prior to this phase of the study, the activities of all personnel in the user area can be readily identified. Those people involved in activities relating to the proposed application form the operating personnel base. If administrative personnel are directly involved in the application and if their numbers may be affected by the change, they should be included. Similarly, personnel who work part-time on the application should be included to the extent of the time dedicated.

If possible, avoid using average rates for personnel and use actual salaries or hourly rates. In the benefit analysis the user will be asked to identify personnel savings and these should be consistent with the costs stated. At a detailed level it may be wise to identify personnel costs by function within the application, since the new system may affect each functional area in a different manner.

Overhead. Overhead should include floor space, utilities, telephones, etc., only if these may change as a result of the new system. Otherwise they should be classed as fixed cost. Employee benefits should, however, always be considered a part of the variable cost. A rate for application to base salaries is used by most companies for budgeting employee benefits and can be obtained from the accounting department.

Computer Costs. If the existing system is an automated system, *computer costs* must be included. Several considerations make this a complex area to treat. First, if the new application will not create a need for additional computer hardware or operating personnel, is it reasonable to consider this cost as variable? In this event, should supplies be the only computer-related variable cost?

Second, although the new application may not, of itself, cause new equipment to be acquired, it may hasten the time when the total workload exceeds capacity. As a result, some other, unrelated application may require an unwarranted amount of justification.

The cost analysis should address all of these. The elements of data processing cost that will change should be identified and shown as a part of the variable cost. These could include supplies, data entry personnel, data entry equipment, and data storage media. If an extra shift of computer operators must be added, this cost may be included.

The cost in terms of computer capacity should be recognized in a separate section from the computation of variable cost. If an internal rate exists for computer time this may be multiplied by the time used for the application. If no internal rate is used, the time utilized by the application should be noted and later compared to the time utilization expected by the alternative methods proposed.

This approach will permit management to exercise some judgment as to the alternative methods of allocating the existing computer resources.

Included in this statement should be a measure of the limitation of the computer resource. The computer has a relatively fixed cost that is responsive to volume changes in fixed increments. Exceeding computer capacity by a small amount may trigger a substantial increase in cost to obtain the next incremental level of capacity. Therefore, a clear understanding on the part of management can only be obtained by showing the present level of use of the computer (either as a percentage of total available time or as a number of hours per month or day compared to the hours available for the same period). This would be compared to the level anticipated by the proposed application.

Maintenance Costs. These are another factor of existing system costs. These may relate to the maintenance of office equipment or facilities. In the case of replacing a courier service with on-line transmission, one company had to consider the cost of maintenance for their fleet of cars.

Maintenance costs may also include the systems and programming effort devoted to maintaining the effectiveness of the existing system. Computer time for this activity should also be included on the same basis as run time (above).

Supplies. This cost may include special forms used, cards, magnetic tape, and similar computer or general office supplies. If accounting records available do not permit analysis for the particular application, estimates of use may be obtained from user personnel, verified by user management, and priced by consultation with purchasing as to average prices or reference to a company "internal supplies catalogue."

The final area of cost to be considered is *amortization*. If the existing system is automated and the firm has had a policy of capitalizing system development, has the existing system been amortized? If not, what portion of the capitalized cost must be written off as expense at the time the new system is implemented? (Even without a policy of capitalizing such expenses, management may want to know how effective this application area has been in achieving its previous goals.)

Office equipment and other capitalized items may carry amortization charges to the application area. These charges should be considered if equipment will be eliminated or changed. Note that these charges will not be eliminated if the company elects to warehouse the equipment for an indefinite period. They will be eliminated if the equipment can be used within a reasonable time to avoid the purchase of such equipment in another area or if sold.

PROJECTING THE COSTS OF THE PRESENT SYSTEM

As previously indicated, the costs of the present system should be projected for sufficient time to cover the life expectancy of the new system or the payback period, whichever is least. In some instances, where the expected increase in cost due to continued use of the present system as compared to replacement would be most dramatically demonstrated by a longer period, or when the benefits obtained from replacement would be most significant near the end of the payback period, it may be appropriate to extend the time period analyzed.

The following factors should be considered when projecting the costs of the existing system:

Operating Personnel

• Impact of increases or decreases in business volume on headcount and type of personnel.

• Impact of regular salary increases and inflation.

• Impact of labor market for the type of personnel required, and consequent salary ranges.

Overhead

• Potential increases in employee benefits resulting from inflation, existing or pending legislation.

• Changes resulting in increases or decreases to floor space, utilities, and telephones from increases or decreases in business volume.

Computer Costs

• Inflation.

• Impact of increases of transaction volume on computer utilization and equipment requirements.

• Increases or decreases of variable cost as affected by changes in volume.

Maintenance

• Increasing cost of maintenance due to required change as a function of system age.

• Increasing cost of equipment maintenance due to inflation and age.

• Cost of replacing worn out equipment.

Supplies

• Inflation.

Amortization

• Normally will not change unless equipment must be replaced, added to, or sold as a result of obsolescence, or increases or decreases in business volume.

Other Considerations

• Business volume may be constrained by the nature of the existing system. This may either be shown as a cost of continuing the present system or as a benefit of the new system.

A key factor in making projections is the recognition that business volume may either increase or decrease in the future. The author has witnessed decisions to implement new systems in two different situations that resulted in substantial cost to the companies involved when business volume declined and the cost of the new systems was too high. This is the result of conversion to systems with a higher fixed cost base than previously existed. By projecting costs for both likely increases and likely decreases in business volume, this potential trap can be avoided.

PROJECTING THE COST OF PROPOSED
ALTERNATIVE SYSTEMS

Projecting costs on the basis of proposed functional specifications for a system is, to a great extent, a guessing game. It is a challenge to the analyst to arrive at the best possible guesses for the operating costs to be expected.

Yet, in order to support the best possible managerial decision, every attempt must be made to reduce the unknowns and the risk in the decision-making process.

The elements of operating cost to be estimated are substantially the same as those determined for the existing system. Differences, if any, are noted below:

Operating Personnel

• Methods of calculation are the same.

• Adjust headcount for personnel that will be terminated or transferred from the application area.

• Adjust for changes in the type of skills or the job classifications of personnel who will be needed to operate the new system.

Overhead

• Calculations are the same.

Computer Costs

• Calculation methods are the same.

• Include any additional peripherals or special equipment that will be dedicated to the new system. For example, if normal growth would require the addition of two disk drives during the next year, but four will be required as a consequence of implementing the new system, then it is reasonable to attribute the cost of the two drives to the new system.

• Follow company practice in capitalizing items over the defined dollar value. The amortization of these purchased items is shown as operating cost for the system.

- Expense items acquired during the implementation period may be charged to the cost of development and implementation. Expense items acquired later should be shown as operating costs.

Maintenance

- Even a new system will require maintenance. This point should be stressed to user management to avoid disappointment. Maintenance during the first six months of a major system may be considered as either operating cost or a part of implementation cost. Thereafter, anticipated maintenance costs should be treated as operating cost.

- Calculation methods are the same.

Supplies

- Calculations are the same.

Amortization

- Calculation methods for new equipment are the same.

- Whether or not corporate policy requires capitalization of system implementation cost, a valid cost/benefit study demands the use of such figures in the comparison. The implementation cost of the new system should be amortized over the expected life of the system and shown as operating costs.

Other Considerations

- The new system may provide capabilities that did not previously exist. The value of such capabilities can be estimated by user management in terms of their contribution to net profit before taxes and shown as earnings resulting from the new system.

In addition to a simple consideration of the above elements of cost, it is necessary to provide management with a view of the alternatives available and some sense of the risk of the estimating process. A comprehensive evaluation would consider these factors by developing, *for each alternative proposed,* the structure of operating costs shown in Figure 5.

For each alternative (including, as previously stated, the existing system), develop optimistic, most likely, and pessimistic estimates of operating cost for the range of possible business volumes (as defined by lowest possible, anticipated, and highest possible volumes).

This approach will illustrate for management the fixed cost base, the maximum costs, and the anticipated costs for each alternative with an insight into the risks of each of these estimates. Later, when benefits are matched to each of these, the resulting charts will provide an indication of the expected feasibility of the system at various business levels.

It is not recommended that all this detail be presented to manage-

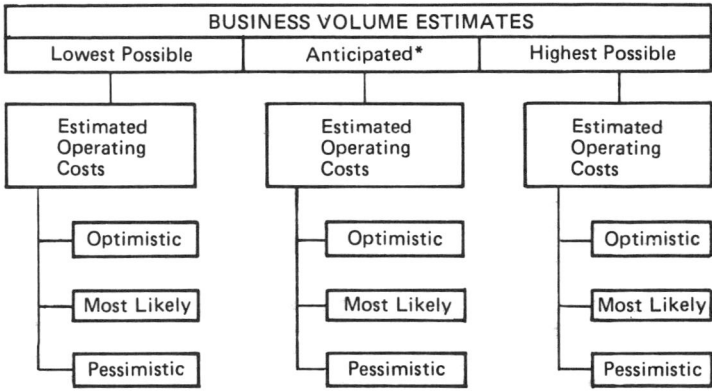

Figure 5.

ment. This is working documentation. Estimates may be summarized for presentation to management by:

- Averaging optimistic, most likely, and pessimistic estimates.
- Weighted averaging.
- Expressing confidence factors or ranges (in terms of plus and minus percentages) to the most likely estimate or to an average.
- Applying probability theory calculations during the estimating process to arrive at a single estimate carrying an expressed level of probability. This method has been used by some large companies for major projects. Whether or not the accuracy of resulting estimates is significantly better than other methods is not conclusive.

No analysis can be considered complete unless it includes the above estimates projected over some time into the future. Unless all implementation costs may be recovered within the first year of operation of the new system, estimates should cover several years. Again, the guide is the estimated life of the system or the time necessary for payback of the implementation cost, whichever is less.

Figure 6 illustrates an operating cost worksheet format that may be used for assembling estimates.

Figure 7 shows a summary of operating costs estimates over a five-year period.

PROJECT DEVELOPMENT AND IMPLEMENTATION COSTS

A detailed examination of techniques for estimating the costs of application development and implementation is presented in another section in this book entitled, "Estimating Project Costs." This section

Elements of Annual Cost	Present System		Alternative System					
			Optimistic		Most Likely		Pessimistic	
	Employees	Amount	Employees	Amount	Employees	Amount	Employees	Amount
Data Processing	14.5	$ 254,600	2.5	$ 30,000	3	$ 36,000	4	$ 48,000
Supplies & Forms		13,300		10,700		11,900		12,800
Operating Personnel	94	583,425	76	482,175	85	527,550	90	561,825
Overhead		252,817		208,942		228,602		243,457
Maintenance Cost:								
Personnel	0.2	4,800	0.3	7,200	0.3	7,200	0.3	7,200
Computer Time		17,000		10,000		11,700		12,300
Other								
Amortization of Special Equipment or Software				7,600		7,600		7,600
Subtotal	108.7	$1,125,942	78.8	$756,617	88.3	$830,552	94.3	$893,682
Amortization of Implementation Cost				26,638		23,034		35,229
Final Total	108.7	$1,125,942	78.8	$783,255	88.3	$853,586	94.3	$928,911

Figure 6.

| | Present System | | Alternative System | | | | | |
| | | | Optimistic | | Most Likely | | Pessimistic | |
Year	Employees	Amount	Employees	Amount	Employees	Amount	Employees	Amount
1	108.7	$1,125,942	78.8	$ 783,255	88.3	$ 853,586	94.3	$ 928,911
2	119.5	1,238,536	81.9	822,418	91.8	904,801	99.9	1,003,224
3	131.4	1,363,389	85.2	863,539	95.5	959,089	105.9	1,083,482
4	144.5	1,498,628	88.6	906,715	99.3	1,016,635	112.3	1,170,160
5	158.9	1,648,491	92.2	1,045,336	103.3	1,077,633	119.1	1,263,773
Total	158.9	$6,873,986	92.2	$4,421,263	103.3	$4,811,744	119.1	$5,449,550
			Capital Expenditure		$88,000			

Figure 7.

will therefore be a brief summary of the content of the estimate and methods of presentation.

The following major areas of implementation cost must be considered.

• System design and programming effort through final systems test. Note: It may be desirable to include in this cost the maintenance effort required for the first few months of operation since this is the "debugging" phase of the project.

• System modifications are treated as a separate item for those instances where the alternative is to purchase a software package.

• Preparation for conversion which includes review and cleanup of existing files (manual and automated). This may also include planning for organizational change or acquisition of temporary help for the conversion period.

• Development and publication of new and revised policies, job descriptions, and manuals of operation for user personnel.

• Conversion of manual files to machine readable form or conversion and reformatting of existing computerized files.

• Training of the personnel who will utilize the system. Special training of analysts or programmers may be included with design and development cost.

• Pilot operation of the new system or parallel operation of the new system concurrently with the old.

• Miscellaneous project tasks.

• Capital expenditures for equipment, software, or specialized forms for conversion.

Figure 8 presents a sample worksheet for a project on which a package was used to implement a new application. These costs may be summarized and spread over the life of the project to provide management with a view of how the project will be budgeted.

Figure 9 shows two ways of summarizing project cost. The summary of total costs includes computer time charges at the in-house rate and approximately half of the project management costs (which would simply be otherwise allocated if this project were not done). This chart is intended to enhance the comparison between alternatives for use of the resources available. The second chart is a summary of variable or out-of-pocket costs which excludes allocated costs and is intended for use in determining the economic feasibility of the project.

The implementation costs appearing in the out-of-pocket cost summary will be used to generate summary figures (by averaging, etc.)

Project Tasks	Cost Elements									Total
	Systems Analysis	Programming	Keypunch	Computer	Forms & Supplies	Outside Contract Services	User Administration	User Personnel	Project Management	
Systems design and programming										
System modifications	$13,500	$16,000		$ 5,200			$ 80			$ 34,780
Preparation for conversion			$ 1,600	1,250		$8,200		$11,860		$ 22,910
Clerical and operating procedures	9,750	750			$1,000			840		12,340
File conversion	2,675	2,050	9,660	16,075			200	3,350		34,010
Training	1,875						240	1,560		3,675
Pilot and parallel operation			900	5,250			540	1,400		8,190
Other project tasks									$14,800	14,800
Subtotal	$27,800	$18,800	$12,160	$27,775	$1,000	$8,200	$1,060	$19,010	$14,800	$130,605
Capital expenditures		38,000								38,000
Final total	$27,800	$56,800	$12,160	$27,775	$1,000	$8,200	$1,060	$19,010	$14,800	$168,605

Figure 8.

Summary of Total Costs						
	First Quarter	Second Quarter	Third Quarter	Fourth Quarter	Fifth Quarter	Total
Optimistic	$39,921	$33,682	$31,346	$36,346	$27,410	$168,705
Most Likely	45,909	38,734	36,044	43,897	30,120	194,704
Pessimistic	52,795	44,544	41,450	52,582	34,050	225,421

Summary of Out-of-Pocket Costs						
	First Quarter	Second Quarter	Third Quarter	Fourth Quarter	Fifth Quarter	Total
Optimistic	$31,545	$27,670	$19,865	$32,945	$21,165	$133,190
Most Likely	36,281	31,820	22,844	37,887	24,340	153,172
Pessimistic	41,723	36,593	26,270	43,570	27,991	176,147

Figure 9.

for amortizing project cost on the operating cost worksheet, for cash flow analysis, and for payback analysis.

Analysis of Benefits

Benefits are usually classified as tangible and intangible. There is a further "grey area" in which intangible benefits may be given some tangible coloring. These three forms of benefits can be determined and presented as described below.

TANGIBLE BENEFITS

Tangible benefits are derived from two sources: cost reduction in operations and profit improvement by access to new sources of revenue. Cost reductions in operations are readily identifiable during the process of projecting the cost of alternative systems for an application. Profit improvement may result from creating new revenues.

Some examples of these sources of revenue are:

• Creating the capacity for handling increased volumes of business which are readily available.

• Creating salable by-products of information generated by the system (name and address listings, property transactions, etc.)

• Creating salable software as a result of developing the system.

• Improving cash management to enable a program of short-term investment (this can be done by improving cash flow, as with a new invoicing system; or conserving cash, as with a new inventory control system that improves inventory turnover).

These kinds of benefits are tangible enough to have been identified and included in the previous operating cost analyses as "earnings."

On this basis, the tangible benefits of proposed alternatives can be determined by comparison of the projected costs of the present system with projected costs of implementing and operating the alternative system over a period of time.

Together, these figures may be used to construct a cash flow analysis comparing the alternatives as illustrated by Figure 10. (Note that the cost of continued operation of the present system is a part of the cash flow of the alternative until the new system has been implemented).

As this example indicates, the tangible benefit of this alternative is $1,785,901 over a five-year period. Where the benefit amounts are large enough, this type of analysis may be sufficient. However, where the benefits determined are smaller in contrast to the investment so that an adequate return on the investment is in question, or where the pattern of cash flow between alternatives is different but the resulting benefits summarize to near the same amount, a technique called present value analysis should be applied to this table. This technique, which uses an internal rate of return to make future cash flows comparable in terms of present dollars, can indicate substantial differences between alternatives.

Finally, a payback analysis should be made. The payback period is determined by the point at which the cumulative savings (loss) amount becomes a positive figure. Figure 11 is an example.

INTANGIBLE BENEFITS

Truly intangible benefits, which may include such items as improved decision-making, more accurate information, improved legibility of reports, and better employee morale should be recognized and

| Year | Present System | Alternative System | | | |
		Imple-mentation	Operation	Earnings	Total
1	$1,125,942	$164,584	$1,125,942	—	$1,290,526
2	1,128,536	30,120	921,676	$ (6,000)	945,796
3	1,362,389	—	891,998	(28,000)	863,998
4	1,498,628	—	945,517	(33,000)	912,517
5	1,648,491	—	1,002,248	(37,000)	965,248
Total	$6,763,986	$194,704	$4,887,381	$(104,000)	$4,978,085

Figure 10

Year	Present System	Alternative System		
		Total Cost	Saving (loss)	Cum. Saving (loss)
1	$1,125,942	$1,290,526	$(164,584)	$(164,584)
2	$1,238,536	$ 945,796	$ 292,740	$ 128,156

Figure 11

presented to management in a separate section of the cost/benefit analysis. This same section should address other intangibles such as potential risks to the success of the project, the impact of potential project personnel turnover, the management guidance necessary to project personnel to assure success and other such factors.

BORDERLINE BENEFITS

The term borderline benefits is here applied to those benefits which are seemingly intangible, but for which a tangible value with some level of reliability can be determined with sufficient effort. Evaluating these benefits may be as simple as identifying areas of potential cost avoidance or as complex as to require operations research techniques.

One of the better techniques (which has the added convenience of being easy to use) is *Bayesian analysis*. In this approach, if the decision maker is uncertain about the value of a parameter, then he:

• Considers the set of possible values the parameter may take on for the period(s) in question.

• Assigns a subjective probability weight to each of the possible values of the parameter. (Remember that the total probability for the occurrence of all possible events in a set (universe) is 1.)

• Calculates the expected value of the parameter and uses this expectation as the estimate.

In practice, suppose that we are trying to derive an estimate for the effect on profit that will result from improved information used in decision-making. The user may feel that three values are possible: no improvement in profit having a probability of .05; $30,000 improvement with a probability of .80; and $50,000 with a probability of .15. The estimate would be the result of summing the products of each value multiplied by its assigned probability:

EXPECTED INCREASE IN PROFIT	PROBABILITY OF OCCURRENCE	EXPECTED RETURN
$ 0	.05	$ 0
$30,000	.80	$24,000
$50,000	.15	$ 7,500
	1.00	$31,500 estimate

If several users are to be consulted on the same estimate, their estimates that result from the Bayesian analysis can be averaged (so long as the report makes clear the process used to construct the estimate).

Individual estimates can be further refined (as part of a group of estimates) by using the Delphi technique. The Delphi method consists of an iterative series of responses from members of the group being interviewed. After the first estimates are obtained, they are collated and the extremes (range) and mean are determined. A second round of interviews is conducted in which each member of the group is separately informed of the collated results obtained in the first round and asked for a new estimate. It has been found that three or four such iterations will result in an increasingly congruent set of responses that have a high degree of probability based on the varied knowledge and viewpoints of the individuals participating.

The estimates created by the above methods (when properly noted as to source and content) may be included as "earnings" or "cost" in the operating cost projections previously described.

Getting It Together

Presentation of the cost/benefit analysis should be made in a concise format oriented toward decision-making. The following structure is suggested:

I. Summary

The summary should be a one- to three-page section that includes, for all desirable alternatives and the continuation of the present system, a cash flow analysis, and computation of the payback period and return on investment (savings plus earnings divided by implementation cost for each year of the projected period) for the proposed new systems alternatives.

II. Cost/Benefit Analysis

This section should contain the supporting detail for:

Present system operating cost projection.

Alternative systems operating cost projection.

Implementation cost for alternatives.

Earnings projected (tangible and "borderline").

Savings projected.

Sources of information.

III. Intangible Benefits

The intangible benefits determined for the alternatives should be noted separately for each alternative and the sources of such information indicated. If some of the intangible benefits are key to the proposal, they may be indicated in the summary section and repeated here with supporting detail.

Summary

The cost/benefit analysis is usually the single most important determinant in the project selection and priority-setting process. A comprehensive approach to cost/benefit analysis can and should influence design considerations, selection of realistic alternatives, and the final management decision-making process.

While technical feasibility and design of the alternatives are usually the province of the analyst and the EDP function, it is in the area of the cost/benefit analysis that company management has the opportunity to exercise their knowledge of corporate goals and objectives and their decision-making powers for the good of the overall organization.

Footnotes

1. Gregory, R. H. and Van Horn, R. L., *Automatic Data Processing Systems: Principles and Procedures*, Belmont, Ca.: Wadsworth Publishing, 1963. Pp. 552–595.
2. This section is derived from J. Emery's *Cost/Benefit Analysis of Information Systems*, The Society for Management Information Systems, 1971, pp. 16–21.
3. *Ibid.*

SECTION 3   ON THE DECEPTIVENESS OF FEASIBILITY STUDIES

During the past fifteen years automation has increasingly been applied to clerical functions in thousands of organizations. During that time many managers have noticed that the application of computer technology to clerical tasks has resulted in increasing costs rather than the cost reductions that were anticipated. With embarrassed expressions, many data processing managers have tried to explain to irate line managers why *their* application now costs more. Some of the usual excuses to explain this phenomenon are:

1. Poor planning.

2. Miscalculation of anticipated results.

3. Lack of user management cooperation.

4. The final design of the system had a larger scope than originally requested.

5. Even though the system costs more, it provides much more capacity for work.

The odds are against the data processing manager being able to produce a satisfactory explanation. These and similar types of excuses miss the essential aspect of the situation. The proper perspective can only be attained through consideration of Fried's Second Law[1]:

> Increased automation of clerical functions results in increased cost of operation.

In order to understand the inevitability of this law it is necessary to briefly explore the environment in which automation generally takes place. This environment can be best illustrated by a topographic model of system implementation (Figure 12). This model consists of three regions identified as:

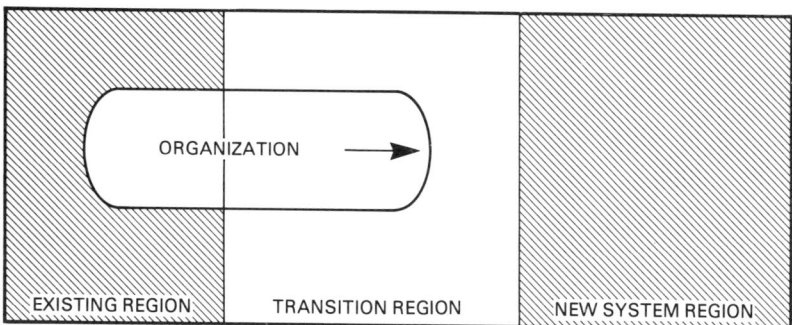

Figure 12. Topographic model of system implementation.

1. The *existing region* which represents the operation of the organization before any changes take place.

2. The *transition region* during which the methods of operation are changed.

3. The *new system region* in which the modifications have been completely implemented.

The organization is shown as moving from the existing region through the transition region to the new system region.

The activities that take place in these regions can be illustrated in their simplest form by the use of a feedback model. Figure 13 shows the simplest feedback model that may be considered as representative of the existing system region. The quality control function is illustrated as controlling the process through a sampling or evaluation of the output. At the point that a need is recognized for drastic modification of the process, the organization moves into the transition region. In most of the transition region the original system must keep operating. However, toward the end of the transition region the new system is installed.

Figure 14 illustrates the system installation feedback model. In this example a major element of effort is added by the required learning process that takes place during installation of the new system. This learning process receives its input from the quality control function and affects both the input and process phases.

It is characteristic of organizations that, once having made a change through an automated system (or having converted to a newer automated system) the process of progressive development of the new system continues indefinitely. Figure 15 indicates the effect of contin-

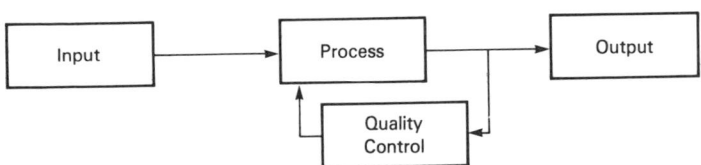

Figure 13. Original system feedback model.

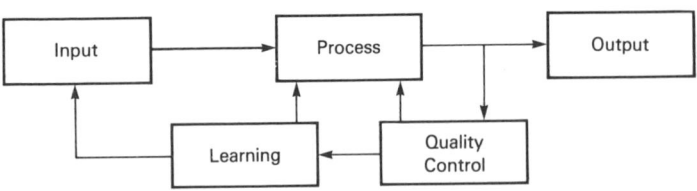

Figure 14. System installation feedback model.

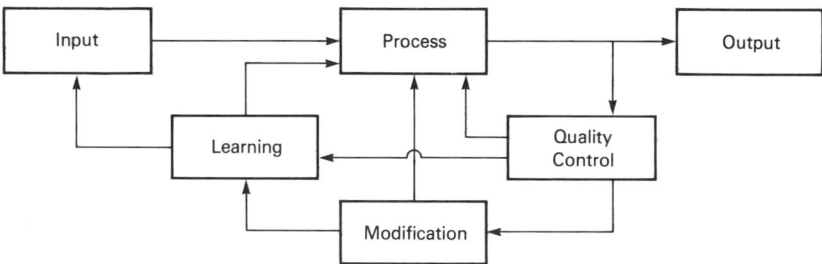

Figure 15. Progressive development feedback model.

ued modifications to the new system. The activity of modification influences the learning effort and the process itself on the basis of continuing information received through the quality control function.

Before entering into a detailed explanation of the reasons underlying the Second Law, further background can be added to our examination of the environment by illustrating the cost profile of system implementation (Figure 16). In the existing region the costs may be rising (providing a motivation for change), they may be level with an increase anticipated, or they may be level with a reduction anticipated as a result of implementing the new system. One of these conditions must occur in the existing region in order to motivate movement to the transition region. The primary element of change occurring in the existing region is recognition of the problem or opportunity.

The transition region is divided into two sections. The first section indicates costs rising as the design and development of the system require the employment of technical personnel and the contribution of

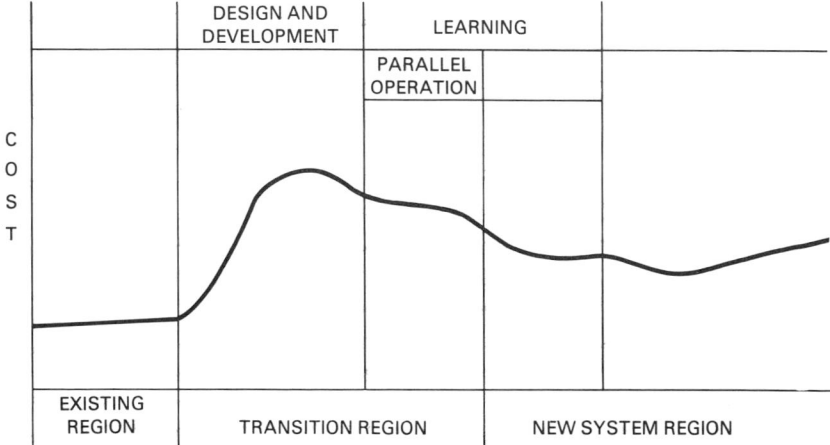

Figure 16. Cost profile of system implementation.

significant amounts of time on the part of user personnel. At the completion of system development costs drop slightly through reduction in the use of technical personnel but remain high while both old and new systems are operated in parallel. This cost level is held high through the parallel operation and the early part of new system operation by the additional effort created in a learning mode.

In the new system region it is assumed that the old system has been discontinued and costs continued to drop as the users become more experienced with the system. Shortly after this point costs again start to rise as the system goes through progressive modification.

Those elements contributing to the cost curve shown in Figure 16 are described below. For convenience, they are organized to correspond with the three regions previously discussed.

Existing System Region

In the profile used as an example the cost of the existing region is presumed to be relatively stable. If this is the pattern, then the impetus for change must arise from other sources. Reasons for change may include the inability of the existing system to keep pace with current workload, demands for faster or more accurate information, and the modification of other systems which have impact on this one. If the cost profile of this region is increasing, this alone generally provides reason for change.

The only activity in this region that is directed toward modification is the recognition of the problem and the definition of a future course of action.

Transition Region

A rapid rise in the cost of operation occurs in the transition region when, in addition to the continuing cost of operating the existing system, a series of entirely new cost elements are encountered. Circumstances differ between those companies already possessing data processing facilities and personnel and those which do not. However, the differences are generally between acquiring *initial* equipment and personnel or *additional* equipment and personnel.

User personnel operating a manual system are frequently naive about data processing systems. The education of user personnel entails an expense; however, an even greater expense is created by the fact that these personnel generally learn by trial and error. As a result, systems requirements and problems are not clearly defined. This may necessitate repeated redefinition of a requirement and consequent redesign and reprogramming of the system in the future.

A group of highly paid personnel are added to the organization in the form of analysts, programmers, and data processing equipment operators. There may even be consultants employed (who are even more highly paid). These people redefine the requirements in their own terms, prepare the specifications for the system, perform the necessary programming and documentation, and frequently assist in the training and conversion required for implementing the new system. Their costs reach a high point during the programming and debugging phase of system implementation and then gradually drop as the installation date approaches.

During this entire period the systems analysts require the help of user personnel. Therefore, some significant amount of user time must be dedicated to reviewing definitions, preparing for conversion, approving input and output designs, and validating test runs.

From the time systems design commences the employees of the user organization are aware that some change is going to take place. Many of them see a threat to their security in this change. Both passive and active forms of resistance are invoked. Active forms of resistance include increased employee turnover, deliberate misinformation, and attempts to sabotage system implementation. Passive resistance may take the forms of not volunteering information beyond that which is precisely asked, work slowdown, or a subconsciously created difficulty with learning to operate the new system.

New systems are generally more sophisticated than their predecessors. As a result, training for use of the new system generally takes

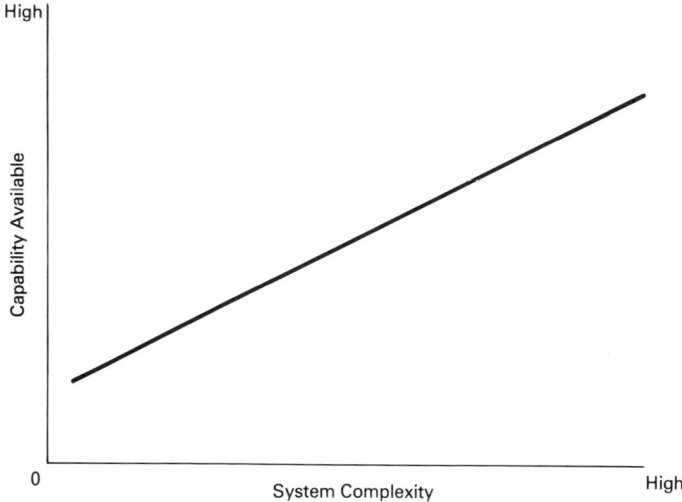

Figure 17. Relationship of capability available to complexity of the system developed.

longer. Frequently more people are required or a higher grade of employee must be hired to replace those using the existing system.

Figure 17 illustrates a corollary to Fried's Second Law that is based on empirical evidence and observation. That corollary is:

> The complexity of any new system is directly proportional to the computer capability and capacity available.

It is obvious that this corollary is also a derivative of Parkinson's observation that "work expands to fill the time available."

Finally, during the development, debugging, and parallel phases of operation an additional burden is placed on existing computer facilities or new facilities must be acquired.

New System Region

A new system normally replaces its predecessor in such a manner that certain areas of the existing system do not change. This is illustrated by the Venn diagram in Figure 18. Aspects of the system such as the functions being performed, the method of collecting data, segments of paperwork flow, and personnel employed will change by varying amounts. Some, such as the personnel being employed, may remain almost constant. The constant area is, by definition, equivalent in both the existing and new systems. This section will endeavor to show that the area not common to both systems is invariably greater for the new system than for the existing system.

The number of employees within a system rarely decreases with the implementation of a new system. Not only is the manager reluctant to shrink his empire (normally measured in headcount), but computer systems are almost never "human engineered." Consequently the learning curve flattens at a lower point of productivity than that of the original system. In addition, with automation many new tasks are

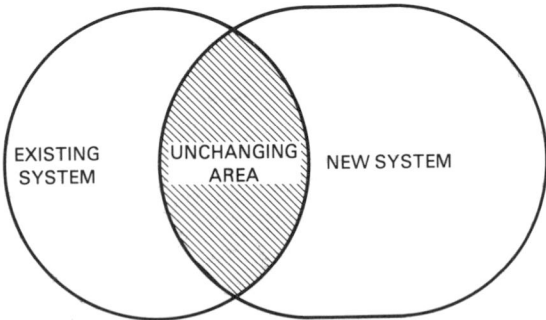

Figure 18. Venn diagram illustrating proportional relationship of areas unchanged by implementation of new system.

pressed upon the organization. Computer input must be created, converted to machine readable form, validated, controlled, and corrected to enable the system to operate.

Computer time normally represents an element of increased cost. This cost may be further inflated by occasional reruns due to input failure, operator failure, program failure, hardware failure, or system design failure.

The output of any automated system creates a demand for readers to assure its validity and personnel for filing and storage activities to retain the reports in an organized fashion. The managers responsible for approving the system feel morally obligated to utilize the outputs. This generates an increased use of managerial time and results in the manager adding staff to analyze and summarize the computer output for his ultimate digestion.

Once the new system has been implemented and the users have become familiar with its operation, there begins an ongoing process of system evolution which corrects deficiencies in the design of the new system and utilizes new techniques which have become apparent through operation of the new system. This cost is added to the basic cost of maintaining the new system. This activity initiates a spiral of continuing and increasing costs of technicians, operators, and computer hardware.

In addition to the above mentioned cost effects, it is necessary to evaluate the impact of new system implementation on management. At an elementary level it is apparent that the addition of new functions and increased personnel resulting from new system implementation will create a requirement for more administrative management. That which is not quite so apparent is the following. The advanced techniques used by the new system create a requirement for the employment of technical managers of increasingly higher skill levels and a requirement for more sophisticated user management. The additional cost of ongoing training must be added to the budget. The misuse of the newly learned techniques adds further to the cost of operation. In addition, once the managers have achieved a high level of sophistication and technical skills they demand higher salaries to remain with the organization.

Finally, the new system has noticeable impact on several areas of the management decision-making process. One characteristic of new automated systems is the increase in information provided to management. As Figure 19 indicates, when the quantity of information available is low, the capacity to absorb additional information is high. Conversely, as the quantity of information available increases, the manager's capacity to absorb additional information rapidly decreases.

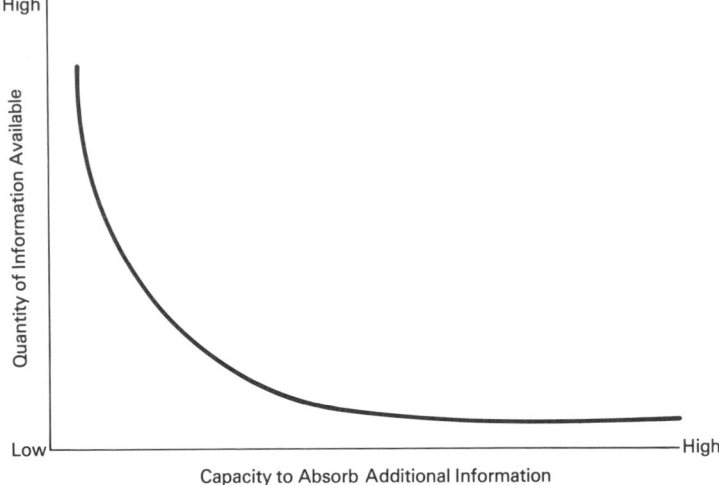

Figure 19. Effect of information available on the capacity to absorb additional information.

In effect, this indicates that there is a limit to each manager's ability to absorb additional information beyond which he will revert to previous decision-making methods.

The volume of information available also affects the time it takes for a manager to make a decision (see Figure 20). Where little information is available, managerial decision-making is done on the basis of intuition and experience. Because of the unknowns and risks, the deci-

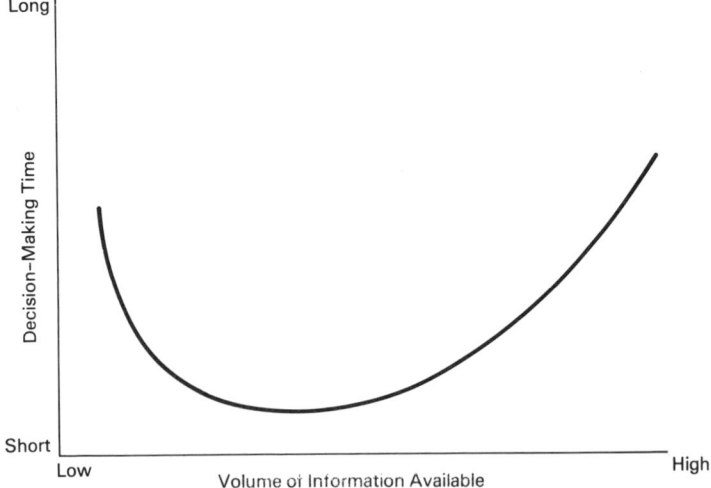

Figure 20. Effect of information volume available on decision-making time.

sion-making time is intermediate under these conditions. As the volume of information available increases the decision-making time rapidly grows shorter. The shortened decision-making time is due to the reduction of risk based on the availability of additional information and to the confidence that this risk reduction brings to the decision maker. As increased amounts of information become available the manager attempts to absorb it. Absorbing the additional information requires increasing amounts of time with a consequent reduction in the capacity to absorb additional information.

The net result is that the manager is overexposed to information produced by the new system and reverts to decision-making based on intuition and experience. His time, however, is further consumed by his attempts to justify his decisions based on analysis of information provided by the new system.

Summary

The decision to automate a clerical function is frequently made in anticipation of reducing costs as a result. As shown, the reverse generally occurs. Automation increases costs in management, technical personnel, equipment, data entry and data processing operators, and frequently in clerical personnel as well.

In addition, an unseen cost may arise due to the loss of customer good will if service is impaired during system implementation.

Fried's Second Law is also substantiated by the almost universal lack of documented evidence of cost savings resulting from automation. In those few reports published, the cost elements reported are frequently incomplete or suspect. There is at least the hint of a conspiracy of silence on the part of the data processing profession to prevent recognition of the Law.

For, once it is openly acknowledged that, "Increased automation of clerical functions results in increased cost of operation," most efforts at automation will *stop*. The impact of this on our economy is almost unimaginable. The vested interests of computer manufacturers, clerical unions, and even national employment policies will be contravened.

Footnotes

1. Fried's First Law is: "There is an inverse relationship between effectiveness (production) and group size in complex technical projects." See: "Don't Smother Your Project In People," *Management Adviser*, March, April 1972. "Project Overpopulation: Productivity's Enemy," *Management Review*, June, 1972.

SECTION 4   A SYSTEMS SPECIFICATION CHECKLIST

Most other sections in this book stress technique. Checklists, by their nature, stress content. They answer the question, "What should be included in this phase of systems development?"

This section is concerned with establishing requirements and specifications within the context of a general systems design. As such, it addresses:

General business requirements

Detailed business requirements

General system design

Some elements of detailed system design

Acceptance test planning

Procedure specifications

Procedure writing

A product-oriented systems development cycle, such as that illustrated in Chapter 3, Section 1, would deliver these products in the research, design and implementation phases. However, there are no discrete boundaries between the activities of analysis, research, systems specification and systems design. Analysis, for example, continues up to the point of detailed program specification.

General Business Requirements (GBR)

By the time this product is to be developed, a significant amount of survey and analysis work should have been performed. This product is designed to recapitulate to management the business parameters of the system development project and to obtain their concurrence and approval to proceed. This is the time to marshal all the descriptive information about the user's problems or goals and combine that information with a proposed solution.

The goal is to document as much as is known about how the business area is being handled, to what depth and extent the problem exists, and whether or not the problems and deficiencies in the existing system are severe enough to warrant the development of a new system. Such information can be seen as final outputs of the research phase.

This product lies at the end of the research phase, but it also marks the beginning of design activities. It is not enough that the problem presents a potential payoff in performance or economy. There must be assurance that the system solution will perform better or cost less, or both, and that the net gain justifies the development investment.

The GBR comes to grips with solutions by listing all the relevant possibilities that may be considered in the design solution. The basic purpose of a general design is to secure agreement on the exact nature and extent of the problems to be solved, the relative importance of design objectives, and the criteria for an acceptable design solution.

- *Problem Restatement*
  This section should serve as an introduction to the document. It should include a restatement of the problems outlined in earlier products. Describe the problem in terms of current performance time, present accuracy and reliability, operation's cost, and business consequences.

- *Related Problems*
  Indicate whether the basic problem causes or results from other problems. These areas could include:
  Staffing needs and training requirements
  Other existing systems or procedures
  Affected customer relations
  Company policy conflicts
  Organization conflicts

- *Constraints*
  List any development or maintenance constraints, such as:
  Production volume
  Cycle or response time
  Processing costs
  Future environment prospects (system life expectancy and growth)
  System reliability
  User-imposed constraints (space, manpower, media, additional training requirements, etc.)

- *Design Considerations*
  Specific preliminary design considerations for the new system or enhancement should be identified. These include:
  Anticipated inputs and outputs
  Required data elements
  Processing algorithms
  Identification format
  Control scheme

- *General Recommendations*
  Pertinent items that should be identified are:
  The EDP or manual system method recommended
  The design recommended and the basis for selecting it

The feasible design alternatives, advantages, disadvantages, and cost

The operations or tasks to be supported

The transactions to be supported

The user options as to output, timing, summarization, and sequencing. Suggest how control is to be exercised.

- *Project Costs/Schedules*

Schedule

Put major development phases into a rough time frame and detail the schedule of the next step, i.e., to produce the detailed business requirements and system design. Include user's commitment requirements.

Cost

Roughly estimate the total system development cost and detailed costs of the next step, the design phase of the project. State the maximum allowable cost and latest acceptable delivery date.

Coordination

Show possibilities for combined development and integration with other systems, and overlaps to be avoided.

Phasing

Suggest the best order in which to develop portions of the system, considering user objectives and EDP organization considerations.

- *Benefit/Value Summary*

Present an updated statement of benefits and cost value analysis.

Present the product to the user for consideration and approval. Obtain the user's concurrence on product content before continuing with the project.

Allow enough time for a technical review. The review should concentrate on the design chosen, the alternatives considered and the cost factors. Upon approval, the next product in project development is undertaken and any corrected or new costs or time estimates are established.

All GBR's should be accompanied by an executive summary if the proposed project cost estimate is sizable enough to warrant top management review.

The summary should include the following:

- A brief description of the system.

- Salient points and conclusions that are important to understanding the subject. This may include comments about alternatives, as appropriate.

• Page number references to particular portions of the GBR that the summary reader should see.

• Whatever action is requested of the reviewer or reviewing body.

• A clear statement indicating the need for specifications to be reviewed in detail by an individual in the user department with the appropriate detailed knowledge and authority to approve or request modification.

Detailed Business Requirements

Delay in the development of a system can be caused by misunderstandings between the user and the project team about what the system is to do. This document, by describing the proposed system in detail in the language of the user, minimizes misunderstandings. It especially ensures that no major differences are unresolved. The emphasis in logical description is on *what* the system is to do rather than on *how* it will be done. The "what" is a cooperative effort of both the analyst and the user representative; this description must be written in sufficient detail to facilitate the design and programming functions. This is the primary reference for the users in understanding the system, and the primary communications link between the users and MIS. It serves as the basis for the detailed design of the system.

Some of the following points may have been covered in previous products. They are included here as information which should be included in the permanent description of the project and system. Expand these points to reflect additional knowledge gained since they were first covered.

Where standard MIS system development forms are appropriate, they should be utilized to define the requirement specifications.

• *Business System Flow*
This section consists of a business system flowchart supported by a narrative description of the system. The flowchart and description show all clerical functions in the flow of information external to any EDP system, and the effect of transactions on the system. It does not show individual components of the system. If an EDP system is a part of the project, it is shown as a "black box."

- *System Outputs*
  This area specifies system reports, CRT screens and any other products. It should include sample layouts and definitions of all the items produced on each product. Definitions should include:
  Title
  Purpose
  Number
  Size
  Frequency (reporting period)
  Page numbers
  Sequence
  Distribution
  Production conditions
- *System Inputs*
  This area specifies system input transactions. This includes any forms that will be utilized in the proposed system. A description of each transaction and the forms being used in the transaction should be outlined. Mockups of each form may be shown. Definitions should follow each form and should contain the following:
  Title of the form
  Form number (if available)
  Function description
  Origin
  Number of copies
  Disposition of copies and responses required, if any
  Transactions that utilize the form
- *Data Elements*
  This section includes the names and description of data elements with indicative keys to associate names with the elements.
- *Processing Schedule*
  Indicate all appropriate processing requirements, such as:
  Batching schedule
  Edit/reporting/updating of input
  Interfacing
  Automatic reporting
  User, on-request runs
  On-line inquiry
- *Control Scheme*
  Identify the requirements for processing controls, such as:
  Out-of-balance input

Rejection and correction of data
Balancing to other files or applications
Validation for the presence of particular files or records
Editing of input data
Run-to-run balancing

Also, identify the organization responsible for ensuring that the above requirements will be satisfied. Controls that are *internal* to an EDP system are the responsibility of those involved in the design and implementation of application programs. Controls that are *external* are the responsibility of the user and data center organizations involved in normal system processing functions.

- *Design Goals*
  The major goals of the system related to system requirement objectives should be shown. This would include identification of information areas, future enhancement possibilities, user areas being served and services being performed.

- *Appendices*
  Include in this section any appropriate figures, forms, tables or statistics that have been referred to in the body of the text, but are not shown.

Present the product to user management for consideration and approval. Obtain the user's concurrence on product content before continuing with the project. In some cases it might be appropriate to present a draft of the product to the user before final consideration. This might eliminate unnecessary retyping of a finalized product.

A reasonable amount of time should be allowed for review. All applications should allow at least seven days for review.

Detailed System Design

This product demonstrates to MIS management that the design meets the needs and constraints of the company's operations as established by the design goals formulated in the detailed business requirements document.

This becomes the baseline system documentation. If a HIPO or SADT ® design technology is used, this set of documents would encompass all levels above detailed program specification. (See Section 5.)

The user would review this document only for assurance that it does not deviate from the established design goals.

The following elements are required:

- *EDP System Flow Chart*
  This chart should show each job step and each data set in the system and their relationships to one another. Include one-time

conversion programs and files to be converted. Accompany this chart with a narrative description and a processing description indicating system flow by charts and decision tables. State the processing which takes place with each job step.

- *File Definition*
  Show the layout of each record on the files. Indicate the physical characteristics of each file and state the purpose of the files and records within the file. Describe file design and explain why it was chosen. The following items should be included in each definition.
  Name of file
  Origin
  Preceding job step or other source (if external)
  Destination (either the next job step or, if external, the recipient)
  Fixed/variable format
  Type of label (standard, unless specifically authorized)
  File organization
  Data base schema and sub-schemas
  Access method
  Sequence
  Block length
  Medium (tape, disk, etc.)
  Estimated volume
  Backup and retention instructions
  File structure
  Name of records in file
  Percentage of file for each record type
  Disposition

- *Record Definition*
  Name of record or data base segment
  Name of associated file
  Fixed/variable format
  Length in bytes
  Sequence of specific records
  Record identifier

- *Field Definition*
  Name of field
  Usage (packed, display)
  Size of field (in bytes)
  Format of the field (A, N, A/N)
  Edit Requirements
  Source

- *EDP Processing Controls*
Describe the internal and external methods that are used to en-sure the accuracy, completeness and authorization of the data being processed. Also, describe what audit trails are to be used to reflect the effects of processing.
This section should describe any special operating controls (di-saster controls, archival storage of master file, security precau-tions to be taken, and the sensitive nature of processed data)

- *Purpose of Each Program*
Each program should be described as to major functions. This would include program action requirements (transactions, sorts, edits, etc.), what is to be processed and appropriate input/output sources.

- *Operating Characteristics*
Outline the primary characteristics of the operation of the ap-plication. Such characteristics would include:
   File transactions
   Tape transactions
   Equipment usage
   Run times (daily, weekly, reports, etc.)
   Operating costs (per run and monthly)
   Tentative system maintenance costs
These totals should be verified by substantiated figures. This basic information, made available to the operations department through the technical review process, often furnishes that de-partment with its first information input on a new system and allows the department to react to this knowledge in a stage of system development where it is most beneficial to both the project and operations, i.e., where modifications are compara-tively easily made.

- *Constraints and Tradeoff*
Describe the effects on system design by any constraints that may exist. Also define the main considerations which resulted in the selection of this design. Examples would be economy of operation, low development costs or fast turnaround. A state-ment should be included on why this design best meets the goals expressed in the detailed business requirements.

- *Costs and Schedules*
This section should include details on several cost and schedule items, primarily:
   Finalized development costs and detailed installation costs.
   Cost of special equipment or upgrades of equipment.

Updated project milestone dates.
Planned costs for data conversion services.
Processing commitments.
Training costs.

- *Appendices*
Include in this section any appropriate figures, forms, tables or statistics that have been referred to in the body of the text but not shown.

This product should be the subject of a technical review or structured walkthrough prior to proceeding with the project.

Acceptance Test Planning

Upon completion of the detailed system design it is advantageous to develop an acceptance test plan for approval by MIS management and the user. This approach builds the quality assurance function into the project.

The purposes of an acceptance test plan are to:

- Ensure that the developed system fulfills the agreed-to user requirements.

- Provide a planned logical sequence of events leading to system acceptance (timetable).

- Serve as a guide for management in judging the adequacy of testing and to measure the progress that is being made.

- Provide the MIS Operations Department with the opportunity to be aware of and prepare for their commitment and participation in the total system effort.

- Provide a tool for user understanding and acceptance of projected test plans and test output.

The basic plan includes the following items:

- *Introduction*

- *Test Structure*
Test objectives
Areas of responsibility
User involvement and commitment

- *Test Controls*
Input controls
Output controls
File controls

- *Test Procedures*
  Submission of tests
  Documentation of test results
  Analysis of test results
  User verification and approval

- *Test Schedule*
  Start date and end date
  Sequence of tests
  Estimated number of tests
  Critical path scheduling

The following items indicate the required information, documents, etc., which constitute the test package. The outline is presented at this point to enable the project manager to plan and schedule the time it will take to produce each test case.

- *Test Case 1**
  Purpose of test.
  Sample input.
  Sample expected output.

- *Test Schedule*

- *User Review Commitment*

- *Conversion Testing* (where applicable)
  Detailed conversion plan.
  Conversion schedule.
  Conversion tables.
  Conversion controls.
  Old master file retention requirements.
  Sample of old and new files.

- *Final Acceptance*
  Detailed list of users who are authorized to validate test results.
  Sign-off procedure.

System test documentation should be organized in the order indicated in the preceding outline. To facilitate changes, each individual topic should be on a separate page.

User concurrence on the plan must be obtained since acceptance testing is designed to satisfy the user system requirements.

* Follow this format for each test case, with tests numbered consecutively, i.e., Test Case 2, Test Case 3. Any test which fails to meet expected results will be rejected and resubmitted as Test Case 1-A, Test Case 1-B, etc., until approved.

Procedure Specifications

The operation of a data processing system is based not only on programs within the system but also on the integration of automated tasks with those performed by people contributing to the operation. This product serves as the plan under which the operating instructions are developed. The plan provides a means to account for the human factor during system development rather than at conversion time, as is often the case.

Specifically, this plan has several purposes. It is a tool for the project team to ensure that all important operations, including training and conversion, are covered by instructions. It defines manpower requirements and serves as a schedule for predicting and measuring progress. It enables management review for adequacy of operating instructions and quality control procedures. It shows the cost of producing operating instructions. Finally, it helps prepare operating personnel for their role in the system.

The plan is produced jointly by members of the MIS development team and the user organization. These plans are reviewed and approved before operating instructions and test cases are written.

The following outline of the procedure plan illustrates the information required for the plan.

- *Introduction*
  Give a brief explanation of the purpose of this product.

- *The System in Operation*
  Operating instructions include the following items:
    List all subjects to be covered by instructions. The organization of the list and the level of detail are determined by the needs of the particular system being defined. Always show the job positions for which instructions are to be written.
    In some cases, instructions vary for similar operations in different areas. If this is so, point it out as a factor affecting the amount of work involved.
    List every subject on which a significant amount of time will be required to produce instructions.
    Include in the plan who has responsibility for writing, publication, distribution and maintenance.
    Explain the scope of the instructions to be written and show the amount of work that is involved. The purpose of this is to help reviewers judge the reasonableness of manpower assignments and of the schedule.

Include in the plan those responsible for designing, proofing and ordering (volume, delivery, etc.) forms.
Schedule the printing and distribution of forms.
Schedule the preparation of data entry instructions.

- *Installation of the System*
Special one-time instructions and procedures are often needed for installation of a new system.
Conversion plan.
Show what files and what cycles are to be converted. Explain provisions to ensure an accurate conversion and to correct errors. Define the responsibilities of personnel in the actual conversion process.
Pilot and parallel operations.
Plan the extent of pilot or parallel operations. State what is included, what data files are to be used, and what the measures are for ensuring accuracy. State the responsibilities of personnel in the actual pilot or parallel operations.
Describe the operating instructions required to maintain the system.

- *Training Plan*
The training plan indicates who is to be trained, where training is to take place and who will perform the training. Plan any special training aids at this time. Much of this need is met by regular operating instructions. But additional aids, such as charts of transactions through the system, may be helpful. Identify training requirements and training aids.

- *Costs*
Show costs to produce the instructions needed to operate the system after installed. Also, show costs to write special instructions for installation and to perform training in system operation.

- *Manpower Requirements*
State who is responsible for writing instructions and performing training and show each person's responsibilities for each task. Show calendar time for production of each portion of the training plan.

Some factors which may be considered in projecting the scheduling and costing of the product are:

Size and complexity of the system.
Size and complexity of the programs.
Quality of documentation required.
Number of different manuals to be produced.

Number of coordination and review points.

Costing formula that includes: drafting rate, technical review, editing, revision, typing and illustrations.

Color and paper stock requirements for documentation.

It is important to obtain user concurrence because this document defines a great portion of user activity and responsibility during the project. This document should be maintained in the project file as the schedule for each of the procedures to be written. Note: Some system designers have found that development of the user manual can be a desirable *first* step in system development since a thoroughly documented user manual is, in effect, a complete statement of detailed business requirements.

Procedure Writing

Based on the procedure specifications, the following activity should take place in development of user documentation.

• Determine who the actual user(s) of the system is and identify the related systems functions.

• Review the user needs/requirements that caused the system to be requested and designed/developed.

• Review the documentation of the system.

• Discuss the functions and capabilities of the system with the designer/developers in terms of satisfaction of user requirements.

• Discuss the above information with the users to determine if this is, in fact, what was requested. If a disagreement is uncovered, direct the user to the appropriate system designer. Note any resulting system changes that would affect or be perceived by the user.

• Determine the level(s) of training required to implement the system and who is to receive the training.

• Develop a procedure/manual outline/organization and present it to user(s) and designers for review and comment. Obtain agreement on which user receives which section(s). Note the number of draft copies required for distribution.

• Determine the level of writing required by various users.

• Perform the research, technical writing and editing necessary to produce user documentation, coordinate the production of material by many contributors and verify the adequacy of the results. Review working drafts with users and designers.

• Coordinate the final drafts of documentation with the user and other appropriate personnel and obtain approval of these items. Determine the number and recipients of final copies.

• Develop a training plan with input from designers, programmers, users, and management. Determine who will do the training, i.e. designer, programmer, writer, consultant, training officer, project manager.

• Assist the trainer(s) in developing training materials and presentations.

• Assist in training user personnel in the use of the system and the documentation.

• Coordinate the printing and distribution of all forms designed for and required by the system being developed. Distribution implies the delivering of all forms to their appropriate locations.

Summary

The checklist presented in this section can be adapted for use in particular organizations or modified to eliminate areas that overlap with other functions. Its primary purpose is to provide a guideline that will help to assure the integrity of systems specifications. Any checklist developed for a particular organization should be established in such a manner as to create quality assurance standards and reduce the potential for project error.

SECTION 5   USING TOP-DOWN AND STRUCTURED DESIGN METHODOLOGIES

Throughout the life of commercial data processing there has been a continual concern with two vital objectives of project development. These are the ability to complete projects on time and within cost, and the ability to deliver the product (system) that the customer really needs.

In order to achieve these objectives, techniques must be developed to solve certain design and development problems. These include:

• Protecting project progress from unanticipated personnel turnover.

• Creating a structure in which work can be subdivided for more flexible scheduling and tighter control.

• Establishing a mechanism for communicating the design concepts to all participants in the development process.

• Developing a means to validate the design prior to investment of programming costs.

• Providing for adequate documentation to assure future ease of maintaining the system.

It is this group of problems that has been addressed by the concepts of structured design and its predecessor, structured programming.

A Brief History of Structured Programming

For over twenty years programming has been viewed more as an art than a science or engineering discipline. A few individual programmers were able to create programs that were relatively "bug free" and easily maintainable while adhering to a budget in terms of both cost and time. For the most part, however, as programs increased in size and complexity, development costs went up, schedules were violated, reliability of programs decreased and maintenance became a major problem.

In 1966, two mathematicians, Bohm and Jacopini, published an article in the Communications of the A.C.M. (Association for Computer Machinery) to the effect that any program having one entry and one exit could be constructed as:

1. A sequence of blocks (non-logical operations).

2. As a structure of IF process ELSE process statements.

3. As a series of DO . . . WHILE to achieve looping.

In the following year, Dr. E. Dijkstra of Eindhoven Technical University, wrote a letter to the A.C.M. declaring that the "GO TO" statement destroyed the capability for writing correct programs. By 1969 Dijkstra had written several papers in which he coined the term "structured programming" and laid out the concept that a program should consist of readable units of code and that the size of these units should be small.

The technique of structured programming was first formally applied by Dr. H. D. Mills of the IBM Federal Systems Division in developing a system for The New York Times. Dr. Mills also evolved the concepts of top-down development and the chief programmer team approach to development.

By 1973, IBM had formalized a concept known as HIPO (Hierarchy, plus Input-Process-Output) and published manuals designed to aid users in creating applications using this concept.

What is Structured Programming?

Structured programming is a technique for simplifying programs in such a manner as to reduce the probability of errors in coding. As such, it depends on dividing the program into easily understood, small segments within a framework (a tree diagram) that clearly defines the relationship of each segment to the others. Each segment is viewed as a process with its own inputs (from other segments) and outputs (to other segments). Segments at all levels are reviewed (both by code reviews and structured walkthroughs) and, as developed, brought into a running system.

The Structured Walkthrough is a formal presentation and discussion, usually conducted by the programmer for a small group of other project members, at which procedures and/or logical structures of program segments are reviewed for the purpose of finding errors in logic.

It was rapidly recognized that the concept of structured programming was too limited and that the program and its documentation existed within the context of a system. Some IBM personnel believed that programming systems documentation emphasizing function could contribute to the efficiency of the program maintenance effort by speeding the location in the code of a function to be modified. They developed the HIPO technique of documenting function to meet this objective.

Hierarchy plus Input-Process-Output (HIPO) addresses the requirements of the people who rely on documentation for many different purposes. A manager or user, for example, may want to obtain an overview of the system. An application programmer needs the documentation to determine program functions for coding purposes. Someone involved in a maintenance activity requires documentation that quickly identifies functions in which changes have to be made. HIPO meets these needs because of its graphical representation of function, its organized nesting of increasing detail, and the depiction of input and output data items at each level.

A HIPO package consists of a set of diagrams that graphically describe function from the general to the detail level. Initially, each major function is identified and then subdivided into lower-level functions; the summation of the lower-level functions equates to the higher-level functions. Programs are then developed starting with the functions described in the topmost level of diagrams. HIPO diagrams can be used from the start of the project through implementation and are useful for program maintenance by easing the identification of the code to be changed.

The major objectives of HIPO as a design and documentation technique are to:

• Provide a structure by which the functions of a system can be understood. The diagrams are organized in a hierarchy structure, much like an organization chart, where each diagram at any level is a subset of a level above it. Complex systems or programs can thereby be broken into manageable pieces.

• State the functions to be accomplished by the program rather than specify the program statements to be used to perform the functions. A section in the diagrams called "extended description" provides additional information about the functions to reduce reliance on other documentation and to provide guidance to programmers.

• Provide a visual description of input to be used and output produced by each function for each level of diagram. Typically, the most important objective in a programming system is to produce output that is technically correct and meets users' requirements. HIPO allows this transformation of input data to output data to be visible.

A typical HIPO package contains three kinds of diagrams: a visual table of contents, an overview and detailed HIPO diagrams.

1. *Visual table of contents.* This diagram contains the names and identification numbers of all the overview and detail HIPO diagrams in the package and shows the structure of the diagram package and relationship of the functions in a hierarchical fashion. It also contains a legend indicating how symbols in the package are to be used. With the visual table of contents, the reader can locate a particular level of information or a specific diagram without thumbing through the entire package.

2. *Overview diagrams.* High-level HIPO diagrams, called overview diagrams, describe the major functions and reference the detail diagrams needed to expand the functions to sufficient detail. The overview diagrams provide, in general terms, the inputs, processes, and outputs. The process section contains a series of numbered steps that describe the function being performed. The input section contains those data items used by the process steps. Arrows connect the input data items to the process steps. The output section contains those data items that are created or modified by the process steps. Arrows connect the process steps to the output data items. An extended description area can amplify the process steps and input and output data items. The extended description also refers to lower-level HIPO diagrams, non-HIPO documentation and code.

3. *Detail diagrams.* Lower-level HIPO diagrams contain the fundamental elements of the package. They describe the specific functions, show specific input and output items, and refer to other detail diagrams. The detail diagrams contain an extended description section that amplifies the process steps and references the code associated with the process steps. They also reference other HIPO diagrams as well as non-HIPO documentation such as flowcharts or decision tables of particularly complicated logic, record layouts, and so forth. The number of levels of detail diagrams is determined by the number of functional subassemblies, the complexity of the material, and the amount of information to be documented.[1]

Data processing professionals who have been in the field since the early 1960s will recognize that structured programming and HIPO are close relatives of modular programming and the tree structure that defined an executive routine supported by and linked to subroutines (in assembly language or symbolic languages) prior to the advent of COBOL.

A Critique of Structured Programming

As of this date, many organizations, both users and vendors, have investigated structured programming. Some have tried the technique. Very few continue to use it.

The initial success of IBM on The New York Times project has been questioned since this project used the chief programmer team concept as well as structured programming. This radical overall change to the project approach did not permit independent evaluation of the benefits of structured programming.

In fact, subsequent experiments have indicated that structured programming alone, using conventional project team approaches, may result in higher project cost, greater main memory requirements for programs, and less effective program operation. Strict avoidance of the "GO TO" statement may result in a proliferation of perform and conditional statements.

Structured programming does have some benefits. It does impose a uniform and universally understood methodology of programming and design standards. It also emphasizes the *review* of coding. Furthermore, if the documentation is properly maintained (a substantial ongoing task), it does make maintenance easier.

The HIPO technique has definite benefits in segmenting the design of the system into easily handled modules which are logically and consistently related. Beyond the design phase, however, the maintenance of HIPO documentation can become burdensome.

The chief programmer team concept, which was unfortunately mixed with the structured programming concept in its early stages, seems to be a major factor in the success of the New York Times Project. The team basically consists of two "superprogrammers" (one designated as chief, the other as backup), several other programmers who code modules, and a project librarian to maintain documentation and coding libraries and support administrative functions.

As most users found out quite rapidly, there are very few "superprogrammers" in the industry. The few that do exist are quite capable of organizing system and program logic and writing clean code without significant amounts of design documentation. (And, in fact, most superprogrammers resist documentation requirements.)

The major benefits derived by industry from the chief programmer team concept have been the creation of the project librarian function and structured walkthroughs.

Allied Concepts

The introduction of, and experiments with, structured programming and HIPO have emphasized the need for creating a *discipline* of programming. While it may not yet be practical to speak in terms of a "programming factory," it is necessary to control the process and results of programming in at least the same manner as engineering.

To this end, the HIPO concept adds benefits in the systems and program design phases. The use of a project librarian aids in control of documentation and programs, and also improves analyst/programmer productivity by relieving them of the burden of administrative detail.

Several other concepts have been found to be of value. Implementing a data dictionary for all systems introduces an element of control and discipline that makes for consistent use of terms in all programs. This enhances maintenance in the future, reduces administrative detail at the project level, and makes it easier to reassign personnel to various projects.

The concept of design review illustrated by the structured walkthrough is valuable in reducing potential errors in code and in the interfaces between modules. However, most programs can be easily checked by the lead programmer on the project with a consequent saving of productive time.

This introduces another alternative which seems to work well in small (under ten people) teams. "Egoless programming" uses the approach of assigning responsibility for success to an entire team rather than to the lead programmer alone. Since all team personnel are aware that their individual performance appraisals are a function of the team's success, they are equally motivated. The lead programmer may distribute segments for coding to individuals, but each programmer is expected to review the code of others in turn. Code does not "belong" to any one programmer. Egoless programming has several benefits:

• It overcomes the lack of superprogrammers by making all code a joint effort.

• It reduces errors in coding by multiple review techniques.

• It makes team members less indispensable to the success of the project by virtue of cross-training.

• It can improve team morale through a greater feeling of participation.

• It can assure the greatest collective effort on the most complex segments of code.

Another technique (closely allied in concept to the data dictionary) is the creation of a module library. This is a way of organizing potentially reusable modules so that they can be easily located, assessed for applicability to a problem, and copied.

The module library contains the source code of each module and is supported by:

• A module index arranged in alphabetical (or key word in context) order and referring to a catalog and folder.

• A module catalog with one-paragraph descriptions of modules by module number or name.

• Module folders containing the source code, history of changes, and test data.

• Module cross-reference listings that indicate where the module is currently being used, which other modules call it, and which modules it calls.

Quality control of programming may be enhanced by the independent "test bed" approach in which a separate team from the programming team designs test data conditions according to the system design specifications. This test bed is then used to prove the logic of the programs and system. Upon project completion, the test bed becomes a part of the overall documentation. The test bed can be created in modules that conform to the modular approach to developing the programs.

Current Trends

In 1972, the Hoskyns Group (London) took a survey of 1770 users of third generation equipment in the United Kingdom. They found that some 53 percent of users had never used modular programming techniques. Of large computer installations, 74 percent had used modular programming to some extent.

The technique has been around for some time and seems to be most commonly used by larger installations for larger programs. Inquiries to hardware and software vendors indicate that, while many have investigated or tried structured programming, few (if any) continue to use it.

However, some have discovered the benefits of using the HIPO approach to systems design and continue to make use of this and some of the other techniques described above.

Structured Analysis

As indicated by the preceding section, the primary benefits from a structured approach appear to be in two areas:

1. System requirements definition and design.

2. Improved documentation for post-implementation maintenance.

In the latter use, there is some concern about the benefits for maintenance as compared to the ongoing cost of updating documentation. Properly applied, the technique does result in comprehensive documentation, which may well be worth the cost in the area of system software (as contrasted to single-user application programs) or systems in which a high rate of modification or growth is expected. It is in the area of system requirements definition and system design that most efforts are now being focused.

Workers at the University of Michigan (on the ISDOS project) have developed a computerized support system for the library functions necessitated by the structured programming techniques.

Another organization, SofTech, has developed and is marketing a structured approach to system analysis. This method, called Structured Analysis and Design Technique (SADT®) (a trademark of SofTech, Inc., Waltham, Mass.) attempts to introduce the clarity and discipline of manufacturing techniques to the design of systems. Since SADT is one of the better approaches, it will be used as a model for this discussion.

SADT provides methods for thinking in a structured way about large and complex problems; for working as a team with effective division and coordination of effort and roles; and for communicating interview, analysis, and design results in clear, precise notation. It also provides for documenting current results and decisions in a way that permits a complete audit of history; for controlling accuracy, completeness, and quality through frequent review and approval procedures; and for planning, managing, and assessing progress of the team effort.

SADT is based on seven fundamental concepts:

1. Complex problems are best attacked by building a model of the problem sufficiently precise to serve as the basis for problem solution.

2. Analysis of any problem should be top-down, modular, hierarchic, and structured.

3. The model should be diagrammed to show component parts, their interfaces, and how they compose a hierarchic structure.

4. The model-building technique must represent both things and happenings, properly related.

5. The analyst should differentiate between an initial functional model of functions to be performed and a subsequent design model of how those functions will be performed.

6. Analysis methods must support disciplined, coordinated teamwork.

7. All analysis and design decisions and comments must be in written form for open review by all team members.

SADT is structured decomposition—the orderly breaking down of a complex subject into its constituent parts. (See Figure 21.) A model is represented through the use of a graphic language designed to expose detail gradually and in a controlled manner, encourage conciseness and accuracy, focus attention on module interfaces, and provide a powerful

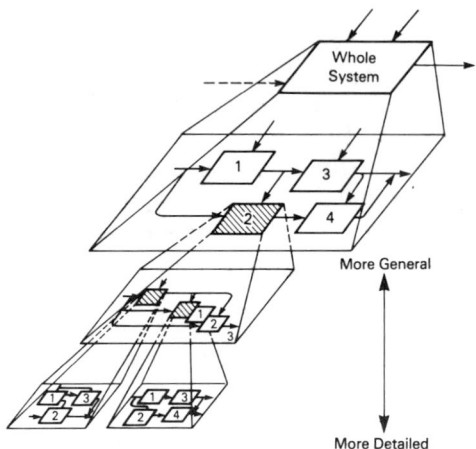

Figure 21. Structured decomposition.

representation of the whole system, thus preserving the logical relationship of each component to the total system.

Application starts with the most general or abstract description of the system contained in a single module or "box." This box is then decomposed into a number of more detailed boxes, each of which represents a major function of the "parent" box. These, in turn, become parent boxes and are decomposed to the next level of detail, and so on.

This top-down approach prevents considering too many details too soon. The number of "child" boxes is no fewer than three nor more than six.

The fact that a child module is a segment of a parent module creates a natural bounded context for the child. It cannot contain any elements which are beyond the scope of its parent. Any interfaces to other children of other parents must have been described between the parents. (See Figure 22.)

SADT develops two complementary models: an activity decomposition and a data decomposition. The activity decomposition details the happenings as activity boxes, while showing the things that interrelate them as data arrows. (See Figure 23.)

The data decomposition details the things of the system as data boxes, with the happenings that interrelate them shown as activity arrows.

The arrow structure on an SADT diagram represents a constraint relationship among the boxes (as contrasted to a flow of control or se-

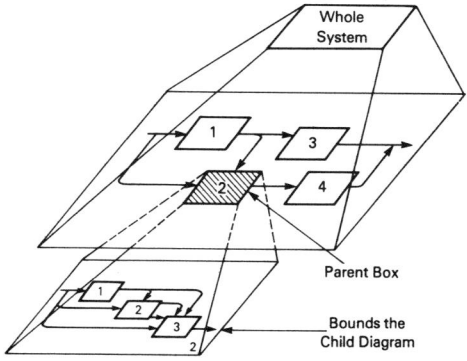

Figure 22. Parent and child relationship.

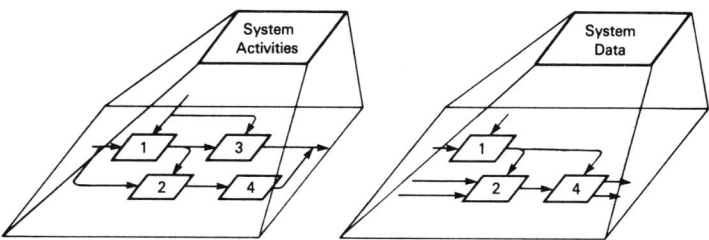

Figure 23. Complementary activity and data decompositions.

quence). The constraint arrows entering a box show all that is needed by the box to fulfill its role. No box can realize its function until preceding boxes have supplied needed results via entering arrows of its interfaces.

Arrows entering the box on the left represent input; arrows leaving on the right represent output; and arrows entering the top of the box represent controls over the way the input/output transformation is accomplished. (See Figure 24.) An output from one box may provide some or all of the inputs and controls required by one or other boxes. (See Figure 25.)

A parent-to-child connection is made by arrows that cross diagram boundaries. The precise matching of these arrows assures that the detail may be developed to its lowest level and remain coordinated with the whole. (See Figure 26.)

In both the analysis and design phases, a final step in the modeling process is to cross-reference the activity and data decomposition. Each model is checked to make sure that it shows all the elements of the other models and that the use of elements is consistent.

Work always begins with a functional model of the problem to

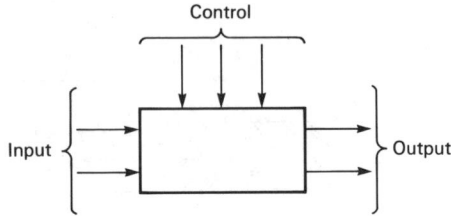

Figure 24. Box-interface arrow definition.

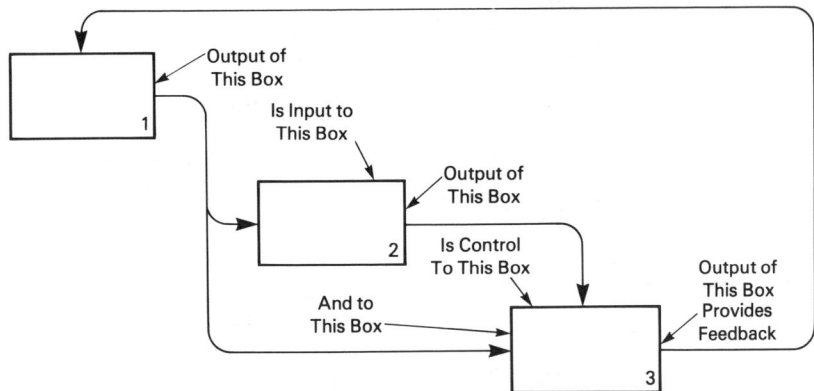

Figure 25. Multiple box-interface definitions.

ensure that the problem will be fully and clearly understood before the details of a solution are decided upon.

Analysis and design require disciplined, coordinated teamwork. The insights and views of project personnel must be communicated effectively at every step and level of analysis to ensure that the models reflect the best thinking of the team.

Because SADT starts with a single black box and proceeds to increasingly detailed diagrams of elements of the problem, documentation becomes available on a continuous basis. Analysis or design decisions can be seen in context at each step and challenged while alternative approaches are available. As changes and corrections are made, all versions of diagrams are entered in the project files—nothing is thrown away. A librarian provides filing, distribution, and record-keeping support, and ensures precise control over the status of the evolving model. A specific coding structure relates all diagrams in the hierarchy of the system model.

The use of SADT also conditions the selection of project personnel in the sense that use of the method requires assigning specific roles to members of the systems development team. A team member may support more than one function, but all functions must be performed.

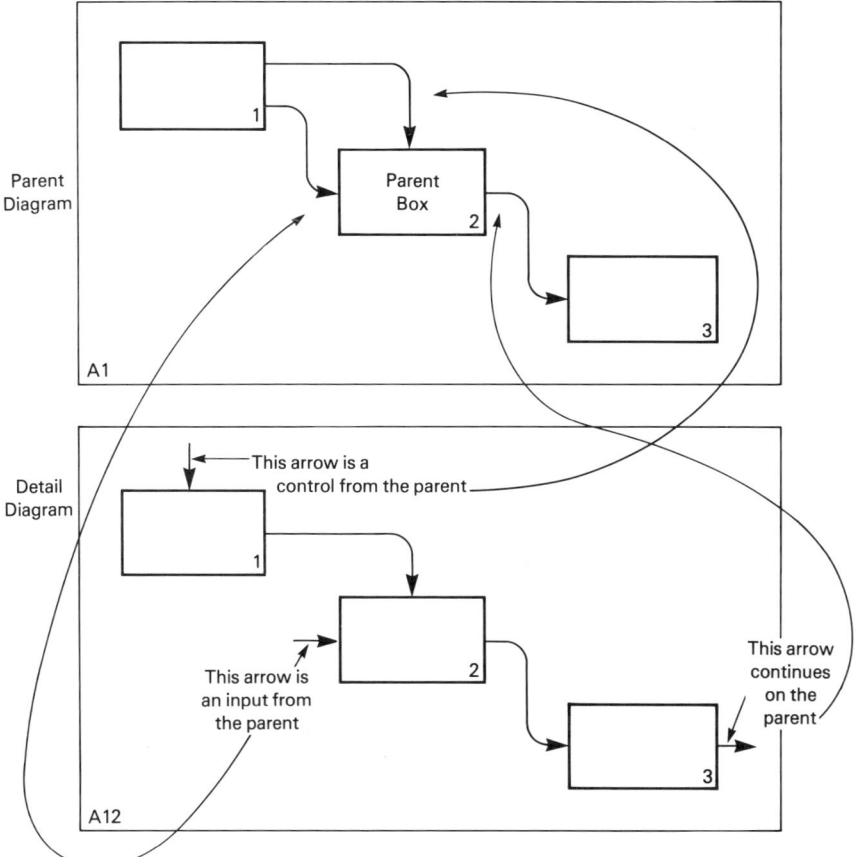

Figure 26.   Arrow continuation across diagram boundaries.

SofTech lists more than 50 organizations that have either adopted SADT as a tool or have used SofTech as a consultant for specific projects using SADT.[2]

SADT and other structured, top-down design techniques may be characterized by several principal features that indicate the trends in systems analysis and design techniques:

1. It is highly formal; everything is *written*.

2. It is tightly structured and all internal elements are "bounded" or constrained.

3. It makes use of a team approach.

4. It emphasizes review and "egoless" design.

5. It emphasizes complete problem definition and requirements analysis prior to any programming.

Name	Function
Authors	Personnel who study requirements and constraints, analyze system functions and represent them by models based on diagrams.
Commenters	Usually authors, who must review and comment in writing on the work of other authors.
Readers	Personnel who read diagrams for information but are not expected to make written comments.
Experts	Persons from whom authors obtain specialized information about requirements and constraints by means of interviews.
Technical Committee	A group of senior technical personnel assigned to review the analysis at every major level of decomposition. They either resolve technical issues or recommend a decision to the project management.
Project Librarian	A person assigned the responsibility of maintaining a centralized file of all project documents, making copies, distributing reader kits, and keeping records.
Project Manager	The member of the project who has the final technical responsibility for carrying out the system analysis and design.

Computer Aided Design

As previously indicated, a major drawback to structured methods is the generation and maintenance of large volumes of documentation.

Some approaches to structured design such as Boeing Computer Services' SSDM method combine a structuring approach and a symbolic representation and coding method with computer programs that ease the task of organizing, cross referencing, and maintaining the systems documentation.

It is expected that other computer aided design techniques will appear in the future as structured methods are increasingly applied to systems design and development.

Summary

Structured design can be a major aid in solving many of the problems that plague systems development projects. However, it is important to remember that structured design dictates certain functional staffing characteristics and operating methods for the development team. Without these, it will not achieve the intended objectives.

Footnotes

1. Descriptions of HIPO have been based on material in IBM publication GC 20-1851-1, "HIPO, A Design Aid and Documentation Technique," 1975.
2. The illustrations for this section are from SofTech, Inc. "An Introduction to SADT," publication number 9022-78R. SADT is a trademark of Sof-Tech, Inc., 460 Totten Pond Road, Waltham, Mass. 02154.

Discussion Topics

1. Why should feasibility studies be performed?
2. What methods are available for quantifying so-called "intangible" benefits?
3. What is the first step in determining the potential benefits of a new system?
4. Are the expected benefits of a new system usually realized?
5. What measures may be taken to improve the chances that proposed benefits will be realized?
6. What major benefits result from using structured design methodologies to develop systems?

MANAGING
DATA PROCESSING

The title of this chapter originates with the premise that those of us who have made a career of data processing have done so because we like it—because, for us, it's more fun than anything else we can do.

In order to keep having that fun, we must remember that, in the view of top corporate management, the primary objective of each function of the organization (including MIS) is to contribute to the ability of the organization to make a profit. In order to do

Chapter 5

this, the MIS manager must create an operation that provides the *necessary* services for the minimum cost consistent with being able to meet the evolving needs of the overall organization as they arise.

The first section of this chapter discusses the development of a long-range plan for data processing. The next three sections are directed toward achieving cost effectiveness and minimizing risk. Both of these considerations support the primary objectives of top management—PROFIT!

SECTION 1   LONG-RANGE PLANNING FOR EDP

Whether it's called Management Information Systems, the Data Processing Department, the Computer Division, or "The IBM Room," the EDP activities of most organizations suffer from one common failing—the lack of long-range planning. Those principles of strategic planning that have been adopted by a majority of the major corporations and which depend heavily on the computer sciences have, for the most part, not been adopted by the computer managers themselves.

The excuses for planning in a short-range, adaptive mode, are numerous. They include the fast pace of changes in hardware and software technology, the high rate of personnel turnover in the field, the constant changes in system requirements, and the frequency of unexpected user demands. All these reasons indicate a clear recognition of the changing environment of which data processing is a part. However, many data processing managers fail to realize that they themselves are the agents of change and should be in the best position to plan how those changes will take place.

A long-range plan for data processing consists of the following elements: 1) the systems plan, 2) the hardware plan, 3) the software plan, 4) the staffing plan, and 5) the control plan.

Before discussing the planning process it is necessary to recognize that some preconditions must exist for successful planning. For the purposes of this section it is assumed that the data processing function is a part of a corporate environment. (However, the basic ideas can be generalized to any organization.)

The data processing function does not exist in an organizational vacuum. As a part of the organizational environment their planning must be consistent with the plans of all other elements of the organization. For example, spending must coincide with the expected earnings of the organization. In addition, no plan for a part of the organization can be designed independently of the overall organization plan. No successful long-range plan for EDP can be developed unless there is a specific corporate long-range plan with stated goals and objectives for the corporation and for the user divisions.

Remember, EDP is usually a service organization working to support the goals and objectives of others. The reason for EDP function has had to "react to unexpected user demands" has frequently been the failure of EDP management to familiarize themselves with the goals and objectives of the rest of the organization.

The following elements of a corporate long-range plan are necessary to provide the environment for successful EDP planning:

1. A statement of corporate socioeconomic purpose.

2. A corporate strategic plan stating major long-range goals and

objectives, major policies, major constraints, and anticipated environmental conditions.

3. A corporate tactical plan stating short-range objectives, and schedules to component parts of the organization.

4. A divisional long-range plan setting forth the detailed methods for meeting the objectives and schedules, and descriptions of specific constraints and environmental conditions.

Incidently, divisional plans are not unrealistically handed down from corporate management but the entire set of corporate long-range plans are the product of a coordinated two-way effort between the separate groups and frequently the result of several iterations of planning drafts.

The second requirement for the EDP long-range plan is to recognize that developing a plan takes both time and effort. A reasonable budget must be established for the planning function.

The third requirement is that a system must be established for charging out the cost of the data processing functions to the users on a basis consistent with their percentage of use. Without such a system no control mechanism can be developed, no true economic feasibility can be determined for system proposals, and no short- or long-range EDP budget can be properly justified.

The fourth prerequisite is a plan for planning. This section is intended primarily to address this last prerequisite.

The Systems Plan

Developing the systems plan is probably the most time consuming and critical portion of the long-range planning effort. The data processing manager and his planners must familiarize themselves with the corporate and divisional plans, the organizational structure, the business methods of the firm and its product lines. They must develop a clear picture of how the various functions of the organization interrelate and how the systems currently operated by the data processing department assist in these functions. One way to establish this picture is by flowcharting the business (see Figure 1). This type of chart can be further enhanced by identifying the organizational responsibility for each function and by clearly identifying which functions are and are not computer supported.

Each present data processing system should be reviewed and described in such a manner as to provide a basis for establishing other parts of the plan. These descriptions may take the form of the sample shown in Figure 2 and should contain at least the following elements:

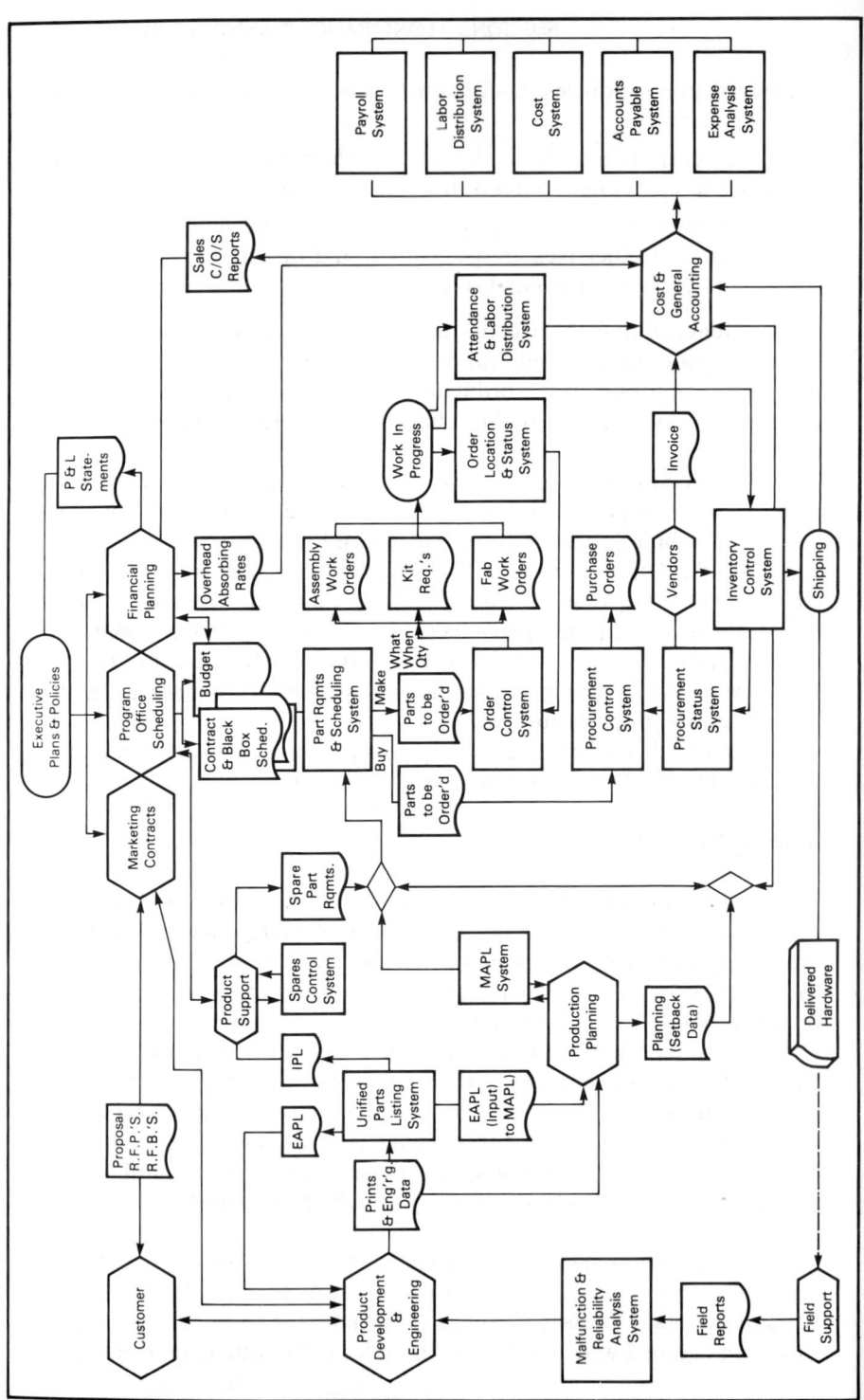

1. A brief summary of the application indicating pertinent features of the system with some indication of the stability of the system and future plans for further development. Each present data processing system should be reviewed with its users to determine areas of potential change or enhancement. If, as frequently is the case, the users are not familiar enough with computer capabilities to assist in this planning, the planning staff may have to define potential changes and enhancements based on their knowledge of the function being supported and computer capabilities. These definitions should then be reviewed with the user groups. This section should also indicate the input method and the record volumes of the most critical files. Volumes should be indicated for the present time and predicted for one year, two years, and five years into the future.

2. Equipment requirements for the system. Memory requirements should be indicated in bytes and represent the largest resident program segment for the system. Peripheral devices should be summarized and not represent the requirements of a single program but the combined requirements of all programs in the system.

Special note should be made as to whether equipment requirements are for a central computer, a minicomputer operating in a distributed processing environment, an intelligent terminal, or a combination of the above. This applies to the other elements of the system description indicated below.

3. File sizes should be stated in terms of characters and represent the greatest number of characters required to be on-line at one time in the system.

4. Computer hours should be stated in terms of schedule requirements. A daily figure representing the number of hours required during one 24-hour period, a weekly figure representing the number of hours required for those portions of the system that are scheduled to run on a weekly basis, and not a summarization of the daily figures and a monthly figure that should represent the time necessary to run jobs that are scheduled on a monthly basis. The computer time should be divided into shifts of activity to permit later analysis of the need for multiprogramming scheduling.

5. The number of programs written and the programming languages in which they are written are provided as an aide to estimating potential conversion problems and costs when considering future hardware plans.

6. The requirement for specialized systems software should be indicated. Examples include terminal control software, telecommunications monitors, data base management systems, data dictionaries, re-

Application: Payroll/Personnel

1. Summary:

    a. Description: System for recording, controlling and reporting all payroll and personnel transactions.

    Functions included are:
    Calculation and printing of paychecks
    Calculation of deductions
       State and federal
       Company required
       Voluntary
    Payroll check reconciliation
    Maintenance of sick leave accrual
    Maintenance of vacation accrual
    Salary statistics
    Skills inventory
    Salary surveys
    Personnel progression and history

    The present system consists of over 140 programs which are questionably documented and written in COBOL, BAL, and RPG. Preliminary studies indicate that the system costs almost twice as much as it should to operate.

    We are currently involved in a project to replace this system and this project should be successfully concluded during the 4th quarter of 1984.

    The new system will include the capability to pay employees in all states and to process work-order- oriented time recording data.

    b. Input method: keypunched cards and magnetic tape.

    c. Volume:
    Current — 14,000 trans./mo
    1 Year — 14,056
    2 Years — 15,176
    5 Years — 16,758

2. Equipment Requirements:

	Current	1 Year	2 Years	5 Years
Core	109K	65K	65K	65K
Card reader	1	1	1	1
Card punch	1	1	1	1
Printers	1	1	1	1
Console typewriter	1	1	1	1
Type drives	4	4	4	4
DASD	1	1	1	1
MSU	0	0	0	0
CRT terminals	0	0	0	0
Typewriter terminals	0	0	0	0

3. File Sizes (Characters):

	Current	1 Year	2 Years	5 Years
DASD	50K	50K	54K	60K
TAPE	12.5M	12.6M	13.6M	15M
Other				

4. Computer Hours:

	Process Day	Night	Current	1 Year	2 Years	5 Years
Daily			0	0	0	0
Biweekly		X	0	10	11	12
Monthly		X	37.1	3	3.5	4

Figure 2.

5. Programs:

Language		Quantity	
		Present	1975 Est.
COBOL	—	43	40
ALC	—	6	0
RPG	—	74	0
Tape sort	—	6	0
Disc sort	—	9	15
Other utilities	—	4	3
Other	—	0	0

Figure 2 (continued).

port generators, and similar software. This is especially significant for planning a distributed processing environment.

7. Telecommunications equipment in use would be described in terms of type of equipment, application use, line configurations, network layouts, line speeds and loads, and so on.

When this section is completed, the planning group must turn its attention to those areas that are not presently computer supported. System forecasting for these functions should take place in the following steps:

1. Review potential changes of these functions with the responsible organization units.

2. Examine the function for technical potential for automation.

3. Rough out a systems concept (perhaps a brief flowchart and five or less pages of narrative).

4. Review the systems concept with the potential user.

5. Prepare a final technical system concept paper.

6. Describe system resource requirements in the same manner as those described for existing systems.

7. Estimate the computer resources necessary for development, testing, and conversion of the new applications.

After documenting the potential changes to existing systems and potential new systems, develop ball park estimates for the cost of development and implementation and the continuing cost of operation for each of these. Considering the present cost of operating the function, the present and future capacities of the systems, the present and future flexibility, and the economic effects of present labor-intensive methods, prepare a chart for each application showing the projected cost of the present methods versus the proposed methods on a five-year basis (see Figures 3A and 3B). Using the same material prepare a payback analysis for each proposed application (see Figure 4).

| | | Alternative No. 1 | | | |
Year	Present System	Implement- ation	Operation	Earnings	Total
1	$1,125,942	$164,584	$1,125,942	$ —	$1,290,526
2	1,238,536	30,120	921,676	(6,000)	945,796
3	1,362,389	—	891,998	(28,000)	863,998
4	1,498,628	—	945,517	(33,000)	912,517
5	1,648,491	—	1,002,248	(37,000)	965,248
Total	$6,873,986	$194,704	$4,887,381	$(104,000)	$4,978,085

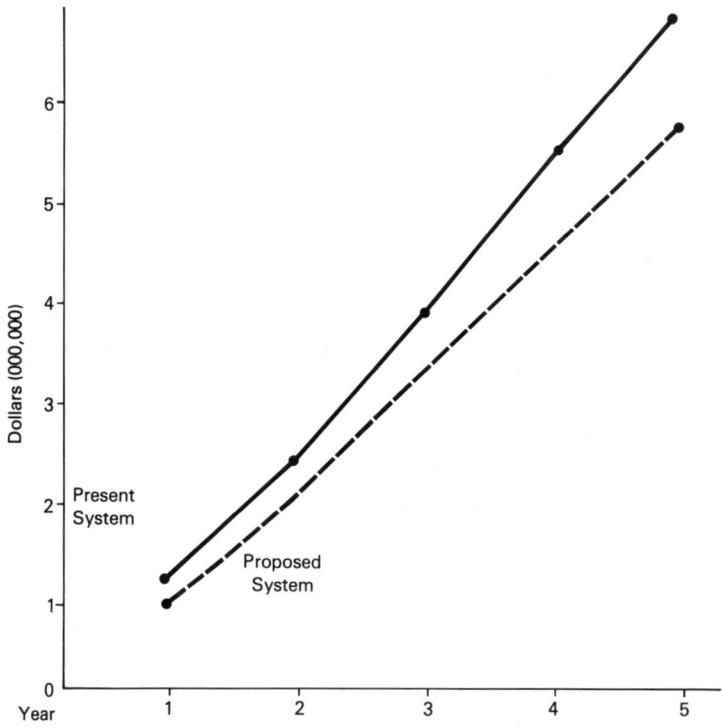

Figure 3. (a) Cash flow analysis; (b) cash flow graph.

Pay Back Analysis

| | | Alternative No. 1 | | |
Year	Present System	Total Cost	Saving (Loss)	Cum. Saving (Loss)
1	$1,125,942	$1,290,526	$(164,584)	$(164,584)
2	$1,238,536	$ 945,796	$ 292,740	$ 128,156

Figure 4.

Separate any potential changes or new applications that do not appear to be economically feasible and that are amenable to noncomputer solutions.

The results of this effort are a list and a description of economically feasible potential applications, or solutions to problems that cannot be solved without the use of a computer, for review with management. These descriptions may take the form of Figure 2.

The selected applications must now be examined for priority of development in terms of cash availability, return on investment, consistency with corporate long-range plans, and anticipated environmental conditions. This is the task of top management.

Experience indicates that the most productive approach is to establish a data processing steering committee. This committee should ideally be established by the president (with himself as chairman) and consist of the heads of all major user organizations. The steering committee should bear not only the responsibility for approving a long-range plan but for reviewing progress against this plan, approving individual segments of the plan, and monitoring the performance of the EDP function.

After the committee has established the priorities of those applications they feel are economically justified, the documentation of the approved applications and their priorities becomes the basic long-range systems plan.

The Hardware Plan

The information provided by the control reports, combined with the future projections of volumes for current systems and the information on new systems to be developed (from the systems plan) provide the basis for forecasting hardware needs.

The hardware plan should address the following items, at a minimum:

- Central computer (model, size, channels)
- Other computers (front ends, minicomputers, special purpose equipment)
- Storage devices (DASD, tape, archival storage)
- Terminals (type, use, location)
- Communications (modems, multiplexors, lines)
- Data entry equipment
- Support equipment (decollators, tape cleaners)

- Facilities (space, power, air conditioning)
- Any other capital or rental equipment requirements

For these items the plan should cover a year-by-year view of capacities, capabilities, location, cost, and the methods of transition from the present configurations to those projected for the future. Transition methods may often require that reference be made to the staffing and software plans. In fact, in order to relate properly to each other, the hardware, software, and staffing plans should be developed concurrently.

The long-range plan has one other principal input that is markedly different from the short-range plan. This is a technical projection of the state-of-the-art of computer hardware, software, and costs.

Within some limits a regular perusal of currently published materials provides adequate indicators to the general trends of changes to be expected in the hardware and software fields for up to five years into the future. For example, virtual memory software was predictable in 1968–69 when it was being developed by all major computer manufacturers and magazine articles on the technique were being published. Remember the IBM 360–67, the Cambridge Monitor System, and CP–67? Those who were familiar with the development of Burroughs software had an even greater ability to predict this development.

Another indicator is simple business economics. We can expect that any computer manufacturer will want to obtain sufficient return on his investment in a new product line before making it comparatively obsolete with a new model. For example, we know that the IBM 360 had a product life of about eight years. We have seen the introduction of substantive changes to the IBM 370 product line after eight years.

With consideration of some "mid-life kickers," we can generally assume that a computer product line will be replaced within eight to ten years by a new offering with greater capacity and capability for less money. The plan should not then anticipate acquisition of a computer at or near the end of its product life cycle without careful study and justification.

Such justification is possible. For example, the *purchase* of used computers near the end of their life cycle can provide substantial savings.

Given various software options and a staffing level consistent with the level of expense authorized by top management, a schedule should be developed for implementing the applications in their order of priority. In addition to indicating manpower and software requirements, this schedule should indicate the computer time necessary for development and operation of the proposed systems and any additional hardware that may be necessary to contain the data base or accommodate the additional time requirements. This schedule becomes a basis for the hardware plan.

Since the planned applications represent an extension or replacement of the current workload, a summarization of the data shown on the descriptions of present applications must be integrated with the expected *additional* workload of planned applications and development work.

This may be charted, showing a baseline established for estimated average computer utilization considering the net effect of replacements of current systems and showing the anticipated impact of future additional applications (see Figure 5.)

To be consistent, estimates should be made in terms of the performance of present hardware. Total anticipated memory and peripheral unit needs should be estimated on the basis of the needs of the systems that are presently, or are expected to be, operating concurrently (in multiprogramming mode).

Having established these requirements, the next step is equipment evaluation. This phase should consider not only the technical evaluation and possible benchmarking of equipment from various manufacturers, but also the single vs. multiple vendor situation, and the buy vs. lease or rent position.

The buy vs. lease or rent decision should consider at least the following major elements:

1. Present age of the product line being considered (or age of the product line at time of anticipated purchase).

2. The estimated sale value of the equipment at the point of the next anticipated equipment change.

3. The cost of money.

4. The cash flow over the expected life of the installation.

5. The present value of future cash flow dollars.

6. Taxes and investment tax credits.

7. The depreciation schedule (for both the company P & L and for tax purposes).

8. Lease termination penalties.

Figure 6 shows a model schedule for calculating the net cost on purchased equipment.

The Software Plan

The software plan, developed concurrently with the hardware and staffing plan, will influence and be influenced by both of these.

The characteristics of the operating system will influence the

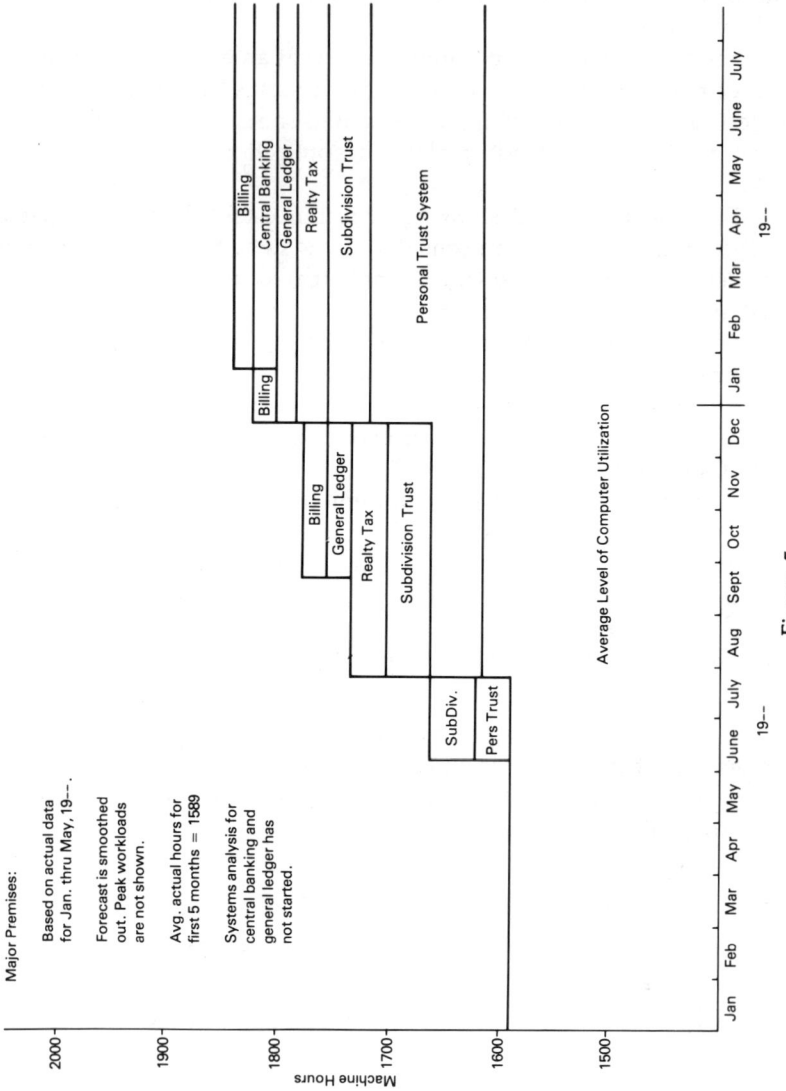

Figure 5.

	Fourth Year	Fifth Year	Sixth Year
Percent of Residual Value	60%	50%	25%
Residual Value	$_____	$_____	$_____
Net Book Value (Tax)	_____	_____	_____
Net Book Value (Books)	_____	_____	_____
Gain — Tax	_____	_____	_____
Less-Recapture of Accelerated Depreciation	(_____)	(_____)	(_____)
Gain — Books	_____	_____	_____
Investment Tax Credit Recapture	_____	_____	_____

I. CUMULATIVE CASH FLOW — In (Out)

	Fourth Year	Fifth Year	Sixth Year
Proceeds from Sale at Residual Value	$_____	$_____	$_____
Taxes Payable:			
1. Depreciation Recapture @ 52%	(_____)	(_____)	(_____)
2. Book Gain @ 25%	(_____)	(_____)	(_____)
Investment Tax Credit Recapture	(_____)	(_____)	(_____)
Loan Principal Balance	(_____)	(_____)	
Net Cash Flow	_____	_____	_____
Present Value Factor	_____	_____	_____
Discounted Cash Flow	_____	_____	_____
Cumulative Discounted Cash Flow to Date	(_____)	(_____)	(_____)
Net Cash Flow After Disposition	$(_____)	$(_____)	$(_____)

II. P & L EXPENSES AFTER TAXES

	Fourth Year	Fifth Year	Sixth Year
Gain — Books	$_____	$_____	$_____
Taxes Payable	(_____)	(_____)	(_____)
Investment Tax Credit Recapture	(_____)	(_____)	(_____)
Cumulative P&L Expenses to Date (After Tax)	(_____)	(_____)	(_____)
Net P&L Expenses After Taxes, After Disposition	$_____	$_____	$_____

Figure 6. Net effect of equipment purchase assuming disposition at residual value.

hardware selection and influence the training and caliber of the staff required for the installation. Some operating systems may require the purchase of significant numbers of auxiliary packages. In addition, an efficient operating system may lower the requirement for hardware.

The operating system must be selected with a view towards the ultimate needs of the systems plan. In order to meet the objectives of the systems plan, a conversion of operating systems may be required. Such a conversion will have a major impact on staffing and must be considered in the schedule of system implementation and hardware delivery.

Systems software must consider application requirements, development requirements and operating requirements. For example, some of the following software may be required under these categories. (Duplication is intentional.)

- Application requirements
  Data communications monitor
  Terminal control software
  Data base management system
  Inquiry system
  Report generator

- Development requirements
  All of above
  Data dictionary system
  Program library management system
  Program performance monitor
  On-line programming system
  Debugging and documentation systems

- Operating requirements
  Program library management system
  Tape library system
  Hardware monitor analysis reports
  Computer time accounting system

These lists are obviously not exhaustive but provide some idea of the considerations for systems software. To these must be added a similar list for any minicomputers in a distributed environment and any demand for network control software.

Documentation and technical standards must be reviewed and plans developed for their maintenance and enhancement. A change of operating systems, for example, will require major changes in the standards of the installation.

The software plan contributes additional cost to the total budget in terms of the anticipated price of software, the anticipated cost of conversions, and estimated amounts for upgrading and maintaining documentation and technical standards.

The Staffing Plan

A staffing plan should be relatively specific for eighteen months into the future and generalized beyond that for at least another twelve months. The end product of this plan should be a chart as illustrated in Figure 7 and supporting documentation.

In allocating time for personnel one would normally expect to budget for maintenance projects, enhancement projects, feasibility studies, and new system projects. This time, which may be considered "chargeable" or productive time should not be budgeted beyond 70 percent of the available time of the personnel dedicated to this work. This will allow for the use of personnel time in training, vacations, sick leave, and organization meetings.

In addition to the above, time should be allocated for such efforts as do not directly result in productive work for the user. For example, budgets should be established for the maintenance of systems software, instruction and training, anticipated loss due to turnover, conversion efforts, and research and planning.

The anticipated outside costs for seminars, schooling, and other training methods should be budgeted. The cost of advertising or employment fees should be budgeted based on anticipated turnover of personnel.

On the basis of the software systems selected, the staffing plan should designate the type of personnel required (development, clerical, or operations) and the caliber of personnel required. Anticipated salaries should be based on the present market for these types of personnel. It may be necessary to consider the use of outside consultants or temporary personnel for peak loads.

A training program should be developed which will permit the continuing development of personnel resources as well as anticipate the advancement and/or "topping out" of personnel.

The ability to meet staffing requirements will have an effect on the schedule of the hardware, software, and systems plans.

The Control Plan

The control plan consists of the policies, procedures, and techniques necessary to provide data processing management and general management with the tools necessary to control the direction and monitor the performance of the data processing organization.

Many of the elements of a good strategic plan are based on

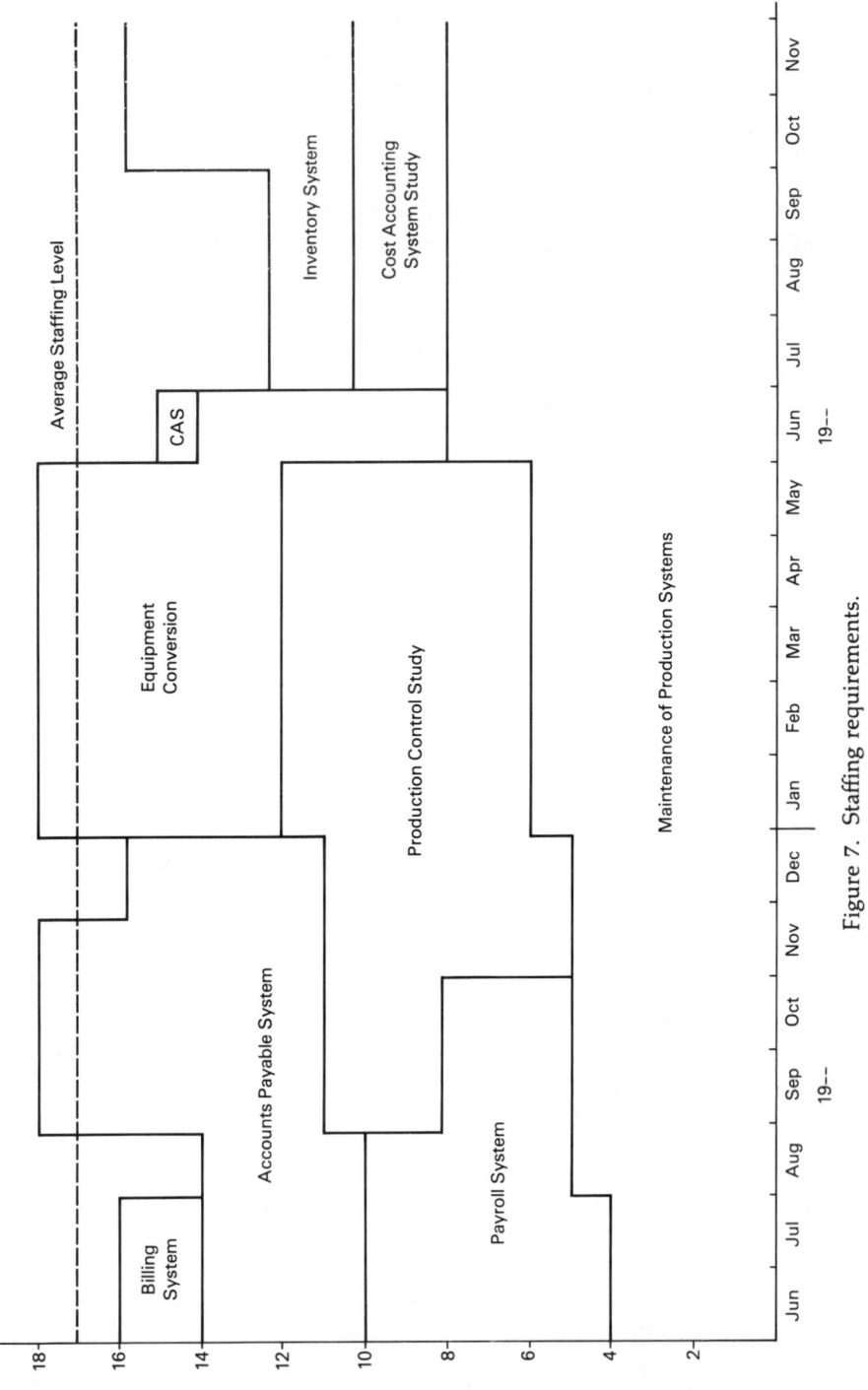

Figure 7. Staffing requirements.

the results of management techniques and performance evaluation methods *in place* prior to the start of strategic planning. These in-place methods provide a substantial part of the information upon which tactical or short-range planning is based, and which can be extended for use in long-range planning.

The management control structure is dependent upon the quality of management reporting which emphasizes performance evaluation and cost effectiveness. Reports should have the following characteristics:

• They should be evaluative, measuring actual performance against a predetermined standard.

• They should be oriented toward the function being measured and reports should exist for all functions.

• They should be predictive in the sense that trends should be clearly indicated.

• They should provide management with a means of anticipating potential problems or unusual expenditures.

• They should be concise and easy to read and interpret, preferably graphic in form where possible.

• Where possible, monthly reports should show a moving thirteen-month period to indicate trends.

• They should support a continuity of structure from the lowest level of the organization through to top management.

• They should be provided with a frequency and promptness that permits management to take any necessary corrective action before serious damage has been done. For example, the Operations manager should receive the following types of reports.

• System downtime report. This report should track system downtime against performance targets by reason (CPU failure, program failure, operator error, peripheral failure, air conditioning or power failure, etc.).

• Rerun time report. This report should track rerun time *chargeable to the data center* by reason in the same manner as the downtime report. Rerun time is defined as the total time required to complete the job minus that time used for the final, good run.

• User-caused rerun time report. This report should track machine time used as a result of user-caused reruns. It is useful in identifying systems problems or training deficiencies. In a timesharing environment the report helps to track down and correct any repeated abuses of the system by terminal users.

- Peripheral performance report. This report should contain the frequency, duration and reasons for downtime for each peripheral device. This helps to identify failure-prone units for better service or replacement. This report should include terminal devices.

- Data entry performance. This report should compare expected performance vs. actual performance in keystrokes for the data entry group. (The data entry manager would need this information by individual to evaluate performance.)

- Data entry volume. This report should show budgeted vs. actual workload in terms of input documents or records keyed by job.

- CPU performance reports. A series of reports may be developed to illustrate the capacity used vs. the capacity available in the CPU. (Note: Such reports should clearly separate the capacity used in the systems state from that used in the problem state.)

- Computer utilization summary. This graphic report should indicate available capacity and its use for productive time, downtime, and rerun time. Trends indicated help with capacity planning.

- DASD capacity summary. This graphic report should track available capacity vs. file space allocated.

Other reports that may prove useful include performance tracking of terminal response time, channel utilization, communications line failures, on-time report distribution, control errors, and so forth.

These reports detect trouble spots that require management action in the short term and provide capacity utilization trends for long-term planning. They also indicate potential staffing and training needs for the long term.

An essential ingredient for the monitoring of performance is a system permitting the charge-out of project development and operation cost to the users. This system should preferably be structured to include overhead factors that result in the recovery of all costs of the data processing organization. Guidelines must be established for the control of project cost and time on a regular basis.

A corporate executive steering committee should establish policies for approval of new projects in a manner similar to approval for capital investment. During the life of a project, various checkpoints should be established at which the steering committee can make "go—no go" decisions for continued investment in the project. In addition, the steering committee should receive regular reports on project progress and review project priorities every six months (or as often as necessary to meet changing environmental conditions).

Putting the LRP Together

The process of long-range planning is described by the flowchart in Figure 8.

As each section of the plan is documented, it should be preceded by a summary of the premises on which it is based. For example, the hardware section should include a list of the sources of data on which predictions are based, a description of anticipated hardware developments, and a review of the vendors who may be able to meet the requirements for the future.

A sample table of contents for the plan may include the following:

I. *Summary of Recommended Action*

II. *The Systems Plan*

    A. Corporate Planning Factors Considered

    B. Systems Plan Premises

    C. Descriptions of Current Applications

    D. Descriptions of Planned Applications

    E. Business Flowchart

    F. Priority for Implementing New Applications

    G. Anticipated Implementation Schedules

III. *The Hardware Plan*

    A. Hardware Planning Premises

    B. Current and Anticipated Computer Use

    C. Current and Anticipated Computer Requirements

    D. Current and Anticipated Hardware Costs

IV. *The Software Plan*

    A. Software Planning Premises

    B. Software Requirements

    C. Current and Anticipated Cost of Software

    D. Technical Standards Plan

    E. Documentation Standards Plan

V. *The Staffing Plan*

    A. Staff Planning Premises

    B. Detailed Staff Requirements

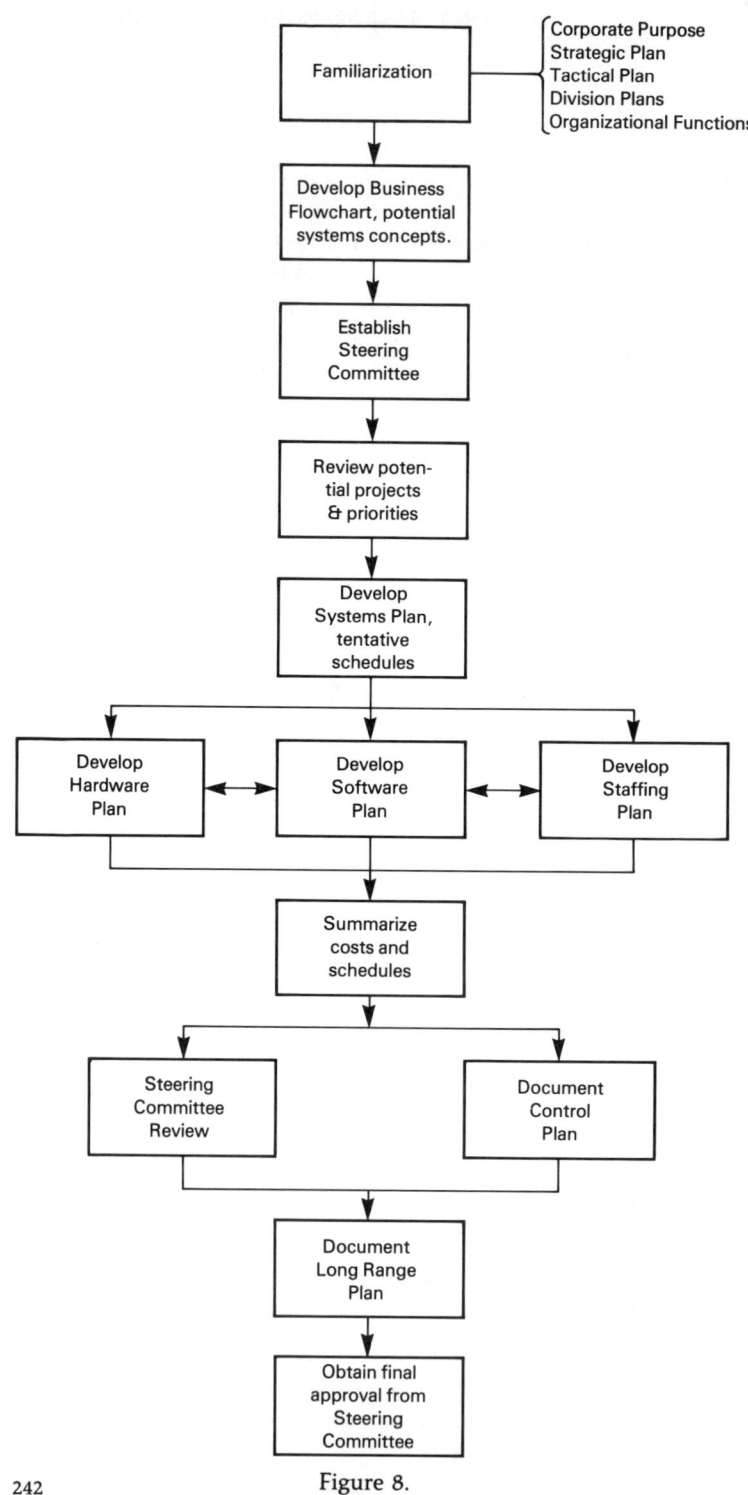

Figure 8.

Maintaining the Long-Range Plan

Those organizations new to long-range planning will find that the first plan will take from six months to a year in development. This of course means that prior to publication some of the information contained in the plan may be as much as one year old. A final prepublication review will be necessary to bring all the information and projections up to date.

Not all parts of the long-range plan can be expected to cover the same span of time. The systems plan should be projected for the same length of time as the hardware plan or through amortization of any purchased equipment. The software plan should project two and one-half years or through amortization of major software changes or conversions. The staffing plan should project a total of two and one-half years. The control plan is, of course, a one-time set up of procedures which may be modified as necessary.

External environmental conditions may have considerable impact on any long-range plan. For that reason it is necessary to maintain a continuous research effort and regular reporting of progress against the plan. At least every six months a progress report to the steering committee should indicate accomplishments and deviations from the long-range plan. At least annually a complete projection should be made for the time spans indicated above.

Summary

The data processing manager will benefit from the long-range plan by being able to reduce his need to react to emergency situations, by a deeper understanding of the company's requirements, and by closer liaison with top management.

Corporate management will benefit from the plan by establishing control over the data processing effort, increasing their familiarity with the uses of the information processing technology, and avoiding the high cost associated with crash programs and unanticipated equipment and software conversions.

SECTION 2   MINIMIZING EDP MANAGEMENT RISK

Those of us who work in EDP management recognize that our environment is continually influenced by external forces. On the surface, it would appear that these influences create a high-risk environment for both the EDP Manager and the organization in which he functions. However, there are elements of risk, which, if they cannot be eliminated, at least can be minimized.

In discussing the subject of EDP management risk, it should be noted that there are two areas, not necessarily congruent, of risk. First, there are the risks to the organization. These risks fall into the category of financial risks, which include unsuccessful project development, project cost overruns, excessive total costs of data processing operation, and potential adverse effects from implementing new systems. There are operating risks which include improper systems implementation, maintaining proper audit trails, potential adverse effects on production, and potential adverse effects on customers (for example in billing systems). Finally, there are risks to the organization connected with the production of reports or completion of systems on time. Second, there are the personal risks for the EDP Manager. These include risks to his credibility, effectiveness in the company, and even to his job, contingent on his failure to adequately minimize the risks to the organization.

There have been many studies done recently on minimizing the risk in computer operations having to do with security, scheduling techniques, backup facilities, and so forth. These areas are all important and highly visible. However, the maximum visibility and maximum risk exposure of the EDP Manager is in the area of systems design and implementation. In this area, there are four ways to approach minimizing risk. These are planning, elimination of risk areas, communication with users in user language, and sharing risk. Let us look at each of these in some detail.

Planning

You might say that talking about planning to EDP people is like talking about motherhood. I believe that it's more like talking about the weather. Everybody talks about it, but nobody does anything about it. The two most criticized phenomena of EDP are project overruns and overreaching computer capacity without warning.

In regard to project planning, it is important to emphasize several specific techniques that tend to minimize risk.

1. Any effective project control system should be oriented to the *product* as well as to the *task*. All of us have had the experience of encountering a project that has been 95 percent complete for six months.

A product required at the completion of each task, and appropriate user acceptance of the product, is a fundamental requirement of good project control.

2. The project structure should contain at least four distinct phases. These are: the definition phase, the detailed design phase, the programming and documentation phase, and the implementation phase. There are two ways in which this structure helps to minimize risk. First the structure imposes specific points of control. Second, and perhaps even more important, the structure permits realistic estimating to take place. We are all familiar with the disastrous results of providing a fixed price bid and schedule at the beginning of a project for the entire project.

The Armed Forces, which for some time have used fixed-price contracting, recognized early in the game that vendors could not properly establish a fixed price based on the requirements issued with the request for quotation. For this reason they established a paid preliminary phase for qualified bidders called the project definition phase. It was during this phase that vendors examined the requirements, developed more detail and finally submitted a quotation. The adoption of this technique considerably minimized project overruns.

In the same manner the definition phase should be used to establish the requirements, develop alternative solutions, and prepare estimates for the alternative solutions.

The second phase, the detailed design phase, should be used to develop the specifications for the alternatives selected and prepare an estimate for project completion of even greater accuracy.

At the conclusion of each of these first two phases, the user should review the estimates with an eye to cancelling or approving continued work on the project in light of his return on investment.

3. A technical review committee should be established for each proposed project. This committee should consist of representatives from systems development, computer operations, systems programming, and the user. At the conclusion of each of the first two phases, this committee should review the definition and estimates and work plan prior to its formal presentation to management. At the conclusion of the second phase a representative of internal audit should participate in the review to assure that control and audit requirements are being met by the design. Finally, after implementation, the system should be the subject of another technical review to determine whether or not the project has met its objectives in the best manner.

4. As previously pointed out, no organization can successfully schedule its people for any extended period of time at 100 percent of

available hours. In the average systems organization, at least 25 percent of each analyst's or programmer's time is required for vacations, sick leave, personal time off, training, coffee breaks, and administrative and organizational meetings. In fact, it is even optimistic in many cases to schedule employees for 75 percent of available time. In addition, a conservative average of probably 10 percent of employee time is spent in nonproductive status due to late completion of activities on which the employee is dependent, poor work scheduling, nonwork-oriented conversation, and other forms of idle time.

All project scheduling should take these factors into account to minimize the risk of project overruns.

In planning for computer capacity, operations should keep a capacity planning document up to date showing current equipment use, expected volume increases, and expected impact of new systems. Technical reviews of systems projects should provide input concerning the impact of additional use on the present equipment and the impact on project costs of additional capacity required.

Elimination of Risk Areas

The next subject concerns eliminating areas of risk. Everytime we contact a company regarding an error in a computerized statement, we get an answer on the order of, "The computer must have fouled up." We in the computer profession know that this *isn't* true. In a different context, most of the time, when a manager calls to find out why his report is late or incorrect, the manager gets told, "Something went wrong with the program." Those of us in the data processing profession know that this *is* true.

When we discuss eliminating areas of risk, one of those areas that we would like to eliminate would be programming. While it may not be feasible to eliminate programming, there are obvious current techniques available to minimize or eliminate those areas of programming subject to risk, and some of the programming effort itself. The recent use of structured programming or HIPO concepts and the use of chief programmer teams as advocated by IBM have indicated that a significant reduction in program bugs can be achieved by these methods.

Another concept is based on hardware cost trends. The implementation of virtual memory concepts on a broader scale will continue to reduce the cost of using main memory. The cost of rapidly accessible peripheral storage devices will continue to drop. The combination of these two items will make data management systems containing multiple file inversions economically feasible. These data management systems will respond to parameter-driven report generators and to on-line inquiry from the user, further reducing the need for programmers.

Hopefully, one major use of programmers in the past can be avoided in the future. That is, conversion of programs due to hardware or operating system change. One of the major reasons for expansion of the number of programmers in the population during the 1960s was this cost of conversion. Systems were designed with programs written in SPS for the IBM 1401. They were then converted to Autocoder for the 1410 or 7010 (some were converted to early conversions of COBOL). With the advent of the 360 operating systems these programs were again converted (to avoid emulation) to Assembly Language, COBOL or PL1 and modified to make use of the operating systems. In spite of manufacturer resistance, users of computers are hopeful that the future will see new releases of equipment that are cross compatible and backward compatible. The lesson we have learned from the 1960s is to avoid conversions like the plague.

Perhaps the single most important development of the recent past is packaged computer software and services. Software packages are marketed for almost every conceivable type of business application. Many companies have been extremely successful in their installation, the secret of such success being avoiding modification of the software.

Fallout from government and university research projects has made several extremely sophisticated software packages available to the computer user. The Air Force and Navy PERT Systems and such packages as the UCLA Bio-Medical Statistics programs are just two examples of the better software available at very low cost from these sources. For more specialized business applications, terminals may be rented for on-line use of proprietary packages for such applications as return on investment analysis, cash flow analysis, on-line program development, and data base management among others. Another product of the recent past is the specialized computer center offering the use of proprietary packages for such applications as payroll, general accounting, check reconciliation, inventory management, accounts receivable and billing, and many other business-oriented applications.

During the past few years, there has been a dramatic increase in the use of minicomputers. Several companies offer the installation of turnkey applications based on the use of minicomputers. These applications already cover the full range of normal business data processing and have been extended into such areas as escrow accounting, message switching, data input devices, and word processing. In looking at these alternatives, the EDP Manager must keep in mind that his task is to meet the organization's needs, not necessarily within an internal EDP structure.

Aside from the use of packaged systems, there are several things an EDP manager can do to help himself. One way to minimize the risk of cost overruns is the use of fixed-price contract programming services. Several companies have been quite successful with this approach which is based on the extensive documentation of analysis and systems specifications. At least one company has gone so far as to contract out all programming and employ only systems analysts on its staff.

Even without so drastic an approach, the application of extensive documentation standards and programming standards is a major step toward cutting the cost of program maintenance. Documentation should always be approached with the assumption that the original programmer will not be available to maintain the program.

Most major installations today have established off-site facilities for backup storage of data base files. Unfortunately, most of these organizations have neglected to similarly protect systems and operating documentation, without which the data base files may be useless. Sorting backup files of the data bases is covering only a small part of the total risk exposure.

As the field of business data processing approaches maturity, a major new method for reducing programming efforts has been discovered. During the initial rush to use computers, many applications were programmed and implemented without regard to their economic justification. The removal of applications that are not cost justified and the refusal to implement new systems that are not cost justified is not only another major step in minimizing risk, but is a significant measure of the EDP manager's true management capability.

Communications

The third approach to minimizing risk is in the area of communications to the user. There have been many discussions concerning the problem of data processing people hiding themselves in a cloud of technical jargon. Fortunately, this situation has been rapidly improving during the past few years. However, there are other problems that still exist.

The attitude still exists on the part of many EDP managers that we should not confuse management with too many facts, that somehow, providing top management with insight into EDP operations will limit the manager's options. On the contrary, providing that visibility to top management is the EDP manager's best method of demonstrating his management skills. Project status reports on all major projects should be distributed monthly. Top management should have a clear, documented understanding of project control methods and chargeback methods.

Above all, remember that the real language of the user is dollars.

Every project proposal should consider alternative methods of achieving the objectives (including non-EDP approaches), comparative cost analyses of the alternatives, and comparative analyses of risk to the business operation.

Sharing Risk

The last approach to minimizing risk is the sharing of risk. There are two methods that should be applied in this area. The first is, whenever possible, to name a member of the user group as project manager. The benefits to this are obvious. They include a higher level of user participation, a clearer understanding of the defined requirements and specifications for the project, and better communications to top management of user satisfaction.

The second involves the establishment and use of the steering committee. A permanent steering committee, acting as a sort of "Board of Directors" for the EDP function, can provide some of the following benefits. The gradual education of management in those factors affecting the cost and efficiency of the data processing function can take place in the committee. The committee can assure the continued conformity of the DP function to the long-range plans of the company. It should review the entire DP budget annually and assist in establishing a budgetary level suitable to the needs of the company. On projects above a certain designated level of cost, it should operate as a board of approval and jointly set priorities among projects that contend for limited resources. It should review projects in progress on a monthly basis to determine their continued feasibility and prevent overcommitment of economic and personnel resources without adequate return. The steering committee also should be responsible for resolution of conflicting political and economic interests at a top level. It should act as a forum where such conflicts can be resolved by group direction or presidential guidance without the DP Manager being the "man in the middle."

Summary

In summary, the EDP manager is not at the mercy of his environment. He is really in a position to control major elements of the environment and minimize risk to both himself and the organization.

SECTION 3   COST EFFECTIVENESS IN EDP

Surveys of general management continue to indicate dissatisfaction with the results of the majority of data processing installations. This dissatisfaction is probably not as vague or ill-defined as many people in EDP suspect. In fact, it may center on the valid question of obtaining value for the money spent. For example, a special report in Dun and Bradstreet's *Dun's Review* concentrated on "Management and the Computer." Among other things, the article pointed out:

> . . . many managers today feel that their computer operations are typified by uncontrolled costs and uncontrolled personnel—in short, that their data-processing operations are not amenable to normal business practices and operations.
> And management is not happy. A study by the Chicago office of accountants Peat, Marwick, Mitchell & Co. showed that fewer than one-third of the respondents were satisfied with the service they were getting from their computer centers. Almost everyone felt that he did not have enough computer capacity and that he couldn't get the job done between 9 at night and 9 in the morning, when the reports were needed, reports Robert Forney, a PMM data-processing consultant.

There is an obvious continuing need to make EDP cost effective. This would involve setting goals for, establishing methods to determine, and implementing techniques to improve cost effectiveness. The goal of cost effectiveness is one of optimizing the use of all available resources within the constraints of the environment and the goals established by general management. This would indicate that there is no fixed point or ultimate goal that can be achieved, but that EDP management must continually strive to make the installation *more* cost effective.

The burden of meeting this goal falls heavily on the EDP manager. The manager alone cannot fulfill all the demands since systems and programming areas must also contribute. However, a comprehensive knowledge is required so that he can guide systems development and programming efforts toward maximizing EDP's cost effectiveness.

Methodology

Cost effectiveness can be determined by an analysis utilizing the following general steps:

1. Objectives must be selected carefully and defined explicitly for both the long and short term.

2. Alternatives for achieving objectives must be identified.

3. Effectiveness measures must be selected. These measures must

be relevant to the objectives and must allow for comparisons between alternatives.

4. Cost estimates for alternatives must be developed with a clear definition of what costs are to be included and how they are to be measured.

5. Decision criteria must be selected. This may include maximizing effectiveness, minimizing cost, some combination of the two, or some other criteria.

6. Models of the available alternatives should be created to relate cost and effectiveness.

The methodology of this type of measurement has certain implications. Valid alternatives must be available. It should be recognized that the present method always represents one alternative. Techniques must exist to obtain good cost estimates and to assure that all relevant cost factors for each alternative are examined.

While real-world situations are such that variables may be almost infinite, they may have to be artificially limited to those having the most impact on the study. The criteria for decision-making must remain constant for the term of the study and in respect to all alternatives. These criteria should not be changed without compelling reasons.

Finally, common values must exist for those measuring cost effectiveness and applying the decision criteria. Differences in values may readily be seen to exist between equipment manufacturers (whose first consideration is sale of their equipment), data processing management (who may be interested in preserving their staff), and general management (who are probably interested in making a profit). There may be more subtle differences in values that should be explored to establish a common ground for decision-making.

Accounting and Control

Cost effectiveness may be analyzed from the accounting and control viewpoint or from the performance audit viewpoint. The accounting and control view establishes the elements of cost that must be accounted for and which may be subject to various degrees of control. These are:

1. Computer rental, lease payment, or amortization or purchase price. (For purchased or leased equipment maintenance costs and taxes are often paid separately and must be included.)

2. Similar expenses for data preparation equipment such as keypunches, key-to-tape devices, on-line terminals, and output handling

devices such as bursters, decollators, or COM (computer output micro-film) equipment.

3. Expendable supplies such as cards, tapes, forms, printer rib-bons, and other similar items.

4. Operating utilities such as electricity and telephone including amortization of the cost of special equipment such as capacitors, regu-lators, or uninterruptable power supply systems.

5. Premises, including rental or amortization of purchase cost, amortization of the cost of special improvements such as double floor-ing and air conditioning, property taxes other than those on computer equipment, and general office space.

6. Amortization of the cost of furniture, typewriters, and other office equipment.

7. Amortization or expense of the cost of specialized purchased software and the cost of contracts for the provision of software support.

8. Salaries, including fringe benefits, for the following personnel:

    a. Management and administrative personnel

    b. Development personnel

    c. Operations analysts (if any)

    d. Maintenance programmers

    e. Systems programmers

    f. Computer operators and other machine room personnel

    g. Control clerks and librarians

    h. Keypunch operators and other data preparation personnel

    i. Maintenance personnel

In addition to identifying the elements of cost there must be a system for collecting these costs or establishing the proper accounts in the chart of accounts for the company. In many organizations it may be necessary to establish an independent cost accounting capability for the EDP installation.

The Performance Audit

The performance audit review is designed to determine whether or not there is effective use of the EDP installation's resources and whether or not an unwarranted excess of these resources is being maintained. To do this the performance audit establishes functional di-visions in the following manner:

1. The *administration audit* is nontechnical and includes a detailed review of the relationship between corporate management and the data

COMPONENT: DATA PROCESSING DIVISION

Acct. No.	Acct. Name	Current Month
300.01	Salaries and Wages—Regular	$ 98,280
300.05	Shift Differential	1,588
300.07	Overtime	1,715
307.00	Tuition and Award Payments	250
320.00	Overtime Meals	159
330.00	Direct Employee Benefits	8,090
350.03	Personnel Training Aids	3,400
350.04	Management Development Expenses	200
360.00	Other Personnel Expenses	3,600
360.01	Cafeteria Cost Allocation	1,665
	Total Personnel Expense	$118,947
400.00	Entertainment	90
410.14	Educational/Research Orgs. Expense	126
410.24	Professional Orgs. Expense	30
421.00	Dues—Professional Organizations	10
	Total Entertainment and Professional Exp.	$ 256
500.00	Rent—Office	6,840
510.00	Insurance—Real Property	129
570.01	Rent—Furniture, Fixtures	162
570.02	Rent—Data Processing Equipment	68,416
572.01	Insurance—Office Contents	27
573.01	Maintenance—Furn., Fixtures, Eqpt.	3,321
575.01	Depreciation—Furniture, Fixtures	580
575.02	Depreciation—Data Processing Eqpt.	3,078
578.01	Personal Property Tax	3,621
	Total Use and Occupancy Expense	$ 86,174
601.01	Postal Expenses	15
630.00	Publications Purchased	114
608.02	Office Copier Machine—Supplies	115
610.01	Stationery—Office Supplies	268
610.99	Forms	4,038
615.01	Telephone/Telegraph	2,219
636.01	Purchasing Services—Allocation	510
640.01	Travel and Company Meetings	110
646.03	Auto Expenses	138
650.00	Other Insurance	62
	Total Other Direct Expense	$ 7,589
	Grand Total	$212,966

Figure 9. Sample chart of accounts.

processing department's management and functions. It examines organizational interfaces, lines of authority and responsibility, planning and budgets, personnel policies, environmental factors, costing methods, and companywide use of data processing capabilities. It concentrates on determining the benefits being realized from the work of the EDP organization.

2. The *operations audit* examines the efficiency of operating the equipment and the flow of work through the production processes.

This audit includes such areas as data recording and preparation, data control, library control, operational procedures, and facilities layout. This audit must be done by someone with extensive EDP experience.

3. The *systems and programming audit* reviews the procedures, techniques, and standards used in developing application systems. This includes project management methods, standards and documentation, testing, and maintenance of systems. The manager must be vitally concerned with the documentation standards, testing methods, and maintenance methods of the systems and programming group.

4. The *application audit* evaluates all systems in operation or being considered or designed for cost performance effectiveness and for economic feasibility. This audit would provide some measure of the degree to which computer applications assist in achieving the company's primary objectives.

5. The *control audit* is designed to determine the effectiveness of different types of control interrelationships. Specific items included are data generation, input controls, processing controls, librarian functions, output controls, scheduling, data security and privacy, and installation security.

Both of these viewpoints must be blended to provide a comprehensive analysis of the cost effectiveness of the EDP installation that would analyze whether or not the tangible benefits of the EDP installation could demonstrate a return on the company's investment. Although it is more difficult, one should also determine whether or not intangible benefits (prestige, competitive position, speed of operation, etc.) are considered by corporate management to have sufficient value as to override purely economic considerations.

Tools

Various tools are available for maintaining and improving cost effectiveness. Standards and guidelines may be developed in some of the following areas.

Operator training has long been a weak area with most equipment vendors. Operators must be trained in both the techniques of computer operation and the detailed capabilities of the operating system with which they are working. Courses are available from the hardware vendors, from firms specializing in education (such as video assisted instruction courses), or may be developed in-house.

Standard methods should exist for documenting operating instructions. These methods will vary for the equipment used, the operating system used, and may vary by application (for example, on-line vs. batch systems).

In order to prevent excessive maintenance cost, standards should be developed for defining and documenting both systems and programs. Good techniques should be developed for analyzing and designing systems (decision tables, etc.) and for minimizing programmer time on repetitively used techniques and routines. Publishing a "programming tips" manual can help in this area.

Standard procedures should be adopted for the control of authorizing projects and determining the economic feasibility of new applications. Such techniques should include payback analyses and cash flow analyses. Whether a system is developed in-house or purchased it should be amortized over the expected life of the system for the purpose of studying economic feasibility.

Approval of new projects or rental of major equipment should be required on the same basis as the authorization of capital expenditures. Firm commitments for achieving cost savings should be established at the time of the feasibility study and should be followed up after system implementation to assure that they actually take place.

The implementation of approved projects should be controlled through methods such as CPM or PERT for planning and the use of cost accounting techniques to monitor project cost and progress. Good project accounting techniques will also provide for analyses of programming performance by task and job against specified objectives. A job would normally be an individual program and a task would normally be a function such as coding, debugging, or logic design.

The failure to use prudent purchasing practice can result in excessive cost. Procurement of supplies, equipment, or software should be done by obtaining two or more bids for each item. Sole source suppliers should be carefully examined (preferably by an attorney) to assure complete vendor commitment to that which has been promised.

Computer utilization should be analyzed to determine whether or not effective use is being made of available resources. The present generation of computers, capable of multiprogramming, requires special hardware or software to determine the actual utilization of the equipment. Frequently, a hardware monitor is really necessary to determine where and how computer resources are used. Such analyses can identify areas for potential performance improvement.

Computer time spent on rerunning jobs should be carefully identified by cause and segregated from the time used for normal production runs. Downtime must be carefully logged for each piece of equipment in order to spot high frequency of failure and alert vendor maintenance personnel.

A master plan for systems development should be prepared and approved by top corporate management. This plan should be reviewed on a regular basis to assure its currency in terms of changing corporate goals. Applications should be developed in terms of their fit with the plan and in sequence of the priorities established by corporate management.

The master-plan approach generally provides for a backlog of work and reduces the high cost of retraining that occurs from fluctuating staff levels. As a major feature, the master plan provides top management with a means of measuring the EDP department's progress toward goals management has selected with resources they have approved. Of principal importance, the master plan provides a basis for anticipating hardware and software needs for the future so that operations can be prepared to support user system requirements.

EDP costs should be distributed to the users in proportion to the amount of use. Data processing production should be charged to users based on some equitable hourly rate. A measure of cost effectiveness is whether or not this rate can recover all installation costs and remain competitive with the rates of service bureaus. (Systems and programming costs should also be charged directly to the requesting user, using rates that include the normal overheads of the department.)

The distribution of cost to the user forces an analysis of the value and effectiveness of the services being provided. Such constant analysis will assist in assuring that the most effective alternatives are chosen for use of the computer. Since effectiveness may be a function of time and of external environmental conditions, priorities for the implementation of systems may change.

Research on hardware and software and the development of improved methods for system implementation and operation are major tools for constant improvement of cost effectiveness and should be considered as an operating cost of the EDP installation.

The EDP department should be established as a *profit center* within the organization. Combined with cost distribution, this makes the EDP department become the most visible part of the business. With cost effectiveness pressure applied by all users as well as top management, the EDP department should develop some of the best management in the organization.

Profit orientation of the department will provide top management with a profit and loss statement and the ability to measure the EDP management's performance on the same basis as other components of the organization.

Alternatives and Tradeoffs

Experience indicates that the productive capacity of experienced personnel in the programming and systems field, as contrasted to less experienced personnel, is generally greater than the relative difference in salaries paid. If an experienced programmer were paid 50 percent more than a comparatively inexperienced man, one could normally expect his productive capacity to be at least twice that of the inexperienced man. Experienced personnel require fewer compilations and test runs, reducing the cost of computer time for program completion. In addition, since work can be performed with fewer personnel, administrative costs are generally lower—fewer supervisors are needed.

In summary, costs of programming specific applications may be reduced by as much as 50 percent by employing qualified personnel at higher salaries. This same is true for systems programmers. A talented systems programmer can often substantially increase the life of existing hardware and software.

Some of the following tradeoffs exist between hardware, software, and people.

Elapsed time to program completion may frequently be shortened by increased use of computer debugging time replacing programmer desk-checking. On-line program debugging techniques such as features of IBM's TSO system permit substitution of computer time for programmer time. Another method for substituting computer time for programmer time is on-line programming and syntax checking. Higher level metalanguages which frequently require double compilation permit a speed up of programming or may allow the effective use of lower cost, less talented programmers.

A few highly skilled technical experts may be hired for the programming of extremely sophisticated techniques while lower salaries may be paid to the balance of the programming staff in which less talent would be required. Excessive computer operating cost can be generated by poor system flow or file organization. This is one area where it pays to make the higher one-time investment in people cost in order to get good system design. Personnel cost should also be expended in the development of good operating documentation which will prevent computer operating errors and minimize rerun cost.

The latest equipment announcements have not succeeded in repealing Grosch's law which states that, "The ratio of the power of two computers is approximately equal to the ratio of their cost squared." Equipment configurations should be carefully reviewed in this context. Two or more computers of like size and configuration in one installation are very likely a sign of poor system design and planning. Adding to major computer capacity can sometimes be less expensive by distributing some of the workload to minicomputers located either in the data center or at remote stations.

Consideration should be given on a regular basis to the improvement of existing computer applications. Systems that are running under emulation on the latest equipment are grossly inefficient in their use of computer time. Poorly designed systems, frequently converted directly from punched card applications, are generally computer time hogs and represent a poor use of the computer in terms of cost effectiveness.

Commercial software packages represent a major opportunity for cost savings. The benefits of a new system are achieved more rapidly because of the reduced time of implementation. Implementation costs may be reduced by 50 percent or more through the use of commercial software packages. Dependence on in-house programmers for maintenance is reduced if the vendor has a capability for maintaining the system.

Staffing levels should be held at a minimum consistent with the average work load. Peak overloads for programming can be contracted out, frequently on a fixed-price basis. Systems design overload can be contracted out, generally on a time and materials basis. Consultants may be used quite effectively for objective appraisals of the cost effectiveness of proposed applications.

If a choice of operating systems exists, the proper selection may frequently be critical to the most effective use of the computer. This is so critical to the future of the installation that outside experts should be consulted if the technical capability of the staff is not equal to the job.

Several alternatives exist to the cost of paying straight rental to a single equipment vendor. Leasing equipment from a third party can result in a 10 to 15 percent reduction in monthly cost. Up to 40 percent of the cost of standard peripherals may be saved by trading them for foreign peripherals compatible with the main frame. Several computer manufacturers offer long-term lease discounts.

Many users have found it profitable to purchase new or used computers.

The purchase or long-term lease of equipment should be approached with care and a full recognition of the consequences. These options are best for organizations with substantial application stability and with predictable long-term horizons.

Key-to-disk equipment may not only increase efficiency of the data entry function, but, with terminals in the user area, may allow the users to pick up the personnel costs of data entry with their own people.

Summary

While it is obvious that many methods to achieve cost effectiveness are dependent on technical expertise, the basic problem remains the same as in any other part of the organization. That is, good management utilizing the definition of goals, measurement of progress, and a knowledge of the field being managed can result in significant continued improvement in the cost effectiveness of EDP installations. Any such improvements should be reported to management as an example of the manager's continuing consciousness of the objectives of the company as a whole.

A checklist is provided as a guide to starting an audit of the data center. While this list is by no means exhaustive, it presents an overview of the type of inquiring required.

The pressure of daily operations frequently is so demanding as to make it difficult to assign personnel to a review of the cost effectiveness of EDP. Furthermore, available personnel may have biases in certain areas. As a result, the EDP manager should consider the use of consultants to perform such a review. (See the section on using consultants.)

COST EFFECTIVENESS CHECKLIST

General Management:

1. Is there a long-range plan for the data center based on anticipated (and validated) user system requirements?

2. Do we build staff expertise or hire an outside consultant for data center planning or for operating problems rather than relying on the computer hardware vendor's personnel?

3. Do we have an effective budgeting and accounting structure for tracking cost?

4. Do we take advantage of volume discounts where they are offered (as in supplies, combining forms, orders, etc.)? Are multiple bids taken?

5. Has our telecommunications network been examined by an expert to assure that lowest feasible tariffs are employed?

6. Do our salary levels prevent hiring the highly experienced personnel necessary for key positions?

7. Are we taking advantage of long-term lease, third party lease, or purchase options on all equipment for potential savings?

Hardware Management:

8. Do we have a formal method for tracking computer utilization, disk utilization, and utilization of other resources?

9. How much more performance could be obtained by augmenting just the most limiting resource?

10. When was the limiting resource last augmented?

11. What is the percentage of time that each major resource in the computer system is active during each shift? Is it reasonable?

12. What is the percentage of downtime for each resource? Is it reasonable?

Systems Software Management:

13. When was the last time that operating system options were reviewed for maximum efficiency?

14. Do systems programmers attend user group meetings (such as SHARE) to obtain the latest information on efficiency improvement?

15. Have software packages other than those supplied by the hardware vendor been considered?

16. Does a clear statement of the installation's performance requirements exist?

17. Is there a standard method for evaluating software alternatives?

18. Would a hardware monitor be useful for performance analysis?

19. Are systems programming projects scheduled and controlled?

Operations Management:

20. Are reruns analyzed to determine and cure the causes?

21. What amount of resources are consumed in all reruns, including job initiation?

22. How often do operators modify the scheduling and resource allocations each shift?

23. Is our operation's physical layout conducive to a logical, easy work flow?

24. Do we have an automated tape library system to reduce library control costs?

25. Are all production systems documented for operators in a standard manner?

26. Do we have a regular operator training program?

Resource User Management:

27. How much resource saving has resulted from application program improvement in the last twelve months?

28. Which application programs are the most logical next candidates for performance improvement? Why are they the ones, and how much monthly savings might result?

29. Which applications use the most of the bottleneck resource in our installation?

30. What portion of all our resources, and at what cost, does online programming consume, including overhead?

31. Are users charged for computer time?

32. How much do on-line application systems actually save the user departments in the company?

33. What is the cost of running our largest application for the current year, and how do we know?

34. How are new projects evaluated prior to undertaking their development, and how do actual benefits compare with projected benefits for the application most recently implemented?

35. What keeps a user group from demanding an unreasonable amount of resources, and what would be an unreasonable amount?

36. Are output distribution lists current?

37. Have users been surveyed recently as to current need for all reports produced?

38. Do users control and provide data input where possible?

Cost/Performance Management:

39. Do we have a budget for research into methods for improving cost effectiveness?

40. Do we have schedules for targeted areas of investigation to improve cost effectiveness?

SECTION 4   HOW TO MINIMIZE RERUNS

While the data center operations manager (DCOM) is beset by a host of problems, few have the overall impact of reruns. Reruns potentially affect not only machine time utilization, but scheduling, file recovery, operator overtime, and other areas within the data center. They also damage the image and reputation of the data center in the view of the user. Time is lost in the distribution of erroneous reports, mailing costs, and user effort in working with and filing reports. The scope of problems associated with reruns can be organized into several categories:

CAUSES:

System failures are those which result from inadequate or improper design of the system. They could include improper data relationships or incorrectly defined processing algorithms.

Program failures are commonly the result of undetected bugs in application programs but may also include bugs in systems software or incorrect use of systems software.

Hardware failures are usually computer component or peripheral failure but may be extended to cover facilities problems such as loss of power or air conditioning.

Control failures are the product of incorrect application of manual control steps or computerized controls that permit incorrect input to be processed or incorrect output to be delivered. These may include not only application controls of data, but also tape library controls or program library controls.

User errors usually result in incorrect input but may also include improper use of terminal-oriented systems even to the point of "crashing" the operating system.

Operator errors are not only those of improper response to or control of the operating system, but including mounting wrong files, and loading incorrect forms into the printer.

Data center management failures cover those failures that result from lack of management taking precautions and establishing procedures to minimize error. As such, they are frequently at the root of many failures attributed to previously cited causes.

CORRECTION:

Recovery methods include the tools, techniques, procedures and personnel assignments established to support the recovery of a system from failure.

263

Duration of time to recovery is a problem in its impact on computer schedules and its impact on users.

User information must be organized so that support for correction efforts which require user assistance are well coordinated.

PREVENTION:

Failure diagnosis includes methods and training for determining the causes of failures in order to correct the failure condition and prevent recurrence.

Rerun follow-up analysis is a longer range tool to prevent recurrence of failure.

Planning for prevention of failure is the management task of implementing proper control, detection, and recovery procedures.

Quality assurance functions are formal methods for assuring system, program, and processing quality

The DCOM's primary problem with reruns is that a substantial number of occurrences are beyond the direct control of Operations. For this reason, the DCOM must actively solicit the aid and cooperation of the systems, programming, technical support and user groups in the recovery process and in the prevention of future failures.

Causes and Correction

This section is primarily addressed to methods for minimizing or preventing reruns. However, a few words on causes and correction are appropriate.

As noted, many of the causes of reruns appear to be beyond the control of the DCOM. System design which does not include sufficient input editing, adequate input and file controls, or adequate user documentation and training can result in reruns. A system design that is incomplete or does not cover all potential data conditions can cause many man-days of recovery work. For new programs or newly modified programs, the risk exposure due to program failure is directly correlated to the adequacy of testing. Hardware failures may create substantial problems and are unpredictable. The DCOM must find some way to protect Operations from these types of failure.

All failures and reruns potentially have an impact on both the data center and the user. A failure that is corrected without delaying user output may have no impact on the user but may have substantial effect on Operations.

The DCOM must consider not only the data center and user cost of recovery, but the image of the data center to corporate management. In this sense, a rerun that is recovered without impact on the user (or is transparent to the user) is second best to not having the rerun at all.

Correction and recovery methods must address the speed of recovery in advance of the occurrence of failure. The following sections therefore address techniques that are primarily aimed at minimizing reruns, but secondarily aimed at minimizing the impact of failure and the time needed to recover. Prevention may be viewed in three categories:

- Those methods which must be implemented by Systems and Programming.

- Those methods which will usually require the work of the technical support function.

- Those methods which the DCOM can install without external aid.

Systems and Programming Failure Prevention Methods

Systems and programs may contain lurking bugs that do not appear until months after implementation. However, the point of greatest risk is on the first run of a system or program after installation or modification. The risk is slightly lower on the second run and from that point diminishes rapidly.

Reducing this first-run risk is dependent on proving validity prior to the run. The process of reducing risk begins during the development cycle of the system. Technical reviews of the system should be conducted at critical points in the design and program specification phases. These technical reviews should include the participation of the DCOM or an Operations appointee to assure that controls and other Operations considerations have been met.

The design review should assure that data input editing and controls are adequate, that suitable disposition is made of invalid input, and that standards for documentation will be observed. (Other points to be checked will appear later.)

Since it is difficult for any task group to objectively perform its own quality assurance function, some organizations have successfully used two additional groups in the EDP organization. The first of these is the system testing group. This group, which may be part of a larger standards and quality assurance function, should report to the EDP Manager. (Quality assurance functions cannot usually be reliable if they are subject to the control or influence of the group whose product is being validated or checked.) It would consist of technical personnel aided by user personnel as appropriate. Working from the system definition and user documentation this group would run the systems test and approve the system for production. Their responsibilities include review for adherence to standards, testing for conformity to design criteria (response time, control elements, etc.), and obtaining user approval of system completion.

A second group used with some success might be termed the system building group. This group may reside in Operations or Technical Support and has the responsibility for constructing the system job streams, assuring that recovery points are documented, arranging for allocation of appropriate disk space, and (if required) cataloging the job control language for the job stream. This group works with the system designers and programmers to make sure that the final job stream corresponds to their intent.

Any change to a system after initial implementation must be the subject of strict control. If a group such as the system building group does not exist, the following safeguards must be operated by someone in the EDP organization.

- Any change to program, whether or not it would require a JCL change, should result in a new version of the program with a new program I.D. number.

- Test programs should reside only in the test library and should not be moved to production libraries until tested and certified.

- Live files should never be used in test unless a backup copy has been created immediately prior to the test. (Live files have further disadvantages for testing, such as the length of the test run and the fact that a live file may not test all program conditions.)

- Production runs should not be made using programs from the test library without the prior approval of the systems manager and the DCOM to assure that all precautions are taken.

- When a program is run for the first time, the operations shift supervisor should be informed. In the event of program failure, the operators will not have to spend time trying to diagnose the problem if this information is available. In addition, the responsible programmer should be on stand-by for a call and Operations should have the programmer's telephone number.

- A further precaution is to require a run time estimate on first run programs. After exceeding this estimate, the programmer may be called to get permission to proceed. This can prevent hours of computer time lost due to a program being in a loop.

- During technical reviews, the DCOM should insist on certain preventative measures and recovery measures being built into the system design.

• Control checkpoints *external* to the computer process should permit the i/o controls group to assure that long-running jobs are continuing in a valid manner. External controls simply imply that formulae (such as input plus balance forward equals output) may be applied to *printed* control totals to assure validity.

• Such controls should exist prior to long-running print jobs to make sure that reports are in balance before being printed from the spool. On-line files should be controlled in some similar manner to assure file validity at the end of each daily process and before the files are used again for the next day's run.

These external "predictive" controls will reduce recovery time in the event of failure by detecting the failure before the run is in the user's hands.

The DCOM should also insist that the system design include clearly designated "recovery" steps so that in the event of failure of a process between such steps the system must only be rerun from the last valid recovery point.

In summary, the cooperation of the system and programming functions is vital to minimizing reruns. Not only is it necessary to address the specific manner in which these functions undertake their projects, but it is necessary to consider organizational issues which may enhance the ability of the entire EDP organization to assure quality products.

Furthermore, it is incumbent upon the DCOM to take an active role in the systems design specification process through the opportunities afforded by technical reviews. The DCOM must also actively participate in the development and approval of project management standards and system implementation and/or change procedures wherever these impact the proper performance of the operations function.

Technical Support Functions

In many organizations, the function of technical support (or systems programming) reports to the DCOM. Where this is the case, establishing certain ground rules and priorities is relatively simple. If technical support does not report to the DCOM, then the DCOM must find some way in which to enforce guidelines and participate in establishing priorities.

First and most obvious, operating system modification or corrections should not be installed without thorough stand-alone testing. This testing should include running of a specially constructed subset of the more complex application programs under the new version of the operating system with some means of assuring that these application programs have functioned correctly. Ideally, this test could be monitored by the previously suggested system testing group.

All potentially affected users of the system (Operations, Programming, RJE stations, on-line terminal users, etc.) should be notified in advance of installation of the date of the change and any possible impact (good or bad) on service or performance. This notice should provide sufficient time for response by any party that would be adversely affected by the planned installation date.

The technical support function should provide the DCOM with a series of measurement tools to avoid the problems associated with unexpectedly exceeding certain capacities or boundaries. For example, file sizes and the allocation of disk space should be monitored to assure that allocated space is not exceeded during a production run. This task goes hand in hand with monitoring channel use and device accesses to balance the channel load and minimize disk drive contention.

Technical Support should also bear responsibility for providing an emergency response service in the event of hardware/software failure during peak production hours. This service must be oriented toward rapid diagnosis of and recovery from system failure.

In some organizations, the position of data base administrator resides in the technical support group. Regardless of its organizational position, the DBA provides substantial support to daily operations. This support includes performance measurement and improvement, security control, consultation to programmers, user training, operational control, and assistance in failure recovery procedures. In the last two activities, the DBA has the responsibility to assure the validity of data and data relationships of the files in use, correct file errors, ensure that lost data can be reconstructed, and ensure that files are protected from inappropriate use. In these activities the DBA participates heavily in failure prevention and recovery activities.

Responsibilities of the DCOM

Within the area of operations, the DCOM can institute policies and procedures that bear directly on rerun prevention. These range from relatively simple rules to fairly complex procedures.

One simple rule used with good results is to forbid any program alterations or new system implementation during peak activity periods or periods where schedules are critical. So, for example, in many installations this moratorium would be effective during the month-end closing period.

For installations having more than 3000 to 5000 tape reels in their library (and depending upon the frequency of activity) a computerized tape library management system is a requirement. The system should provide for managing the library at a level that permits tape reels to be externally labelled with only the reel number. This will enhance the security of the library as well as improve efficiency and control. Some tape library systems offer a restart feature that expedites recovery by designating the tapes required for the last recovery point in the job stream and scratching those tapes created in subsequent programs.

The tape library system can also manage archival storage. Given file retention requirements for the IRS and other government agencies, archive management can be critical to the company. This may be especially important for multinational companies that ship products and assemblies through customs points. Negotiations of customs fees may require several years of product cost and shipment information. File retention rules should be clearly designated for each system and the archive content should be periodically audited.

Comprehensive tape library management also requires that tapes be rotated through a cleaning and certification cycle to eliminate bad tapes and reduce read/write failures. A program of education on tape handling can help to reduce costs and minimize reruns.

The subject of operating documentation is invariably a sore point to the DCOM. A thorough audit of operating documentation usually reveals numerous deficiencies. Such deficiencies as missing or obsolete documentation are invitations to failure. The following steps should be followed to improve operating documentation.

• Establish documentation standards.

• Review and update documentation making sure that all recovery points are designated and control procedures are included.

• Ensure that documentation includes recovery procedures.

• Examine all procedures and request modifications to reduce work steps, minimize operator intervention, minimize file handling and optimize workflow.

• Periodically, or on a rotating basis, perform an audit of operating documentation to assure continued quality of maintenance.

As a further aid in minimizing operator intervention, where possible the JCL should be catalogued to the procedure library and access to jobs should be limited to prevent unauthorized changes (which can result in reruns.)

From the people standpoint, much of the success of operations is due to trained, motivated operators, control and support personnel. The skills of each of these people should be reviewed with the intent of developing individualized training programs to enhance their performance in present positions and qualify them for further advancement.

Suggestion programs should operate on a basis that will ensure consideration and a *reasoned response* to each suggestion. If possible, a reward system should become a part of the suggestion program. Motivated people help to spot potential problems and prevent possible failures.

The DCOM is increasingly becoming a "resource manager" for people using the computer system from outside the computer center. Such users, operating from RJE stations and terminals of various types, are difficult to manage. However, certain measures are required to prevent such users from affecting the system to the detriment of all other users.

The DCOM, either directly or through the use of the technical support function, must establish rules and procedures for use of the computer resource and publish these as a user manual. The user manual should contain information regarding the facilities and resources available, constraints on their use, approval procedures for use, operating policies, security considerations, access methods, schedule availability, priority allocation, operating procedures, and cost allocation or charging rules.

If possible, the DCOM should arrange for periodic training classes for these users to aid in improving their performance and reducing reruns or failures.

As much as possible, technical support should build or obtain programmed constraints to prevent violation of user rules or at least detect such violation. Uncontrolled outside use of the computer center resources can damage the ability of the center to recover from failure in a timely manner. (Not to mention increasing the requirements for, and cost of, resources.)

Security of the data center must also be considered since destruction of data files or processing resources can involve substantial costs for recovery. Major areas to be reviewed include:

- Water damage exposure
- Fire
- Air conditioning
- Access control
- Electrical service
- Housekeeping

- Personnel
- Hardware maintenance
- Software security
- Service personnel control
- File storage
- Internal audit controls
- Contingency plans

Many of the concerns reviewed for security are overlapping with those applicable to prevention of reruns. These include observation of the physical conditions of media and equipment. For example, as previously mentioned, tapes and disks should be cleaned regularly and records of read/write errors reviewed to eliminate faulty media from the libraries.

A trouble report and follow-up system should be established. The trouble report should contain a description of the problem, a preliminary diagnosis, a description of the action taken to solve the problem, a final diagnosis (if necessary), and a description of the action taken to prevent the problem from recurring. There should be authorized signatures for each of the above sections.

From the trouble reports, certain information can be charted to identify areas of weakness that require attention. Abnormal program terminations (ABENDS) can be charted for frequency and lost time by reason (operator, device failure, program failure, software, etc.). A high frequency of ABENDS due to operator error (for example) may indicate a need for operator training or some personnel problem.

Failure of hardware should also be tracked for frequency and duration of lost time by unit and by reason. The failure of a peripheral device can often cause a rerun not only for the job using that device, but for all jobs running at the time. Repeated failure of a unit signals a problem in maintenance or need for replacement of that unit.

Some operations groups have established the position of operations analyst. This person (or persons) becomes familiar with the operation and control of critical systems and provides a "first line of defense" in the event of failure. Using his knowledge of the application, he can diagnose the problem and expedite recovery without waiting for the application programmer to respond to a call. Any work done by the operations analyst would, of course, be recorded on the trouble report and reviewed during the follow-up procedure.

Rerun statistics developed from the trouble reports should also document reruns caused by users through bad input or improper use of terminals, etc. These statistics should be reported regularly to user management to obtain aid in control and reduction of this cause of failure.

If the data center uses a charge-out system for time on the computer, determination of the cause for reruns becomes extremely important. User-caused reruns may legitimately be charged to users; however, reruns caused by failures internal to the EDP function must generally be absorbed. This system provides an added incentive to failure prevention.

The rerun statistics relative to hardware or communications failure are useful for continuing follow-up with vendors to assure proper maintenance. The DCOM should establish a "call hierarchy" within the vendor organization and set up an agreement by which calls will be made to increasingly higher levels of vendor management based on frequency of failure and/or duration of failure. This approach commands the attention of vendor maintenance personnel.

The DCOM has an additional responsibility in the area of hardware and systems software selection. The DCOM must participate in the evaluation and selection process to assure that selected products have at least the following:

- A record of user satisfaction by other users.
- An adequate and competent maintenance organization for the response required.
- Easily understood operating documentation.
- Human engineering for ease of use.
- Sufficient financial stability to assure long-term support.
- Adequate training and education facilities for users.
- Contractual guarantees of the agreed-upon performance and support.

The above considerations in the selection process are a form of failure prevention that can have a long-term impact on the data center, any terminal equipment linked to the data center, and the communications media.

Summary

The DCOM should create an "internal audit" program to review the above areas of concern. One approach is to assign specific responsibility for audit and reporting to members of the operations group for designated potential problem areas. Another approach might be to bring in a consultant to perform the audit and report on existing practices and recommended improvements.

It is important to recognize that the DCOM alone cannot solve all problems relating to failure prevention. Cooperation between operations and other functions such as systems, technical support, data base administration, users, and internal audit will often be required. The DCOM will often have to be a clever tactician and a diplomat to gain the assistance necessary to improve operations by minimizing reruns.

Discussion Topics

1. How can a long-range EDP plan be directed toward meeting the future requirements of the overall organization?
2. Should an MIS Director have a technical EDP background?
3. How does managing the MIS function differ from managing other departments in a company?
4. Does cost effectiveness for EDP really mean spending the least amount of money on data processing?
5. What are the risk exposures of the EDP or MIS manager and how can these risks be reduced?

PERSONNEL
AND PERSONAL
MANAGEMENT

With all the modern techniques of automation spearheaded by computer people, it seems a paradox that data processing itself remains extremely labor intensive. Every EDP manager is acutely aware of his dependence on people. Systems development and maintenance, operations, controls,—all of them are people-dependent activities. In a 1978 Auerbach survey of the concerns of EDP managers, two of the top five concerns expressed had to do with personnel and the management of personnel.

The EDP manager must recruit and retain a staff in an environment constantly beset by change and the pressures of production and project deadlines. Furthermore, the EDP manager is often the principal agent of change in the rest of the company— and change alone is a disturbing factor for most people.

This chapter addresses several of the critical issues dis-

Chapter 6

cussed above. The first section deals with recruiting personnel for EDP. The second deals with how, why, and when to use consultants. The third section addresses the impact of change on both user and EDP organizations and how to resolve the problems arising from change. The fourth section discusses the sensitive area of conducting a performance evaluation review of personnel.

The latter part of the chapter takes a different perspective—that of the EDP manager's personal needs and opportunities. The fifth section presents some ideas for techniques that lead to the personal advancement of the EDP manager. Last, the sixth section covers managerial and leadership concepts that provide avenues for self-improvement on the part of the EDP manager.

SECTION 1   RECRUITING EDP PEOPLE

The EDP manager's problems often seem to center on schedules, controls, hardware availability and capacity, systems software, and similar concerns. In the normal daily onslaught of problems, there is sometimes a tendency to forget that the basic ingredient of every organization is people. This section is concerned with finding, recruiting, and introducing the best available personnel to the data processing organization.

Prerequisites for the Recruiting Effort

Before any attempt at recruiting is made, several organization and management considerations must be addressed.

First, what are the needs of the organization? Can they be solved in another way? For example, increased use of overtime, modifying schedules, modifying and reassigning job duties, changing operating methods or equipment.

If other alternatives are not available, is the additional position justified? What are the penalties for not filling the position? Will filling the position cause the department to exceed its budget? Is there a job description for the position? Is the job description up to date? To whom will the new employee report? What level of performance is expected of the new employee? Does the position require a junior, intermediate, or senior person?

Is the salary range for this position classification adequate in terms of the labor market and the experience level desired? Is there further room for advancement either in the classification range or in higher-level classifications? What is the starting salary the company is willing to pay? Will it create any conflicts due to comparison with the salaries of current employees? Is the proposed salary competitive?

These questions should be answered satisfactorily prior to any recruitment effort. If any answers are unsatisfactory, that situation may act as an impediment to recruiting either through lack of management approval for the proposed position or through the inability to conduct a successful recruiting effort.

Identifying Specific Requirements

Once the prerequisites have been met, the next task is to clearly describe, in writing, the characteristics of the employee desired for the position. Assuming that a job description exists, it must be supplemented by specific requirements for the information of the personnel department and recruiting agencies, for use in conducting interviews, and to establish a baseline for future performance measurement of the new employee.

The following requirements should be specifically described:

- *Job description.*

- *Specific skills required.* These would include such skills as clerical and accounting for a control clerk, clerical or cataloging skills for a tape librarian, typing skills for a secretary, and programming language skills for a programmer. Where specific performance measures can be used, they should be specified.

- *Experience.* Does the position require specific experience with certain hardware? Is knowledge of an operating system needed, and at what level? Is experience with certain kinds of applications necessary? Are programming skills required? For each of the identified areas of experience, how much experience and at what previous levels is required? Does the experience stated as a requirement correlate with the job description?

- *Educational qualifications.* What level of education is necessary— high school, college, trade school, industry courses?

- *Management or leadership skills.* If the job requires supervising others, what evidence of management or leadership skills will be acceptable?

- *Personal characteristics.* This area must be treated carefully to avoid conflict with any antidiscrimination legislation. However, certain requirements of the job that bear on personal characteristics may be specified. For example:

> The job requires dealing with the public and a neat appearance is desirable.
>
> The job requires lifting paper or card cases weighing 50 pounds and adequate physical strength is required.
>
> The job requires up to sixteen hours of overtime per week on a regular basis.
>
> The job requires a security clearance of a certain level.

Determining the needs accurately is vital to prevent employment of an overqualified or underqualified person. Varying either way from the real needs can result in dissatisfaction on the part of both employee and employer and can contribute to excessive turnover. A clear statement of needs and goals is of obvious value in measuring future employee performance.

Finding People

For some reason it always seems that the ideal person to fill any given opening is already satisfactorily employed somewhere else. Finding the right person for the position is a function of finding the right group of people from which an individual can be selected. The following methods are arranged in a sequence that indicates those which have produced the most favorable results.

The first preference is reference. A recommendation by a present employee (who is considered to be a reliable performer) is extremely desirable. Employees who come into the organization in this way are frequently easier to introduce into the organization's methods and more closely fitted to the organization's requirements (because of the recommender's knowledge). As a result, these employees become productive faster. A further consideration is that a reliable present employee will rarely recommend someone that he considers unable to perform the required task. As a result of this good experience, many companies offer a "finder's fee" to employees for recommending people who are subsequently hired.

Professional recruiters are next best preferred if they are capable of screening to meet defined needs. The requirements must be defined with extra care and precision or a professional recruiter will be ineffective. Although the fee of many recruiters may cause some hesitation in their use, it is frequently profitable to utilize their services. This is not because of any great savings on the part of the organization in screening resumés to the requirements. Instead, it is that recruiters provide a specific advantage in having access to personnel who may not be actively seeking employment and who therefore could not be reached through usual advertising media.

Advertising in trade journals is another way of reaching a broad segment of that group of people who are not actively looking for employment. Since many trade journals have a weekly or monthly publication cycle, it is necessary to recognize manpower requirements some time in advance to properly utilize this media.

Advertising in regular community newspapers is normally a last choice since it is indiscriminate in nature. That is, it reaches a broad spectrum of the public and usually results in an extensive amount of work in screening resumés. Also, it frequently does not reach that group of people who are currently employed. However, it is frequently the least expensive approach in terms of out-of-pocket costs. If this type of advertising is used, it is most effective to use a display ad (at least six column inches) placed in the "Career Opportunities" or some other specialized section for professionals or in the "Computer" section of the classified ads for nonprofessionals. Display ads are more effective because, quite frankly, they don't look cheap and this ad is the first impression that a prospective employee will have of the organization. The space available in a display ad should not be wasted. It should be used to clearly spell out the qualifications, the nature of the position, and the nature of the company. This will aid in minimizing the number of inappropriate responses.

Radio and television advertising have occasionally been used. Because of time slot problems, this is a very expensive media if measured by response per dollar spent.

If the requirement is for entry level personnel, direct contact with schools may provide a list of candidates. An especially good experience has been noted with graduates of the Urban League school in the Los Angeles area. Similar public or private schools are quite happy to provide candidate lists and arrange interviews.

Screening

If the organization has a personnel department, it should be used. Not just because the personnel department objects if it is bypassed, but because they can provide several valuable aids in the recruiting process. One of the most valuable of these is preliminary screening.

The personnel recruiter who is assigned the preliminary screening should be carefully briefed in person to make sure he or she knows exactly what to look for. They should be provided with a written list of specific requirements but should not be expected to do any technical screening unless the interviewer has a technical background. The list of requirements or "preliminary screening level" should be set so as to accomplish the real purpose. For example, if the purpose of preliminary screening is to eliminate all but a specific narrow range of applicants, then only those few resumés passing the preliminary screening will require final review. On the other hand, if several openings exist at various levels, the screening level should be defined in broader terms and the resumés classified into specific ranges.

One danger in setting too tight a screening level is that of excluding the possibility of serendipitously locating talent you might be able to use in another position.

If pre-employment testing is used, there are certain ground rules to follow. Pre-employment tests must be validated by the Equal Employment Opportunity Commission. They should be used in a manner that applies the same test to all applicants for a given position. Tests should evaluate only technical ability required for the position. (This obviously could include even a vocabulary test if it is required for the position.) So-called personality tests and IQ tests are coming under increasing fire for being ethnically biased. All test results and interview records should be retained for several months after the interview.

Many employers are concerned about potential problems with the EEOC. The easiest way to avoid these problems is to avoid discrimination or any appearance of discrimination in testing and interviewing practices and to develop a history of equal employment practice. It should be remembered that testing alone is not a defensible method of selection.

Final screening of applicants should be done by the person to whom the employee will report. Frequently it is beneficial to have two equally qualified persons review the same set of resumés to catch anything that may have been missed.

Interviewing

Interviewing is a very subjective process. Many books have been written on the subject, but it still remains a mystery to many managers. As a result, they haphazardly develop approaches which frequently do not accomplish the purpose of selecting the most desirable applicant. Even considering that they may be applied with the individual manager's distinctive flair, some general rules for interviewing should be followed.

The interviewer should prepare in advance a list of questions that will aid in determining whether or not the applicant is qualified for the position. If several people are interviewed for the position, a written record of the quality of their responses and the interviewer's general impressions should be kept for comparative analysis before final selection.

The applicant should be provided with clear directions for getting to the interviewer's office and someone should be prepared to meet the applicant. A prospective employee's first impressions may determine whether or not he or she is willing to work for the organization. A specific time should be set aside for the interview, and it should be conducted in an environment where there will be no interruptions or disturbance.

If the applicant is qualified and is to be seriously considered, he or she should be told about the job, to whom the position reports, what he or she will be expected to do, and how his or her performance will be measured. Such applicants should also be shown the facility where they will work and any questions they may have should be answered.

Only in rare circumstances should the applicant be made an immediate offer. If there is serious interest, the employee should be informed by the personnel department about the company, its business, and the employee benefits available.

Making an Offer

Prior to making an offer, the personnel department or the manager should make a thorough background check of the employee. This background check should verify the information provided on the application and serve to assure the interviewers of their personal impressions. This background check will also bring to light any evidence of job hopping or unaccounted for time periods.

A minimum and maximum figure should be determined for the offer. The minimum should not be designed to take advantage of the prospective employee. Salary information within an organization readily becomes available to everyone. If the employee's salary is significantly below what others in his category are receiving, he will be dissatisfied. On the other hand, the maximum salary offer should consider the salaries of equally qualified employees already in the organization. Starting a new employee at a salary higher than that of equally qualified present employees could result in widespread dissatisfaction and a rejection of the new employee.

If possible, have the personnel department extend the offer to the applicant. This provides an area for negotiation if the initial offer is not accepted. When agreement is reached, the personnel department should verify the offer in writing, clearly stating the terms, conditions, and position for which the offer is made. If some probationary period is established, this should be also clearly defined in the letter.

Introduction to the Organization

The method used to introduce the new employee to the organization can have long-term effects. The following actions should be considered in such an introduction.

Time should be taken to introduce new employees to the company, its products and services, and to the other employees with whom they will be directly working. Reporting relationships within the organization should be clearly delineated.

There should be an adequate program for training the new employees to any special tasks or skills required and sufficient time should be allocated for the average employee to master these skills.

It is very important that a specific assignment be available for the new employees in order that they may demonstrate their ability and in order that they become rapidly assimilated by the group. When the assignment is provided, the manager should review the department's expectations with the new employee and how the employee's performance will be measured.

Finally, standards and procedures in the data processing environment tend to be relatively complex and to vary from one installation to another. If new employees are to be productive, they should be given training in those procedures and standards as soon as they are introduced to the organization.

Meeting Expectations

Whether or not it is formally specified, the first three to six months is really a probationary period for the new employee. This period accomplishes the employee's acclimatization to the organization and determines the extent to which the employee meets the needs of the function for which he or she was employed. For this reason, it is worth considering this period along with other concerns of the recruiting process.

As previously indicated, the new employee should be informed of performance expectations during the introductory process. Experience has shown that this is not only good general practice, but in the case of hiring disadvantaged personnel, it is crucial. Such employees may not have had the average exposure to company life and may therefore need information that ordinarily would appear to be common knowledge.

One example is that of a disadvantaged employee who was constantly tardy. Only in the exit interview was it discovered that the employee did not understand the necessity for being on time for shift turnover.

Performance expectations should cover some of the following items and be quantified where possible.

- Duties and responsibilities of the position.
- Working hours and overtime requirements.
- Interpersonal and reporting relationships.
- Timing of performance review.
- Work elements that will be reviewed.
- Levels of performance expected for each work element.

A few final thoughts on expectations must concern the possibility that the new employee fails to meet the agreed-upon performance criteria.

If this should occur, rules usually established by the personnel department should be carefully observed. These rules usually include:

1. An oral warning at the time that failure to perform is noticed.

2. A written warning upon a second occurrence. This warning should describe the failure and the potential penalty for another repetition. Copies should be sent to personnel, inserted in the employee folder, and handed to the employee. Many companies require that the employee acknowledge receipt of the warning by signing all copies.

3. Dismissal or suspension according to company procedures.

Several matters of equity or fairness must be considered in these situations. After all, the fault may not be in the employee alone, but in the selection process or in the organization. It is possible that the employee is simply mismatched to the job or organization.

It is only fair that a failure to perform be called to the attention of the employee as soon as possible to provide the opportunity for corrective action. If the employee cannot perform the job, consider the possibility of transfer to a more appropriate position. Finally, if no alternative exists, do not simply allow the employee to remain in the position with little or no advancement. This is an abdication of managerial responsibility that can only harm the employee, the manager, and the organization.

Summary

Recruiting activity is not simple. Properly addressed it requires planning, attention to organization and work methods, and the sensitivity to people that is the hallmark of the good manager.

The definition of success in recruiting is placing the right person in the right job to attain the desired level of performance and employee satisfaction. The guidelines set forth in this section should help in creating a successful recruiting endeavor.

SECTION 2   CONSULTANTS AND HOW TO USE THEM

Are consultants a threat to in-house EDP personnel? Are consultants worth the money? Is a consultant someone who borrows your watch to tell you what time it is?

There are many questions and even more bad jokes about using consultants. This section is intended to address the issues of:

- When to use consultants

- How to select consultants

- How to get the most out of consultants.

These issues are worth addressing because consultants can be valuable to almost any organization, under the proper circumstances.

What Is a Consultant?

Jerome H. Fuchs, President of the Society of Professional Management Consultants, defines management consultants as:

> ... problem solvers with special training and broad experience in all types of enterprises. They apply sound and proved methodology and objectivity to solving managerial problems and maximizing economic opportunity. Most companies improve operations through an evolutionary process. Since management must necessarily assign priority to administration of day-to-day activities, significant improvements are effected through implementation of short- and long-range plans. However, the constraints of daily pressures tend to delay actions planned to bring about these changes.
> The consultant can provide valuable adjunct support by speeding this process. Unencumbered by internal constraints, the skilled professional consultant can systematically gather facts, analyze the problem and arrive at a sound constructive solution. Management consultants not only have broader exposure to similar situations, they must remain at the forefront in the state-of-the-art within their area of expertise. This is evidenced by their substantial contribution to the body of knowledge employed by the business community. They have been instrumental in creating a need for, and accelerated growth in, applications such as organization planning and manpower forecasting, management development, executive compensation, profit planning, cost and budgetary control, materials management and strategic business planning. Consultants have been at the cutting edge of innovative and advanced techniques such as operations research, PERT and critical path analysis, management information systems and manufacturing automation.[1]

In the specialized field of data processing we find, in addition to the management consultant, systems analysts, programmers, and con-

sultants who specialize in such fields as computer performance enhancement, computer security, project management, hardware and
software selection, data base management, telecommunications, and
other more esoteric areas.

In summary, the consultant should be one who provides a specialized skill or knowledge supported by broad experience to supplement
the skills and experience of the organization. The consultant provides
these skills for a fee and on an *objective* basis. This last sentence is important because it identifies one critical point. A consultant must *not*
have any vested interest or conflict of interest that would render his
service anything less than objective. (For example, a consultant employed to evaluate and select hardware should have no connection with
any of the manufacturers of hardware being evaluated.)

When To Use a Consultant

The practice of using consultants goes as far back as the time of
Moses, when Jethro, his father-in-law, advised him on the manner in
which the Israelites should be organized for their journey to Canaan.

In more modern times, consulting traces its roots to the development of management theory and industrial engineering in the late nine-
teenth century and early twentieth century. Such men as Frederick
Winslow Taylor, Henry Laurence Gantt, Henri Fayol, Frank Bunker
Gilbreth, and George Elton Mayo pioneered in these fields and began
the development of expertise in advisory management.

As technology and society became more complex, the need for
specialized expertise to solve specific problems became more intense.
The field of consulting, as we know it today, is a product of the 1940s
and 1950s.

Ira S. Gottfried, President of Gottfried Consultants, Inc., in his article "Consulting Consultants" in *Data Management*, points out that,
"Interestingly enough, consulting firms find their clients to be mainly
the successful companies rather than companies who are in trouble.
The growing, profitable corporation recognizes its limitations and is
able to spend the money to gain additional assistance from outside the
company."[2]

There are many reasons to use consultants. The following are
some of the major ones:

• *Specialized Expertise.* With the complexity and variety of current
management and computer technology there is an occasional requirement for highly specialized skills to solve specific problems. These
skills may not be available on the open job market, but consultants may
have such special talent available. This situation often arises in such

areas as high technology development or projects that require unusual combinations of experience across industries.

• *Limited Use of Special Skills.* Intermittent needs arise for specialized skills to solve problems of a specific nature. An organization cannot justify retaining full-time staff for such occasional use when it is less costly to hire consulting assistance as necessary. Consulting assistance may also be used to supplement the regular staff during peak load periods. A prime example of this is the use of contract programming personnel for major development projects. This permits temporary expansion of the regular staff capacity while relieving the company of the need to make permanent employment commitments.

• *Avoiding Wage Inequities:* Some specialized skills are in such high demand that the wages for permanent personnel with these qualifications are disproportionate to the wages of other personnel on the company's staff. Rather than employ a person whose salary would distort the organization's wage and salary plan or create apparent wage inequities, it may be better to hire outside consultants to meet these needs until internal skills can be developed.

• *Shortage of Skills in the Marketplace.* In some areas the organization would like to hire full-time personnel with specific qualifications. However, the demand for these skills may exceed the current supply in the general market (or in a particular geographic area). A consultant may be used until such full-time personnel can be acquired.

• *Providing an Objective Viewpoint.* One of the most frequently noted uses of an outside consultant is to provide an objective view of an internal situation. While there may be personnel with equivalent skills in the regular organization, they may actually have (or be accused of having) vested interests in certain methods or decisions. An outside consultant may approach the problem without any prior commitment resulting from its history or from internal political influences.

• *Providing Outside Information.* Consultants tend to work for many clients and have the opportunity to gain a broad exposure to methods, markets, and sources of information. As a result, consultants may be used to provide specific services such as finding merger or acquisition possibilities, locating sources of financing or performing market surveys. They may also be useful in helping to identify alternative problem solutions or strategies based on similar situations faced by other companies. The varied exposure of the consultant and the ability to rapidly identify nonproductive courses of action may save a company considerable time and money.

• *Saving Executive Time.* One of the major problems of management is finding enough time to both handle day-to-day administration and develop and implement innovative methods or perform special assignments. Very frequently these managers have the experience and talent to accomplish their assignments, but not the time. A consultant, working under the direction of the manager, can provide the "extra time" and a similar level of skills. Consultants frequently assist in such projects as long-range planning.

• *Training and Education.* Many companies utilize consultants to assist management and technical personnel to improve their skills or acquire new skills. Some examples are in the teaching of project management methods, work flow methodology and systems design or programming techniques.

• *Performance Appraisal.* Appraising the performance of technically specialized groups within a company is often difficult for general management personnel lacking the specific technical expertise. Consultants may aid in this appraisal process by providing both the necessary level of expertise and objectivity.

• *Respected Opinions.* While it may appear to be unfair, top management frequently respects an outsider's opinion more than the same, equally qualified person's opinion from within the company. Perhaps some of this is due to the implicit objectivity of the outsider, an established reputation, or the fact that management has to pay a fee for the opinion. In any event, this aspect of consulting is something that a manager can use for leverage to test ideas from within the company and bolster those that prove sound. The respect for outside opinion also leads executives to use consultants as "sounding boards" or confidants when premature exposure of thought processes and ideas might only serve to disturb employees. Consultants can also use their position as outsiders to aid in organization planning and resolving differences between contending executives in an objective manner.

It may appear that a consultant is expensive in comparison to a regular employee; however, the major reasons for use of a consultant that are listed above point out that the consultant's experience often permits a faster reaction to problems at critical times.

How To Select a Consultant

Consultants may generally be classified into four categories: individual "freelance" specialists; small firms with staffs of specialists; large, combined practice companies (such as the "Big Eight" accounting firms); and large, multidisciplinary, research and consulting organizations (such as SRI International and Arthur D. Little, Inc.).

In many ways consulting is a very personal business. The "chemistry" between the consultant and his employer is a significant part of a successful relationship. It is therefore extremely important that the employer meet and get to know the consultant(s) who will actually be doing the work. In dealing with the individual consultant or with the small firm (up to ten members), one may expect that the person interviewed for the assignment will actually do the work. During the interview it is possible to gain a clear picture of the consultant's experience, personality, and performance. Surprisingly, this may also be true of the large, multidisciplinary research and consulting organization. These organizations are frequently made up of relatively small departments of specialists, each operating as a separate profit center.

Other large consulting firms often utilize sales representatives or managers for selling. These people may retain an administrative interest in the proposed project, but will not do the actual consulting work. The "seller" will handle preliminary talks, define the approach, set the scope and extent of the job and set the size and qualifications of the project team. They may also supervise the work to some extent.

It is important for the potential client to recognize this distinction between "sellers" and "doers," between "administrators" and "workers." The client should insist on meeting the critical consulting staff members with whom he will interface.

Usually, consultants will attach to their proposals a list of "qualifications" (examples of similar projects and client references) and the biographies of some of the members of their staff. Some things to watch out for in these qualification statements and biographies are:

• Biographies are generally brief and summarized. They do not indicate the actual extent of participation of the person in the projects shown. They may emphasize or highlight those areas of competence best suited to the needs of the proposed project, but this emphasis may not be commensurate with the individual's actual depth of experience.

• The biographies listed may include consultants whose skill and expertise have led them to managerial levels. These individuals may not be available to actually work on the proposed project.

• Confidentiality of the client must be respected by consultants. For this reason many of the qualification statements will not indicate the name of the client company. However, a prospective client is entitled to ask for a confidential verbal identification of some previous clients and a more explicit explanation of the work done and results achieved than that which can usually be included in the brochure or proposal.

• Some previous jobs described may have been performed by consultants who will not be available to work on the proposed project.

The client should find out how the consultant proposes to apply the knowledge gained on prior projects to the proposed task.

Once the decision to retain outside consultants has been made, the process of selecting the right consultant must be undertaken. While the right firm can be of great value to the organization, the wrong one can create problems that may take years to solve.

The first step is to define the problem area or assignment for which a consultant is needed and determine the specific skills that will be required. Keep in mind that the initial results of the project may modify the definition of the assignment. For this reason the skills expected should not be too narrowly defined.

There are several sources that may be used to locate prospective consultants. Key executives of the firm are often familiar with consulting organizations. In addition, there are associations such as the Association of Consulting Management Engineers, the Society of Professional Management Consultants, and the Association of Management Consultants; there are advertisements in trade magazines and telephone directories; and there is the word-of-mouth recommendations of staff members and contacts in other companies. If the specific skills of candidate consulting firms are not known, write for a brochure, indicating the type of assignment proposed.

Assuming that the list can be narrowed down to three competing firms, it is advisable to request a personal visit to your company. This visit serves the dual purpose of allowing the consultant to "scope" the proposed project and allowing the client to get to know the consultant. During this interview, delve into each firm's personality. Review their willingness to present direct recommendations vs. only alternatives, the personalities of the managing principals or partners that will be serving your company, their history and experience of achievement, the type of specific supervision provided to the consultants that will be working at the company, the level of experience of the individual consultants suggested for the assignment, whether they will assist in actual implementation or will only present a report of recommendations, and their initial reactions to the stated problem.

In addition to considering the above items, explore the type of end product normally provided such as a written report, a slide presentation or an oral report only. Consulting firms will offer a variety of approaches to a specific problem. Some prefer to use a team effort composed of consultants and company personnel, while others prefer to do the job only with consultants.

Inquire about the commitment of time the firm is willing to make to the specific assignment. Will the consultants be working full time or only part time? What other commitments will they have and at what locations? Should there be idle time, will the client be charged for it or will they be able to absorb this time in other work? Where will they actually perform research and indirect effort? What type of research and reference library do they have to assure good backup, when needed?

The next item to explore is the methods used for progress reporting. Ask for a sample of a progress report. Explore how frequently they desire to keep the client apprised of both progress and problems.

At the end of this initial interview, request specific references. These references should include companies and industries similar to the clients as well as companies where assignments similar to this one have been performed satisfactorily. It is good practice to personally check these references. At this time, a secondary interview may be requested to actually meet the specific consultants who would be assigned to the task.

Utilizing the above interview techniques, one will find the selection process is almost automatic. Out of the three potential candidates, it is usual that only one of the firms will significantly impress the client with their professionalism and experience. Obviously, their methods and motivations must match the client's expectations and a rapport must exist with the consultants.

The consultant should be evaluated in the same manner as a prospective employee. The emphasis must be on appropriate experience assigned to the task and on a mutual feeling of trust and respect.

An individual or small consulting firm may be just right for a specific assignment. However, if varied areas of expertise are involved, the small consulting organization may not be able to provide them. In such a case, the small consultant may subcontract some of the work. This can dilute the client's control over the project.

The large research and consulting organization may provide all the areas of expertise necessary, but the prospective client should carefully review the qualifications of the individuals who will be assigned to the team. These organizations generally provide the multidisciplinary capability necessary in many current complex projects, but tend to avoid services other than research or consulting so as to avoid conflict of interest situations.

The "Big Eight" and other large audit firms tend to provide a "supermarket" of outside services that frequently include not only auditing but EDP consulting, financial systems design, executive search, and employee benefits consulting.

James H. Kennedy, editor of *Consultants News*, reports on consultants' conflict of interest concerns in the March 1978 *Dun's Review*.[3] He points out that the Senate Subcommittee on Reports, Accounting, and Management has recommended to the Securities and Exchange Commission that CPAs reduce their management advisory service to a narrow band of computer and systems work. This would eliminate such nonaccounting services as executive recruiting, market analysis, plant layout, site selection, actuarial services, and other potential conflict of interest situations. In addition, Kennedy recommends looking at abuses such as:

• *Serving on the Board of Directors.* Can a director whose consulting firm serves the company be totally objective?

• *Combining recruiting and consulting.* Should the management consultant who recommends sacking the president be given the executive search assignment to fill that very slot?

• *Reporting client crimes.* Is the management consultant responsible primarily to the client or the general public?

Finally, the question of independence is important. Would the outside auditors criticize the weakness in a company's internal controls when the system was designed by their own consulting department? Can they be truly objective when they highlight the need for new administrative procedures or a new inventory control system which their consulting department can help to install?

The best advice seems to be: ". . . never use the same firm for both auditing and management consulting at the same time," according to J. P. Frankenhuis in the *Harvard Business Review.*[4]

How To Get the Most Out of Consultants

Consultants to EDP organizations offer a variety of specialized services. These may be categorized as follows:

• *Management-oriented services.* This area includes market research, product planning, project management, management training, installation guidance, recruiting, and management information systems development.

• *Integrated services.* This includes installation evaluation, requirements analysis, equipment selection, conversion management, and facilities management.

• *Technical services.* This area includes systems design, programming, documentation, performance analysis, technical training, computer time, network planning and so forth.

Few, if any, organizations offer *all* these services. The largest variety of services is generally offered by the multidisciplinary research and consulting organizations.

It is critical to the prospective client that the assignment be clearly identified and that consulting firms with the appropriate experience and skills be selected to offer proposals.

Control of the assignment largely depends on the client having a clear definition of the job. Such job specifications should include:

- *Statement of Work.* Complete technical job specifications of the project. This should cover the scope of the assignment, specific tasks involved, estimated man-days for each type of task, and total estimated cost.

- *Responsibility.* Specify the degree of responsibility that the consulting firm will assume. This must be fair and reasonable based on the scope and content of the project.

- *Reporting.* Stipulate the frequency and method of reporting expected. Normally, this consists of weekly oral reports to the consultant's in-house counterpart, and a monthly written progress report to executive management.

- *Objectives.* This is the most important factor and should be developed in consonance with overall corporate profit planning goals. Objectives should clearly and concisely state the purpose of the undertaking.

- *Results.* This differs from objectives in terms of degree. Results usually are more definitive and indicate expectations of the assignment. Although the consultant's commitment is limited by the built-in uncertainties in a project, he nevertheless should indicate what can be expected so that one can measure the outcome of his services against the cost involved.

Depending on the nature of the assignment, some of the above specifications may not be capable of definition. In fact, defining them may be a part of a consulting assignment. If this is true, the definition phase should be planned as a separate assignment. Satisfactory completion of this phase may then lead to further work or put the client in a better position to evaluate alternatives.

Some companies have achieved excellent results by contracting with two or three consulting firms for a definition phase of the same problem, the contract for the major project then going to the firm that produced the best results from the definition phase.

Regardless of the method used and the extent of specifications developed, these specifications form a part of the agreement between the consultant and the client. It is extremely important to the relationship between these parties that a formal contract be drawn up to assure that there is no future misunderstanding between them. The contract should include the following items:

- *Scope of Work.* A specification of the assignment. Any change to this specification during the course of the project should be written and agreed to by both parties.

- *Approach to the Project.* A definition of how the consultant will work with company personnel and a work plan of how the project will be conducted and controlled.

- *Products or Deliverables.* A list (and brief description) of what the consultant is expected to deliver to the client. This may include items as simple as presentations to management or as complex as a complete system. In the latter case, an addendum to the contract specifying standards to be used and acceptance testing criteria should be included.

- *Assignment Start Date and Elapsed Time.* The contract should include the start date for the assignment and a completion date. Many professional firms will quote the number of actual consulting days separately from the total elapsed time of the assignment, the difference in timing being attributable to delays caused by interviews, holidays, and clerical support.

- *Charges.* Many consulting contracts are written for a fixed price. Where the work assignment can be clearly specified, this approach provides the maximum protection to the client. Where the nature of the assignment prohibits fixed-price contracting, the following issues should be addressed:

Per diem: What specific professional fees will be charged for each member of the consulting team? How many hours per day are covered by this per diem? Is there a daily minimum of hours that the consultants will bill? Does this per diem include travel time, and how is overtime billed?

Out-of-pocket costs: What specific type of costs are included in the professional fees? At what rate is local travel to be charged? Will the company be billed for telephone calls, secretarial assistance, reproduction costs? What other costs will likely be billed under this contract? It is suggested that the company ask the consulting firm for an approximation of these costs. Often, such services can be provided by the company at a cost lower than that for which they otherwise would be billed.

Estimated range of fees: Request that the consulting firm give both a high and low range of fees at which they expect to complete the assignment. This range should cover both professional fees and costs. What notice will the company receive if it appears that these fees will exceed the estimate?

• *Billing Terms.* Clarify the frequency and details that will be received on the billing statement. Will audits of expense and time reports be allowed and where can this be performed? Is payment required within a specific number of days after receipt of statement? What actions will the consulting firm take if the client is unhappy with the statement?

• *Employee Protection.* The contract may have a clause that specifies that the consulting firm may not hire company employees for a given period of time after completion of the assignment. In addition, many consulting firms request that the client similarly refrain from raiding the consultant's staff.

• *Confidentiality of Information.* There should be a protective clause assuring that the consultant will maintain full confidentiality of information provided by the company.

• *Guarantees.* Although most consulting firms refrain from providing specific guarantees of performance, certain coverage is proper. This includes coverage regarding necessary workmen's compensation insurance, replacement of unsatisfactory consultants, guarantee that consultant fees will not be increased during a reasonable period of time, obligation of the consulting firm to redo unsatisfactory portions of the assignment (without charge) and a guarantee that the specific consultants assigned to the company will not be placed on other assignments that might tend to change the completion date.

Prior to the start of the assignment the company should designate an internal liaison representative to work with the consultants. It is also important to allocate sufficient time of those individuals with which the consultants must interface. This allocation of time will assure that the consultants are able to proceed without unnecessary delays. Internal personnel should normally be assigned to the project at a level that will ensure that the knowledge gained during the project will remain with the company at the conclusion of the project (and not disappear when the consultant leaves). The consultants should be asked to interview several candidates for the liaison roles and select those with whom they feel they can best work.

As much information as possible relating to the project should be gathered in advance by internal personnel. This will further minimize the time and cost of the consultant.

It is also important that the company provide an adequate work area that can be used by the consultants. This should be a closed office containing adequate desks, chairs, and phones. It is also helpful if a conference room is provided that contains a blackboard and easel. Many companies have found it advantageous to provide a stenotypist on a full- or part-time basis. It is also appropriate for the liaison representative to advise the switchboard and mailroom of the location and mail station for the consultant team.

Unless there are overriding reasons for confidentiality, the consulting team should be introduced to senior staff members with whom they will interface at a staff meeting. It is also advisable to distribute a letter to all organization personnel informing them of the project purpose and scope, the names of the team members (both consultants and company personnel) and their location.

Liaison personnel should provide an introductory tour of the facilities to the consultants and make sure that proper identification badges or passes are provided.

During the course of the assignment, it is important that the company be assured that adequate progress is being made. This can be accomplished by establishing a schedule for progress meetings. At these meetings, the company representatives should be given assurance that the consultants are on the main path and not being sidetracked with new problems. Specific discussions should be held regarding delays due to lack of availability of company personnel and/or information, progress vs. schedule and schedule vs. budget. Preliminary conclusions should be reviewed to assure that the consultants are receiving complete information from company personnel. As appropriate, written progress reports should be obtained for review by top company management.

During the course of these progress meetings, it is extremely important that the company representatives be honest if they are doubtful or unhappy with the progress of the assignment. It is at this time that company representatives should advise the consulting team leader of any negative reactions to team personnel or methods.

As the assignment progresses, the progress meetings should reveal any recommendations upon which the client can act immediately to receive the benefits, rather than waiting for a final report. These meetings should also serve to shape the emphasis and character of the final report or presentation. If the assignment is for development or implementation, the progress meetings will assure that time/cost objectives are being met and that the work product is meeting acceptance criteria.

The client, in conjunction with the consulting team leader, will have to determine the final format for presenting the results of the project. Many consulting assignments conclude in a report and presentation.

An approach to scheduling these, which has been very successful, is to make a "final" project presentation concluding with distribution of the report. About a week to ten days later, another meeting is scheduled to review the results of the report and answer any questions raised by the report.

In addition, a private informal meeting between the consulting team leader and the key executives of the company should be held to review the project and identify any problem areas found by the consultants which were outside the scope of the original assignment. The information imparted in this meeting can be of great value to the company management.

Evaluating Consultants' Performance

A client should expect to receive value for the money paid to a consultant in the same manner as any other investment made by the company. Three methods may be used effectively to measure performance. Jerome Fuchs identifies these as:

> The first method is to compare the consultant's performance against the job specifications stated in the contract. This item-by-item review of each section of the proposal ascertains whether the consultant complied in all respects to the work statement and other project requirements. It should be an objective appraisal aimed at determining the quality of the job. The approach should be consistent with the handling of other outside contracted services or with the criteria used to evaluate an in-house person's standard of performance.
>
> The second method is to measure the consultant's contribution toward improving the financial position of the company. Normally, there is a cause-and-effect relationship between his successful completion of the assignment and certain direct benefits. Since the consultant was retained expressly to bring about constructive change, the impact of his work activity should be reflected directly in the income statement and, to a lesser extent, in the balance sheet. Although certain assignments are more difficult to measure than others, each should add some degree of finite value to the company.
>
> The third method for measuring the consultant's performance is in the long-term benefits expected from his presence. This would involve the 'rub-off' effect on in-house personnel from exposure to his approach to problem solving and his specialized knowledge. Therefore, your appraisal of the consultant should be based on how he assists in establishing a sound foundation for future growth, as well as on his near-term achievements.[5]

It should be noted that the failure to achieve the objectives desired is not necessarily the fault of the consultant. Some companies have defined project specifications that are inappropriate or overestimated the benefits they expected to receive. If the consultant, during the course of the project, discovers such inconsistencies, they should be reported to the client. If the client still desires to proceed without changing the scope of the project then some of the above performance measures will not be meaningful.

Summary

Consultants can provide a valuable supplement to the internal capabilities of a company. For best results, they should be used in a clearly specified assignment covered by appropriate contractual commitments and controls. Where possible, projects should include both consulting personnel and company personnel to ensure that the skills, experience and knowledge gained from the project remain with the company.

Footnotes

1. Fuchs, Jerome H., "Management Consulting Services Reduce Costs," *The Office*, January, 1978. p. 130.
2. Gottfried, Ira S., "Consulting Consultants," *Data Management*, June, 1969. p. 44.
3. Kennedy, James H., "Management Consultants and Conflict of Interest," *Dun's Review*, March, 1978. p. 117.
4. Frankenhuis, J. P., "How to Get a Good Consultant," *Harvard Business Review*, Nov.–Dec., 1977. p. 138.
5. Fuchs, p. 131.

SECTION 3   MANAGING THE PROBLEMS
OF ORGANIZATIONAL CHANGE

Managers of data processing, systems development, and systems projects are required by the nature of their jobs and the industry to cope with the effects of change. Not only are they personally affected by change, but they are agents of change in their own or in client (user) organizations.

Whenever there is a significant change in an organization, there exists a potential for arousing a hostile, aggressive response from members of the group. Some changes are more likely to arouse aggressive response than others. These types of change would include:

1. The merger of two organizations into one.

2. The firing or demotion and subsequent replacement of an organization head.

3. Improperly introduced major changes in work rules, equipment, or methods (this excludes the type of changes characterized by the Hawthorne experiments).

Recently, it has become popular to maintain that man is instinctively aggressive and that this is his natural state. Several best-selling books contend that humans only work together when their needs overpower their basic aggressive instincts. It does not seem necessary, however, to go so far afield to find the genesis of aggression and hostility arising in the context of organizational change. The purpose of this section is to examine why aggression and hostility arise in the process of organization change, how they manifest themselves, what are the underlying reasons for the different forms they take, and how management can avoid or combat them.

The Structure of Aggressive Action

The structure of aggressive action has several layers (Figure 1), and we must recognize that there is a mental and emotional inertia in both individuals and groups. Robert Tannenbaum says that the most characteristic individual and group reaction to change is resistance. Even before the nature of the change can be determined it appears that change itself is charged with negative valences.

The obvious manifestation of hostility is overt aggressive action. This may take several forms, ranging from reduced job efficiency to leaving the organization. The type of action taken by the individual is, of course, a product of his lifelong conditioning coupled with his understanding of the nature of the change. Each person interprets change differently, so that the change is not precisely recognized for what management intends it to be, but what the employee perceives it to be.

The proximate cause of overt aggressive action is frustration. Frustration results when an external barrier stands between a motivated individual and his goal. These goals may be rational, consciously recognized objectives or they may be human needs far down on Abraham Maslow's "need hierarchy" list.

Frustration is born of the conflicts that arise between the requirement to accept the externally imposed change and the forces driving the individual to reject the change. The intensity of the conflict depends on what the individual perceives the impact of the change to be on his goals or needs.

The central reason for aggressive resistance to change, is the threat to the satisfaction of human needs. Maslow has described the pattern of human needs as being a hierarchy or pyramid, the base of which represents such physiological needs as food, rest, clothing, and shelter.

The hierarchy of these needs is:

Second Level—Security

Third Level—Social

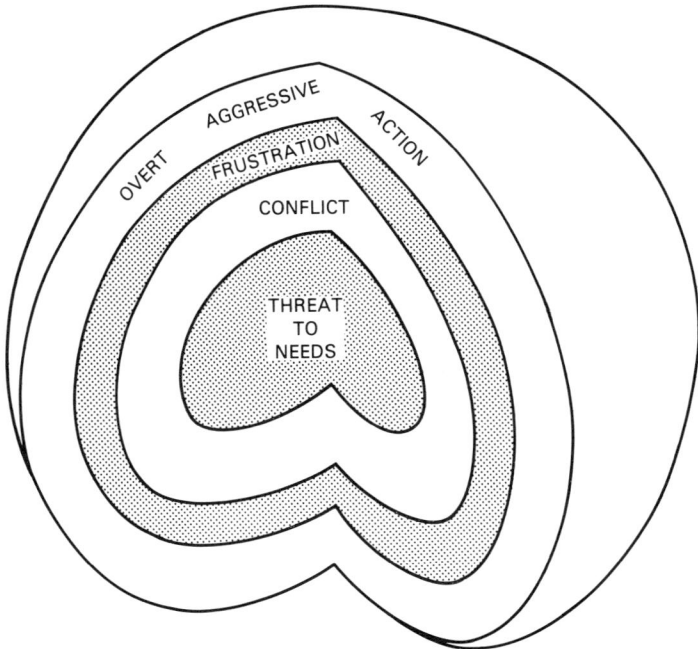

Figure 1.

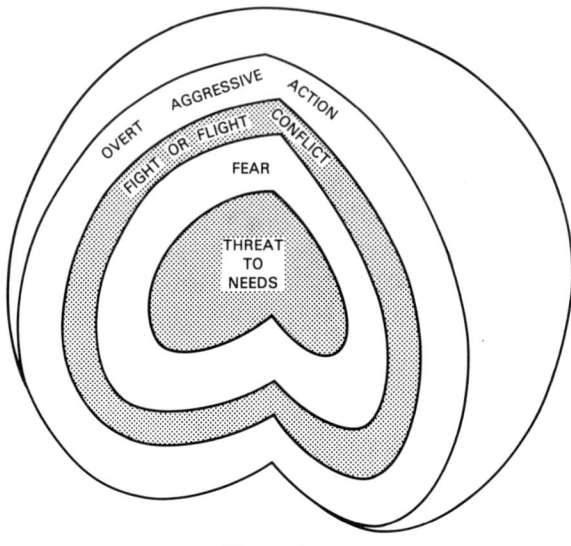

Figure 2.

Fourth Level—Status, recognition

Fifth Level—Self-actualization, fulfillment

As each level of needs is satisfied, the next level emerges. Until these needs are satisfied (at least temporarily) no higher-level needs will appear. It is interesting to observe that the threat of change seems first to attack the highest level needs and gradually work its way down the pyramid.

Prior to examining specific types of activity, there is a second model to keep in mind. (See Figure 2.) Change is strange, threatening, and full of uncertainties. In fact, uncertainty itself is always threatening. This generates fear. The fear syndrome generates a "fight or flight" conflict which leads directly to overt aggressive activity or departure from the organization.

Both models exhibit the common characteristic of conflict. This conflict is normally resolved before any action is taken by the individual. All goal-directed activity involves some degree of conflict, but usually there is no frustration as long as satisfactory progress is made toward the goal. The employee who remains with the organization may adapt to frustration by regressing, by becoming aggressive and hostile, by developing a tendency to blame others, or remain frustrated by doing nothing (which leads to more tension).

Regression

Individual resistance to change may be indicated by reduced job efficiency. Frustration may result in the reduction of psychological efficiency, a syndrome called "regression." Unconsciously, the individual's efficiency is reduced because he diverts energy from the task at hand to the mental process of worrying about the change. This worry increases his emotional imbalance, which increases the effect of his emotions on the efficiency of the personality. In addition to worrying about the impact of change on his position, he now worries about his recognizable loss of efficiency. In a continuing feedback loop, the person "regresses" to a more primitive, childlike state, where efficiency is much lower. In this primitive state he tends to defend his security needs by falling back on the informal organization for reinforcement. We have seen people in both EDP and user organizations that increase their time away from the job, create and pass on rumors, and become involved in factional activities as regressive reactions.

Each person is influenced by his attitude toward the objectives of the organization, by his group loyalties, and by his personal relationships. According to the way he perceives the impact of change on himself, the individual's positive or negative feeling about the change may dominate his attitude. Within the existing social system of the organization, factional splits may arise based upon the clash of attitudes and beliefs of different kinds.

At this point the regressed individual is sunk in a morass of ineffectuality. He has now reached a point of protracted regression at which it is frequently converted to active aggression and hostility. His aggression may be expressed verbally, through griping or rumor mongering, or it may take physical form. Frustration can be temporarily alleviated by overt aggression. Hostility and aggression are generally directed toward anyone perceived to be the cause of the frustration, or anyone supporting those perceived to be the cause. This perceived source of his frustration may be attacked physically or symbolically. If it is invulnerable to attack, however, the aggression may be displaced to an innocent but more vulnerable bystander. Domestic problems may arise in this manner.

Of special importance to EDP managers, where the change is one of work method and the organization consists of old, trusted management, aggression may be displaced to the "efficiency experts" or to minority groups attempting to enter the work environment.

Defending Status

The individual's fifth level needs for self-realization and self-fulfillment are the first to be threatened by the process of regression. At this point he will fall back to defend his needs for status, recognition, and respect. Those members of the organization most likely to manifest concern are in the middle range of status, compensation, and capability. They are the ones aspiring to advancement and who view themselves as capable of advancement.

Those who feel that they cannot advance, either because they are relatively secure in their positions, or because their self-image is one of having reached their maximum development, tend to accept organization change with relative equanimity.

The individual who stays with the organization and cannot accommodate the changes is, as we have seen, subject to exhibiting responses such as regression, overt physical or verbal aggressiveness, and impaired efficiency.

Other symptoms also characterized the individual involved in resistance to change. The individual may escape the situation through apathy. Another form of escape is chronic absenteeism and tardiness. Tardiness may also represent a physical method of indicating aggression. Furthermore, we have seen that change disrupts the sense of security and induces anxiety. Under these conditions, change may induce psychosomatic illness such as heart disease, ulcers, and nervous breakdowns.

In another type of hostile activity, the employee sets out to "punish" the organization for his imagined maltreatment. He may do this by withdrawing from contact with management and sometimes other employees, in an attempt to deny them the benefits of his association. The final, and most complete form of resistance to change is leaving the organization.

Turnover results not only from frustration produced by conflict, but also from a direct attempt to escape from the region of negative valences. This would seem to indicate that the employee envisions the future to be as hopeless as the present. The inability to resolve the conflicts underlying his frustration may lead the individual to a potentially self-destructive rage. He seeks the opportunity to strike out against the organization as the symbol of his frustration in a manner that will bring the most attention to his situation and do the most damage to the organization. In what amounts to a kamikaze attempt to damage the organization regardless of personal cost, the employee may quit. This, in effect, is a symbolic suicide of protest.

Introducing Change

Up to this point, this section has examined the causes and effects of fear and frustration arising from organization change and how these are manifested in the syndrome of aggression and hostility. Having absorbed this background, the manager is now faced with the problem of moving from the general to the particular, from the theory to the reality.

Organization changes resulting from other reasons can encounter similar problems, however, those types of change specified in the beginning of this section have one element in common: *they are introduced because of the desire of the organization's top management to improve the performance of the organization.* Those who have been the prime movers for change have the right to expect their appointed executive to successfully implement the changes designated.

The organization manager, therefore, encounters two sets of pressures. One, from below, is a strong resistance to change. The other, from above, is the pressure to successfully implement the change or lose his position. He must somehow convince his subordinates that the change is right and proper, and that the change is going to be good for them.

He must face the fact that there are generally accepted legitimate norms about the rights and responsibilities of both managers and subordinates. These norms are established by a procedure of implicit bargaining. Change, however, violates the implicit bargain and will be regarded as illegitimate unless carefully introduced. Assuredly, changes will be resisted more if they ignore established values and habits.

In the problem of introducing changes to work methods and rules (either within the EDP group or the user group), we are faced with the question of timing. The *established* manager must consider that fast changes may lead to violent resistance and disrupt the entire organization. On the other hand, slow changes may invoke some resistance, but it will be less intense at any given time. Even the slow change must be clearly communicated to all employees or exaggerated fears will arise about where the change is leading.

Volatile EDP organizations are the subject of frequent reorganization. It is sometimes desirable that a *new* manager should make all his changes at once rather than let them drag on. This has the virtue of clearly defining the new "rules of the game" to all members of the organization. The abruptness of this method does incur the risk of losing some employees. However, this risk is a normal part of the management considerations involved in introducing any change.

Even so, it is often wise for a new manager to wait before taking action until he knows more about the organization and the people with whom he is dealing. Reality dictates that this waiting period may often be short, since the manager cannot ignore top management pressure for rapid change to improve the performance of the organization.

One general characteristic of changes in methods and work rules, or in the mergers of two organizations into one, is that they can be introduced gradually to the members of the organization. Almost all sources agree that changes are invariably resisted if the staff is not previously advised or conditioned, and that resistance to change that springs from fear of the unknown can be reduced by providing appropriate information. Employees who are concerned about meeting their needs are the chief contributors to the "rumor mill."

The new manager has one preliminary organizational decision to make. He must decide if he will keep or replace all or part of the present staff. If complete replacement is intended, then his path is clear. He must move as rapidly as possible to accomplish that objective, and may, for the most part disregard the present staff. However, new staff members should be either carefully indoctrinated by the manager personally or segregated from the old staff members to prevent communicating the poor morale of the original organization members to the new organization.

If, however, he intends to retain all or part of the original organization members, then he must find some way to use (or give the illusion of using) participative decision-making techniques. *He must make them feel involved in the decision to make the changes and the methodology for implementing the changes.*

Group Decision-Making

The members of an organization will feel less threatened if it appears that they have some degree of control over their own destiny. However, group decision-making is a dangerous tool in the hands of the inexperienced manager. The group may decide on a course of action completely opposite to that desired by the manager. He must, therefore, ultimately demonstrate his authority to the group. One way to prevent this ultimate exercise of authority from being too obvious is to return decisions to the group for further consideration of pertinent points until the decision that emerges from the group is either that which the manager desired or an equivalent or better substitute.

Sayles and Strauss feel that when individuals are permitted to participate in making the final decision on a change, it is sometimes useful to ask the group to accept the change on a tentative, trial basis.

This technique is most appropriate to the EDP organization. It enables employees to test their reactions and provides them with more facts on which to base their decision. It may also help to unfreeze their attitudes and think objectively about the proposed change. A tentative change appears less threatening and generates less resistance than a permanent change. They also feel that where individuals do not participate in making the final decision, tentative changes may be unwise since they prolong the period of uncertainty and tension. There is also always the chance that employees may affect the final decision by resisting or sabotaging the tentative change. If the group's participation in the decision-making is only illusory, then the technique of the tentative change is probably unwise. The manager risks being forced to show his hand if the group rejects the change after the trial period.

There are several fringe benefits associated with the use of the group decision-making technique. Participation of the individuals generally results in diminishing the time required to establish new group norms.

Individuals who fail to live up to standards of proper conduct as redefined by the group are subjected to pressure to conform. Group decision-making commits each member of the group to carry out the decision that is agreed on. It is, therefore, very useful in introducing change to user groups by having broad participation in the system definition phase. It also serves to improve the group member's image of the group manager.

The group decision-making techniques runs the risk of incurring some disadvantages. The decision of the involved groups may be contrary to the good of the entire organization, differ from the intentions of higher management, or be inconsistent with the organization's long-range plans.

Group decision-making in a shrinking organization environment is probably inappropriate. Because needs for security are much more obviously threatened, one should expect greater resistance to change in a company which is contracting or stationary in size than one which is expanding and providing a greater number of opportunities, even though more changes may be taking place in the latter organization.

In the contracting organization the group may be forced to decide on preserving or eliminating the job of one of its members. This is not only a decision which it is ill-equipped to make, but also a decision that is unfair for management to ask.

Three difficult-to-manage and frequently interrelated conditions do not lend themselves to group decision-making. These are decisions relating to the contracting organization as described above, decisions on which management cannot provide group members with all of the appropriate information even though it is known, and those in which the head of the organization is to be terminated and replaced.

It is in the extremely sensitive area of terminating and replacing a group head that group decision-making cannot be used. Many reasons for this are apparent. Most obviously, no successful business organization can be run as a democracy. Unlike a government, a business organization cannot afford to be operated by a hierarchy of individuals who have achieved their position through winning a popularity contest. No matter how well disguised throughout, it is at this point that the business organization ultimately reveals its dictatorial nature. Because in North America the concept of dictatorship is alien to native citizens, it is the ultimate sticking point.

No manager can relinquish the decision or the responsibility for naming the subordinate to whom he will delegate authority and whom he expects to hold responsible for its appropriate exercise. Furthermore, no manager can be expected to operate efficiently if each decision must be conditioned by his need to maintain personal popularity with the group.

Each executive, due to the limitations of his span of control, is forced to delegate some of his authority. He shapes the entire character of the organization under him by the appointments he makes to those positions reporting to him. Each appointee subsequently constitutes his own staff of members with whom he can comfortably communicate and in whom he has trust.

An important corollary to this is that the follower must be able to identify with the leader. Control cannot be exercised if those who wish to control are too different from those who are to be controlled.

In recognition of this, the appointment of a top caliber manager to a group whose previous performance was unsatisfactory, will generally result in the manager reconstituting the group with personnel closer to his ideals. It will furthermore cause members of the original group to be extremely restive since they cannot adequately communicate with their new supervisor.

Given then that the group cannot participate in this decision, that no information will be provided by higher management to the group or its original manager prior to his termination, and that no information can be provided to the group relating to the actions of the new manager, this becomes the most difficult introduction of change imaginable. How then, can it be handled?

Introducing the New Manager

Observation of many changes indicates that most managers intuitively feel that where no information can be provided to group members, as little material for conjecture as possible should be allowed to reach the "rumor mill." For this reason many will approach a termination so that once the news has been made public, the terminated group head will be removed from contact with the group as rapidly as possible. This condition assumes, of course, normal popularity of the group head with his subordinates and some reasonable question as to whether or not his performance has been inadequate. If the group head is terminated for obvious cause, or he had been unpopular with his subordinates, no such minimizing of publicity is necessary.

Some brief announcement of the reasons for the manager's removal must be made to the group. This announcement should be as brief, objective, and unambiguous as possible. It should provide as little room for misinterpretation as possible. If the organization desires to retain the members of the affected group, the terminated manager's superior must clearly state to the group the effect of this change on their individual positions.

Several possible courses of action are open to management. They may break up the group and distribute its members through other groups in the organization, they may appoint an interim manager, or they may appoint an immediate permanent replacement for the terminated manager.

Breaking up the group could normally be expected to result in the loss of some of the group members to the organization. The symbolic death of a group with which they identified may so shatter the identification of the individual with the organization that he might be unable to adjust to other groups.

The appointment of an interim manager suffers from the same drawbacks as the introduction of interim change when the group will not be responsible for the decision. In addition, the interim manager cannot be expected to make any but extremely short-range decisions. His immediate supervisor would be required to make most of the decisions for the group. The personal relationships within the group have been disrupted, the goals of the group are ambivalent, and the temporary manager must face some loss of status when he returns to being an ordinary member of the group. Under these circumstances, very little productive work will get done.

It appears that the best possible circumstance is the appointment of a new manager as soon as possible after termination of the original manager.

How the New Manager Assumes Control

The ease with which the new manager can assume his role is directly proportional to the briefness of the time between these events. The group which has suffered the shock of losing its leader can absorb the appointment of his replacement as a part of the same event. The norms and patterns of personal relations within the group have only been disrupted one time. On the other hand, if an extended period of time has elapsed, the group has adapted to the circumstances and established a new set of norms and interpersonal relations. These are disrupted again when the permanent appointment is made after some time has elapsed.

It is also difficult, at that time, for the new appointee to say anything reassuring to members of the group regarding the security of their personal position. He does not have enough first-hand knowledge to reliably evaluate group members, and they know it. Almost anything he says regarding group member security will be questioned. It is therefore incumbent upon his superior to make any such statements deemed necessary.

The newly appointed manager requires some time before he can be expected to deal appropriately and believably with the problems of group members. With the personal expectations of the new manager being an unknown quantity, the level of frustration within the group can be expected to rise. This frustration is generally undirected and will be manifested in many of the ways previously described.

Until he is prepared to make some believable definitive statements as to his own expectations for group member performance and as to meeting the needs of the group members individually, he should probably avoid meetings of the total group. Such meetings might only serve to provide the group with a focal point for its hostility and aggression.

The new manager's first requirement is time—time to evaluate the members of his staff and time to absorb the situation and the organizational environment. The manager is generally required to maintain at least as good performance as the group had before, even though he may not be able to improve it immediately. It is necessary for him to resist higher management pressures for rapid results until he can make sound, well-considered moves. Assuming that he has the necessary management support and has convinced them of the need (and his ability) to establish his own timetable, he must then find a way to buy the necessary amount of time from the members of the group.

If there existed any group cohesion in the past, it has probably been severely damaged by the management changes. However, a large part of the informal organization must still exist. This informal organization has its leaders and high status members. The key to maintaining group performance is the informal leaders. By identifying and forming a working relationship with these leaders, the new manager can generally prevent a drastic reduction in the group's performance level.

Reestablishing individual cooperation and group cohesion is extremely important. If these informal leaders do not react in a positive fashion to the manager's approach, they represent a major threat to the effective performance of the new manager. For this reason, if he cannot obtain their cooperation, his only recourse is to remove them from the organization. While their removal might temporarily create an added disturbance, it will allow group hostility to diminish in a shorter time, since some major elements fueling that hostility will be removed.

The new manager must make every effort to get acquainted with his key personnel as soon as possible. While the formal structure of a group meeting should be avoided, individual informal talks provide an excellent method for both evaluating employees and forming interpersonal relations. As soon as possible, those people who can form the cadre of a rebuilt organization should be identified. This cadre and all those whom the manager determines are of value to the organization should be apprised of the manager's opinion as soon as possible. This feedback will help to satisfy their needs for reassuring their security.

Such a selected cadre should be made to feel that they are the manager's "chosen" group. This cadre, whose needs have been met through the highest levels, as well as any new members of the organization hired by the new manager, have a vested psychological interest in supporting him.

In the formation of new group norms, and in creating the new implicit bargain between the group and the manager, these people form a "voting block" to support the manager. This must be done carefully in order to avoid formation of a clique. The objective is to have all members of the group join the cadre rather than to form separate opposing forces.

As previously discussed, original group members have suffered a blow to their self-image which was modeled on the previous group leadership. It is important that these people change the locus of the image with whom they identify. Those who are to remain with the organization must be "imprinted" with a new image in keeping with the objectives of new management. Imprinting must be done with someone not too remote from the group members, someone with whom they can identify or choose as an ideal image.

Because of this need for identification, there may be too much difference between the group members and the manager for such imprinting to take place. Those selected for membership in the cadre must be carefully chosen for those qualities the manager would like to see spread throughout the group. Screening of new applicants is very important at this stage. Outsiders brought in must be technically competent enough to rapidly earn the respect of the original group members and to demonstrate the good judgment of the new manager.

Members of the restructured group need to enhance their prestige and demonstrate their ability to function successfully as a group. Discreetly managed participative goal setting should be introduced for the purpose of establishing short-term objectives. Long-term objectives and projects do not provide the immediate reward necessary. Short-term objectives that can be readily accomplished provide a rapid, rewarding experience to group members.

After the psychological damage to their self-image, group members badly need the victory that goal accomplishment provides; or a token of recognition for their contribution, coming from higher management; or some bettering of the organizational position of the group. Another method could be winning a long-standing argument with another group. These events can often be arranged without too much trouble.

Minimizing the Impact of Change

Since the problems have been created by change, it is necessary to minimize or eliminate any forms of change that are not absolutely required. Unless it is the intention to replace the group, the manager should not change the offices or the physical location of the group. Even when such a change would appear to enhance the prestige of the group, the slightest disadvantage of the new location will create another focal point of controversy.

Under these circumstances any change appears to be an attack against the previous norm. While a given change may not really be an attack against the previous norm, the group accepts the change as a symbol of such an attack. For example, changing the time of a coffee break is not an attack on the entire previous system, but it may be taken as such. The manager must try to preserve some of the "institutions" of the previous system.

Until all possible imprinting is completed and the manager is secure in the support of his "voting block," it is unwise to directly criticize prior management. This criticism has been implied most severely by the management change itself. The new manager may not be directly associated as yet with the organizational elements that caused the change. He can maintain a neutral position with members of the group by criticizing "circumstances" and "the environment" or he can blame changing needs on the part of the organization for the failure of the prior manager. This would be taken as less of a personal affront to group members and gives them a "way out."

The generally pessimistic attitude that exists immediately after the organization change is emphasized by critical interpretation of the new manager's most innocent comments. The group member who feels that he has been dealt with unfairly by higher management expects duplicity on the part of the new manager. The manager must be scrupulously fair and open to the greatest extent possible. He must be especially candid in reviewing the performance of staff members and in appraising their future opportunities within the group. Any action taken that is contrary to his expressed intent will be taken as further evidence of duplicity.

For this reason, he should be concise in his discussions with group members. Until he is fully accepted, he should not "philosophize" with members of the group and risk being misinterpreted.

On the other hand, he should slowly build increased association with group members through brief informal contact whenever possible. Such contact can serve to reduce tension and reinforce the manager's "human" image.

Charges of duplicity can also arise from skipping the chain of command. Such action makes an already insecure subordinate become even more insecure. The supervisor who has been skipped over is pushed into regressive action which actually does decrease his efficiency. In this, the manager who suspects inefficiency on the part of the supervisor can actually create it. Furthermore, he demonstrates to group members that he has a low regard for the skipped-over supervisor. While this may not actually be true, it is the way group members are most likely to interpret the action.

Should it be necessary to review all current work or work methods, remaining members of the original group must be dealt with in a manner that will allow them to feel secure and save face. If a project must be temporarily stopped, it is important to find other tasks to keep those people formerly on the project busy. The manager must be careful to avoid insulting the creators or the product itself directly. He can permit face saving by such devices as crediting poor past performance to improper direction, changing company needs, technical obsolescence, or new factors making the previous approach uneconomical.

Incidentally, keeping people busy has a fringe benefit. It reduces the time available for generating and propagating rumors. The more creative and self directing the group members, the more it is necessary to keep a good backlog of work available and continue the pressure to produce.

Summary

Despite the manager's best efforts, he will probably lose some group members who for one reason or another he would prefer to keep. The manager who tries to keep an employee who is resigning is probably making a mistake. The employee has reached a point of frustration at which nothing will permanently satisfy him. While a promotion or a salary increase may temporarily dissuade him from leaving, it also denies him the satisfaction of "getting even," which further frustrates him.

The manager can expect to lose those employees who have suffered a loss of authority, status, or prestige as a result of the change. He must carefully reinforce the authority of those that he wants to retain in the organization.

One must remember that each person and each environment is different. While studies in group psychology and in individual reactions to frustration may point to some generalized causes and effects, and may permit the establishment of some guidelines for overcoming hostility and aggression that result from organization change, there is no "cook book" answer, and there is no clearcut list of "do's and don't's." We can, however, be sure of one thing: we must get used to handling change because change will probably be the hallmark of the organization of the future. This is emphasized by observation of one of the more effective methods of handling change. Today's aerospace, electronic, and fashion industries have handled the problem of change by making change a constant part of the organization environment. This may be the ultimate answer for the organization of the future. It is certainly key to the rapidly changing world of data processing practitioners and their clients.

The techniques outlined above are relevant to introducing change in both the EDP group and the user environment.

Footnotes

1. C. Argyris, *Personality and Organization,* New York: Harper and Row, 1957.
2. B. Berelson and G. A. Steiner, *Human Behavior,* New York: Harcourt, Brace and World, Inc., 1964.

3. A. Maslow, "The Need Hierarchy," *Management and the Behavioral Sciences,* Boston: Allyn and Bacon, 1968.

4. J. B. Miner, *Personnel Psychology,* Toronto: MacMillan Co., 1969.

5. L. R. Sayles and G. Strauss, *Human Behavior in Organizations,* New Jersey: Prentice-Hall, Inc., 1966, p. 304; and Tannenbaum.

6. R. Tannenbaum, I. R. Weschler, and F. Massarik, *Leadership and Organization,* New York: McGraw Hill, 1961.

SECTION 4   THE PERFORMANCE EVALUATION REVIEW

In popular use the performance evaluation is often called the "review." The review has become a   euphemism for an annual salary increase. Many managers make the mistake of allowing the amount of the salary increase to speak for them in telling their employee what they think of his or her performance. It is my belief that the people in the data processing field are usually of higher intelligence and greater awareness than the average. As a result, they are more likely to benefit from a fair critical appraisal of their performance.

Considering the plethora of papers and books on behavior and motivation that have appeared during the last few years, it is no wonder that the average manager is afraid to discuss any possible "demotivator" with an employee. This, however, is no more than a convenient rationalization. It is used to disguise the fact that no sensitive manager wants to hurt the feelings or livelihood of his employees. More than one organization has become a haven for mediocre to incompetent performers as a result.

Standards

Next to a production line worker it is probably easier to develop standards for data processing people than for most other fields. Yet the development of performance standards, the key to employee appraisal, has remained a mystic art in most data processing organizations.

Clearly, a computer operator can be evaluated on his ability to perform certain specific tasks without error. Operator error in a computer operation is highly visible. Console logs tell a complete story of the errors, restarts, and utilization of the machine. A wealth of experience is available for measuring the keystrokes and error rates of data entry operators.

Standards for the programming and systems analysis functions are less tangible, but they can be created. These standards may be divided into five areas of performance: production, technical competence, project organization, project management, and sales ability. Within these areas performance standards should include the following.

Production:

Is the project completed on time and within budget (based on reasonable estimates prepared by the employee and his supervisor)?

Technical Competence:

Do the system and/or programs work with minimum error and require minimum maintenance?

314

Do the programs operate efficiently?

Does the system meet the user's objectives?

Project Organization:

Is the project well planned using appropriate planning tools (flowcharts, bar charts, PERT, cost breakdowns, etc.)?

Have the requirements for the system or program been clearly defined?

Has the project team been well organized to include user personnel, with clearly specified areas of responsibility?

Project Management:

Does the employee demonstrate the ability to motivate other employees?

Is the effort well coordinated?

Is friction between team members or between the project team and the user at a minimum?

Does the employee display a cooperative attitude?

Are concise, understandable progress reports submitted on time?

Sales Ability:

Does the analyst or programmer view the user properly as a *customer?*

Are his presentations clear, concise and polished?

Is he ready with the answers to users' questions?

Do the presentations achieve their desired result?

Evaluation

There are really two aspects to the evaluation: *when* and *how.*

Evaluation should be performed whenever necessary. There is no need to wait for a predetermined period to expire. In fact, waiting may endanger a project. It is also unfair to the employee to allow him to continue an undesirable course of action without warning. An evaluation review with the employee should take place *at least* once a year.

No manager hesitates to review an employee when his evaluation is favorable. Managers do, however, procrastinate where unfavorable aspects exist. Delays may only exacerbate the current problems and result in an irremediable situation. There are also no problems with *how* to give a performance review when the manager can say, "Everything is great. Keep up the good work!" All the problems arise in presenting criticism.

When a critical review is necessary, don't be chicken. Confer with the employee, reminding him of the standards against which he is being evaluated and telling him of your appraisal of his performance. Document the appraisal since such documentation is a valuable tool for future action with the employee. Approach the conversation with the idea that the employee (presumably) wants to remain employed and to advance to the limits of his ability while you, in turn, want his best performance. Let him know what he needs to do to improve and how you can help him.

Summary

The time for EDP managers to prove that they are *managers* is long past due. The quality of your staff directly affects your own performance and the appraisal you will receive. Developing your staff to meet the standards you set is a matter of enlightened self-interest. Such development can only take place through the proper use of the performance evaluation review. Delay or failure in providing critical evaluation reviews is a disservice to both the manager and the employee.

SECTION 5 "IF YOU'RE SO SMART, WHY AIN'T YOU RICH?"

We data processing managers are really very brilliant. Our educational background is equal to or better than that of most other company executives. No one in the company knows more about how it works and no one is a better integrator of the company's various systems.

So why, as a recent survey shows, are we frequently the second-lowest paid executive in the company? And why is our salary frequently less than 25 percent that of the company president?

In the past, top executives frequently came from the ranks of manufacturing and engineering. More recently, a large percentage of top executives have been recruited from the accounting and sales management ranks. When will it be our turn? Not all of our present group of top executives are related to the boss nor are they all able to selectively lose the proper golf games. For the most part, they have built on a base of being superqualified in their own professions before moving up. For this reason it is worth a brief look at what it takes to be a superqualified data processing manager.

In the area of education, an MBA or its equivalent is extremely valuable. An accounting major is a real plus. While a CDP may be helpful, nothing could equal being a CPA. In the technical area, the data processing manager should have a familiarity with programming and with organization of the programming effort. He or she should have even more familiarity with systems analysis. Some knowledge of computer operations is extremely helpful and he or she should at least know what to expect from his or her operations manager.

The data processing manager must be an expert in project control. It is this function in which results are most evident to management and on which performance will most likely be evaluated. He or she should have had direct experience in controlling projects. He or she should know and be able to use such project scheduling and control techniques as PERT or CPM. He or she should have a thorough knowledge of project financial control methods.

Recognizing that business systems always have people interfaces, the DP manager should be competent in the fields of manual methods, policy and procedure development, and forms design, control, and procurement. A high level of skill in dealing with people is mandatory. The ability to communicate both orally and in writing with all levels of personnel within and outside of the organization is a prime requisite.

It is incumbent on the DP manager to translate the jargon of the computer world to the customer. For this, a familiarity with the concepts of sales and service, financial techniques, manufacturing and engineering, accounting, personnel management, and general business management is required. In addition, a knowledge of long-range planning methods may be of significant importance.

Assuming that our hero, the data processing manager, is super-qualified and highly efficient, we are still faced with the problem of getting promoted.

First, it is necessary to map a career strategy setting achievable goals within realistic time frames. This involves a process of self questioning. Am I smarter than my competition? Do I know more about the operation of my company than anyone else? Am I deficient in any area of skill or knowledge that may be critical? Am I satisfied with my present position in the company? Do I really want to advance? Am I really willing to take on more responsibility? If all the answers are not satisfactory, am I willing to work to overcome the deficiencies?

Most executives from other disciplines are wary of computer-oriented personnel. They tend to view the data processing manager as a specialist or technician, much the same as the accountant was viewed a few years ago. As the head of a staff organization, the data processing manager is thought to have been sheltered from the realities of the business world. The entrepreneurial drive is lacking. How can you run a company when you've never been responsible for making a profit? What do you really know about marketing? Your perspective is limited to only what takes place inside the company.

In the face of these kinds of opinions, it's obvious that an image change is needed. This image change has two prime ingredients: visibility and exposure. More correctly, high visibility and low, selective exposure, visibility being defined as being seen by the right people. Exposure, on the other hand, is being left open to view under circumstances with negative implications. For example, every decision involves some risk. Proper risktaking is a part of our entrepreneurial scheme. If the risk is taken and the conclusion is successful, showing the results is visibility. If the results of the risktaking are disastrous, then a clear view of the results is exposure. This is not to advocate hiding failures, because the proper presentation of a failure can demonstrate the maturity of the manager and be converted to visibility.

Several steps can be taken to add to visibility. All of them involve risk. So obviously, they lead either up or out of the organization.

1. *Take authority.* If authority is not specified for a given area, assume that it belongs to you. Once you have taken it, others will assume that it was yours anyway. If you are stopped by someone else you can always plead ignorance or "emergency conditions." Even in an organization, "nature abhors a vacuum." If you don't do it, someone else will.

2. *Make decisions.* All the better if they concern areas outside the data processing function. This is another way of expanding your authority.

3. *Report your activities.* Regular reports on the operation of your department should be provided to all members of top management. Don't try to hide problems or failures, but do include proposed solutions when reporting a problem. Always make sure you report your own problems before someone else does.

4. *Sell your services.* Propose ideas for *profitable* new applications. Suggest ways in which you or your staff can help (methods studies, economic analyses, etc.).

5. *Take over new functions.* When some functions are automated, the residue of staff may logically be associated with your organization. Some administrative tasks are not wanted by others but provide opportunities for you to demonstrate your abilities (managing the motor pool, the building and facilities, the mail room, etc.).

In addition, there are two other valuable rules to remember. First, always train your replacement. The indispensable person can't be moved when a promotional opportunity exists. Second, know when to leave the company. If all avenues for advancement are blocked, get out.

If you don't wind up rich, at least you will get to travel a lot.

The newly appointed manager or the analyst who takes on the job of project leader for the first time is entering a new world that will demand different skills, a different perspective, and different interpersonal relationships from those to which he has become accustomed. The analyst, as an analyst, has usually had numerous opportunities to observe (and criticize) managers in both the systems function and user operations. Now the chance exists to demonstrate the validity of observations and judgments made in the past.

But the standards by which an analyst's performance is judged and those by which a project leader or manager are judged are very different. Unfortunately, the failure rate among project managers is fairly high. Since analysts as a group are observant, intelligent individuals, it must be some other factor that creates the problem.

The standards by which an analyst is evaluated include:

Completion of tasks on time and within budget

Productivity

Problem-solving ability

Compatability with others

Attitude

At first glance these seem to be the same standards that would be applied to a manager. In a sense, they are. But while the analyst is evaluated on his own performance, the manager is evaluated on the performance of the group. The group consists of individuals over whom the manager has limited control.

In today's business systems organizations an increasing number of analysts and project managers have had the benefit of some college or university business training—enough to recognize that management is an acquired skill. However, several authorities in the field of management insist that it is a skill that can be learned, but cannot be taught.

This section will make no pretentions to *teach* management. Rather, it will present basic concepts of management as a reminder and a self-checking device for both the novice and the experienced project manager or EDP manager.

The Management Task

Classical theories of management had evolved, by the 1950s, a list of management functions that included:

planning	supervising
organizing	motivating

directing   decision-making

controlling   coordinating

Starting in the 1940s, management theory was invaded by a new group, the behavioral theorists and researchers. Their approach to defining the role of management has been summarized by Ralph Stogdill as:[1]

Defining objectives and maintaining goal direction.

Providing means for goal attainment.

Providing and maintaining group structure.

Facilitating group action and interaction.

Maintaining group cohesiveness and member satisfaction.

Facilitating group task performance.

Quite obviously, then, the project manager is going to be evaluated for areas of performance over and above those applied to the analyst functions performed.

The project manager's position is especially demanding in that it requires both the skills of the analyst and the skills of the manager. In addition, it requires the discretion to determine the appropriate circumstances for the use of these two skills.

In a broad sense, the project manager will be evaluated on the ability to get the job done on time, within budget, to the satisfaction of the user, and in a manner that maintains or enhances the cohesiveness of the project team and the relationship of the project team to the rest of the company so that there exists a continuing ability to produce results. For the project manager, this boils down to one thing: motivating the people with whom he interacts to contribute to the goals of the project.

Modern Management Theory

Most of the history of management theory, starting in 1812, had been dominated by economic principles applied to the firm and to the worker alike. It was only in the 1920s that noneconomic values began to receive some attention. First with Elton Mayo's 1924 study of a textile mill near Philadelphia, then with the famous study of the Western Electric Company plant at Hawthorne in 1929 by F. J. Roethlisberger and W. J. Dickson. From that time to the present, management theory has evolved to the point that its primary considerations are noneconomic.

Once it was recognized that economic incentives were not

enough, the seminal thinkers in the management field became interested in exploring any behavioral attribute that could motivate the worker to align his goals with the goals of management. Some of the concepts of modern management theory, which are rapidly becoming classics themselves, are summarized below.

Chris Argyris: There is a lack of congruency between the needs of healthy individuals and the demands of the formal organization. This condition frustrates the individual and forces him into adaptive behavior within the informal organization. Job/role enlargement may decrease the degree of incongruency if the adaptive behavior has not become too entrenched in the organization culture and self-concept of the individuals.[2]

Frederick Herzberg: All men are motivated by work. Man needs autonomy to accomplish his job. Work should not be fragmented. Man's work life is influenced by two categories of behavioral constraints:

Hygiene factors, which include company policy, working conditions, benefits and salary, titles and security, and which can produce negative effects.

Motivating factors, which include achievement, meaningful work, recognition, responsibility for making decisions, and advancement and growth opportunities.[3]

Abraham Maslow: Each individual has a hierarchy of needs that range from basic physiological needs to purely psychological needs. The higher needs appear only after the lower ones have been satisfied. Individuals can be motivated to strive for organizational goals in order to satisfy their present level of need. Management must recognize and attempt to satisfy the need level of the individual. These need levels are (from highest to lowest):

1. Self actualization. The need to realize one's own potential.

2. Esteem. The need for recognition by associates and authority (generally measured by the authority and responsibility vested in the individual).

3. Social need. The desire to belong to certain groups and be loved by its members.

4. Safety. The desire for security and survival.

5. Physiological needs. The fundamental motivators such as hunger, shelter, sex, etc.[4]

Couched in terms of manager-worker or leader-follower relationships, the consistent pattern displayed by most modern studies is that all person-oriented behaviors are related to follower satisfaction. Work-oriented behaviors on the part of management (autocratic, restrictive, task-oriented, socially distant, directive, structured) tend to inhibit group productivity, cohesiveness, and satisfaction. The only work-oriented behavior that consistently relates to group productivity is that which maintains role differentiation and lets followers know what to expect.

Person-oriented behaviors (democratic, permissive, follower-oriented, participative, and considerate) all relate positively to group satisfaction, the last two relate positively to group cohesion. But person-oriented behaviors alone do not consistently relate to productivity.[5]

Management of Systems Personnel

As though the complexity of management were not enough, it presents even greater problems when applied to the area of creative groups. In the usual line organization the manager represents management, and employees (within some tolerable range of behavior) perform according to the manager's requests. In a creative function this is, to some extent, reversed. The manager is looked upon as a fellow professional and is expected to represent the group to management. Studies of research workers have shown that the manager is expected to establish conditions that are conducive to initiative and independent judgment, and to take an active interest in the work.

While it would be dangerous to generalize from a study of research workers to systems analysts, Richard French has derived some implications from these studies to the motivation of systems personnel:

1. Systems analysts get a great deal of satisfaction out of seeing a job through from start to finish.

2. Systems analysts do not want to stagnate. They want to have the opportunity to keep up with the state of the art. Many will be attracted by the latest kind of equipment/software, etc.

3. They do not like detailed supervision. They like responsibility as long as it is defined and they are measured against the definition.

4. Systems analysts tend to look for growth opportunities and avenues of promotion (even beyond the systems organization itself).[6]

Studies of research workers, engineers, and project-oriented groups have resulted in a surge of interest in *team building*. Some organizations have used transactional analysis concepts to improve internal communication within groups as a device for improving group cohesiveness. This is based on the assumption (not proven) that group cohesiveness relates positively to production. The best that can be said of this approach at this time is that it's like chicken soup—it may help, and it certainly can't hurt.

Participative management, which does more to satisfy the need for esteem (a level above the social needs met by group cohesiveness) seems to work better with systems people. This technique invites all who can meaningfully contribute to a problem solution or management decision to provide their input to the decision-making process in terms of advice, reservations, alternatives, and/or consent.

Participative management can be a good motivator, but it must be used carefully. The author has observed several situations in which this technique, improperly applied, has had a bad impact on projects. In some instances the technique was applied to decisions that the group members were not qualified or authorized to make. (For example, whether or not certain functions should be included in the system design or whether or not certain departmental standards for documentation should be used.) Another case was that of a project manager who was unable to control the extent of discussion on topics. This, combined with the fact that several members of the group used the opportunity presented to vent personal piques, turned the group into a debating society that could not get any work done.

In several instances the technique was attempted by a project leader who was basically authoritarian. It was not long before group members recognized that their participation in decision-making was a sham. Morale plunged, and productive capacity dropped with the lack of interest in the project. The project leader also lost the potentially valuable contributions of experienced personnel on the team.

From these examples we can derive certain guidelines for the use of participative management.

1. The intention to utilize participative management should be introduced to the group in a meeting that will permit a statement and appropriate discussion of the concept and the ground rules for its use.

2. Participation in decisions should be limited to those affected by the decision and those with appropriate expertise.

3. Subjects beyond the decision-making authority of the group should be clearly designated at the outset to avoid wasting time on consideration of such matters. These excluded subjects may include personnel actions, priority setting for projects (which should be done by the user), and technical standards below the requirements of the installation. Suitable subjects for participation should also be outlined. These may include preparation of estimates, division of labor, internal project priorities, project standards, and working schedules (if company policy permits).

4. Participative management techniques require the time of all personnel on the team. It is expected that an improved understanding of goals and improved group communication and cohesion will raise

production to more than offset the lost time. However, to assure that excessive time will not be lost, some format for the process should be established. One method is to require any member who determines the need for a decision to briefly document the problem and a proposed solution. Copies of the document are distributed to participants and they are allowed sufficient time, according to the complexity or impact of the problem, for consideration of the proposed solution. A meeting is then called for discussion. At the conclusion of the meeting the decision (or recommendation to management) is documented and distributed to all members of the group and to the manager to whom the project leader reports.

5. It is generally understood by people working in industry that corporations are not democracies. If the project manager must bear full responsibility for the success or failure of the project, then final decision-making authority rests with the responsibility. Yet a course of action on the project manager's part that consistently rejects or overrides the consensus of the group will frustrate the intent of the participative process. Decisions which are not acceptable are frequently the product of a lack of information on the part of the group members. The project leader must be sure that any information that he possesses is brought to the attention of the group during their consideration of the problem. In those instances where the decision is not acceptable to the project manager, the manager must make clear to the group those factors which make the decision incorrect or unfeasible.

Another approach to team building is the concept of *egoless programming* or *egoless design*. Gerald Weinberg, in his book *The Psychology of Computer Programming*, says that the most successful software firms use this principle.[7]

The egoless group is the result of getting every member of the team to recognize his humanity (and fallibility). On this basis, all members of the team are equally responsible for the success of the project. They are expected to review each other's work for possible error. Products of the group are shared in the sense that all members get credit. The reverse of this is also true, so that an error in design or coding is not the error of an individual, but a group error, since it has passed by another member for review.

The prerequisite for establishing an egoless group is rooted in participative management. This group depends on a common understanding of its goals and constraints and a common view of design considerations. An interesting sidelight on this approach is that egoless groups are self policing in the sense that each member is expected to contribute to the maximum of his ability in his assigned role. Peer pressure is exerted strongly on any who shirk their task or act in a manner disruptive to the group.

The concepts of modern management theory and experience with team building combine two major elements necessary for successful teams: good internal communications among team members and between the project manager and team members, and a system of providing worker satisfaction and rewards.

The communications system must not only carry information quickly and freely to all members of the group, but must also:

• Explain problems, purposes and goals that affect the group.

• Describe procedures and let each member know what is expected of him.

• Outline responsibilities and authority.

• Outline rights and privileges.

• Explain accountability and rewards.

The system of satisfaction of needs, or rewards, must provide for:

• Individual respect.

• Equality of working conditions.

• Control over own affairs.

• Knowledge of environmental constraints.

• Opportunity to use individual ability and capacity.

• A feeling of participation.

• A feeling of equity and consistency in management of the group.

In addition to team building and motivation, it is implicit in the title of the project leader or manager that *leadership* is expected.

Volumes have been written on leadership styles and considerable research has been done. Leadership styles have been classified as productive and nonproductive. Nonproductive styles range from the merely ineffectual to the absolutely destructive. James Cribbin has classified these styles or patterns of leadership into five categories.[8] They include the domineering manager, the pseudodemocratic manager, the accommodative manager, the paternalistic manager, and the bureaucratic manager.

Similarly, Cribbin has described three productive leadership patterns: the directive, the collaborative, and the collegial.[9]

Selection of an appropriate management style should be a conscious decision. Unfortunately, that rarely happens. However, the opportunity to make such a conscious selection always exists. Factors that influence this selection include:

• *The personality of the manager.* With what style will the manager be comfortable?

• *The ethical sensitivity of the manager.*

• *The characteristics of the work group.* Are they assembly line workers? Professionals? Creative? Dependent? Independent? Unionized?

• *The existing relationship between the manager and the workers.* Is the chemistry good?

• *The managers position of power and influence in the organization.* Several studies have shown that people prefer to work for managers who have "clout."

• *The constraints of the work and work environment.* A style appropriate to a university staff is different from that for a machine shop. Also, each organization has rules and policies that may dictate the style of management that will be rewarded.

• *The style of leadership acceptable by society.* Outside of military organizations, a dictatorial style of management cannot be successful for long in the American society, as an example.

Motivating the work force, building an effective and productive group, and leading that group do not completely fulfill the duties of the manager. The manager has an obligation to the firm, to group members, and to self in the area of developing subordinates. This obligation exists to the company, so that the group can continue in the absence of the manager; to the employee, so that the employee can experience opportunities for challenge and qualify for advancement; and to self, because people who are indispensable in their positions cannot be promoted. The following techniques are some that may be used for developing subordinates.

Realistic achievement goals should be set through negotiation between the worker and supervisor. They should be fair goals, but designed to "stretch" the worker's ability and knowledge. They should be quantifiable in terms of number or a definite product. They should cover a definite time period before being reviewed. (Short interval scheduling is a good development tool.) They should be meaningful to the employee and the organization.

Individual coaching may be a useful tool if an employee recognizes the need. It is rarely successful if imposed. Coaching also depends on the employee being motivated to improve and seeing some reward to himself in it. It should be performed in an environment that permits fast feedback to the employee and the coach must be respected by the employee.

While coaching is designed to make the employee a more productive worker, *counseling* is directed toward helping the employee to become a better adjusted human being in the work environment. Counseling may be directed toward facets of adjustment such as performance and achievement, career, job adjustment, social adjustment, and personal adjustment. Managers are usually well advised to avoid counseling activities, much as a psychiatrist would avoid a personal relationship with a patient. However, it is the manager's job to recognize the need for counseling and request the help of the personnel department with the employee. Given the right relationship between the manager and employee, the manager may sometimes suggest that the employee seek outside help or counseling.

Delegation is perhaps one of the strongest development tools. Delegation should be done systematically. The manager should understand the strengths and limitations of the employee. The delegation should be part of a development plan, and the ground rules should be spelled out. The employee should be informed of the limits of responsibility and authority, what can be decided autonomously, what must be referred for final decision, which decisions require special permission, and what is reserved to the manager for decision. Performance should be reviewed frequently with the objective of moving the employee from the position of being monitored to being independent.

This last point introduces the key element in employee development programs: the performance review. Performance reviews that occur annually or semiannually are closely associated with salary adjustments. As such, they distract the employee from the content of the review itself. A development program should set up performance reviews at shorter intervals to provide critiques of progress and other rewards than salary (such as praise or public recognition). Not only can progress be tracked more closely in this manner, but the employee can adjust his actions within a shorter time span and receive psychological rewards more frequently. This approach motivates the employee to greater progress.

Finally, the manager has one more duty, that of self-improvement. The project manager has the difficult task of maintaining both management and technical skills, of learning to manage personal time so as to meet individual commitments and aid staff members, of remaining open, patient, communicative, and friendly. Yet there must be time for self-improvement because the manager is, to a great extent, a model for the employees.

Management of User Personnel

Many of the skills discussed in the previous section can be applied to assure project success with user personnel. However, there is one substantial difference: user personnel rarely report directly to the project manager of the systems group.

The management skills described in this section are used in two ways with user groups: (1) in an advisory capacity to the managers and supervisors of user areas, and (2) in those instances of direct interaction between project management or systems analysts and users.

It is vital to recognize that the project will create change for the user. From the time that a systems project is first conceived until it has become the norm of operation, user personnel are affected. Change, even change to something "better," creates feelings of apprehension. There is no way in which some resulting disruption can be avoided; it can only be minimized.[10]

User management has the job of minimizing that disruption. The project manager, with a greater knowledge of the new system and the actual changes anticipated, must use this knowledge, combined with good management techniques, to assist the user personnel and supervision (through user management) to make the transition as smooth as possible.

The team building and employee development methods applied to the project team can be adapted for use in the user group. Certainly, participative management will be helpful in alleviating the fear of change.

One area in which the project manager can be of exceptional help is in the development of new standards for employee performance under the new system.

Standards for performance are often grossly misunderstood. One study indicated that only a 35 percent correlation existed between the managers interviewed and their subordinates as to what performance was expected of the subordinate.[11]

The project manager should be prepared to assist user management at three points during the life of the project. First, in developing the feasibility study and economic justification for the system, certain expectations of efficiency are created which imply a difference in standards. Second, between final design and implementation, a tentative standard must be developed for the user to ascertain whether or not the system is operating according to expectations. Third, after the system has been in operation for some time and all unknowns (or the major ones) have been resolved, a permanent standard for measuring employee performance must be created for ongoing operations.

Performance standards are invariably more successful in application when they are constructed with the participation of those whose performance will be measured.

The opportunity to redesign or replace an existing system is also the opportunity to improve the working environment. Systems design should take into consideration the people who will use the system. Systems should be designed with a view toward "human engineering."

Human engineering means making the system easy to learn and use. It means reducing the possibilities for human error, and getting the users "turned on" to the system. This is done by satisfying some needs of the employees.

We have previously discussed Maslow's *need hierarchy* and the satisfaction of those needs. In one study, workers and supervisors were interviewed to rank those things that they felt make a job desirable, with the following results:

	ORDER OF PREFERENCE BY:	
	Workers	*Supervisors*
Recognition for being a skillful worker	7	1
Liking for persons I work with closely	2	8
Job security, retirement, insurance, seniority, etc.	3	2
Salary or wages	4	1
Having interesting work	5	5
Professional advancement	6	3
Satisfactory supervision	7	6
Satisfactory working conditions	8	4

This study was factor analyzed and it was concluded that those desiring advancement and responsibility cared little about job security, those liking advancement and salary cared little about their coworkers, and those liking advancement and recognition were negative about job security.[12]

We may reasonably conclude that there is frequently a difference between the perceived needs of workers and those of supervisors and managers. The design of systems should take this into account. The design should further create opportunities for satisfying those perceived needs.

Several methods can be explored with user management for taking advantage of the opportunities afforded by the project. These include job enlargement, increasing responsibility, increasing decision-making authority, restructuring work flow, reorganizing and regrouping workers, and building in feedback mechanisms to provide for frequent self-appraisal and psychic reward.

Working through user management, the project manager may use some of the following approaches to increase employee's feelings of achievement, responsibility, and recognition, thus increasing their identification with the goals of the project.

Remove some of the more obvious and irritating controls on employees, adding to their feeling of personal dignity. Some companies have sharply improved morale and production by eliminating time clocks.

Increase employee accountability by making them responsible for certain quality levels, outputs, or expense controls. Have reports of these activities routed to the manager so that recognition can be granted.

Provide information to the employee on the whole system, even though the employee may only be working with a small part. Show them how they interact with others in the system.

Devise programs for employee self-improvement. Examples: in-house training may be used, changing jobs for cross-training, outside seminars or visits to other companies using similar systems, coaching, and career counseling.

Look for job enrichment possibilities. These should not simply add to the employee's workload, but should provide the employee with an opportunity to use his talent and mind.

Assign employees to become experts in certain facets of the system so that they can coach and train others.

Try to increase the delegation of management functions from the user management to employees and supervisors.

Although the above sounds like the project manager giving a lot of "advice" (perhaps unwelcome) to user management, it can be done without irritation to user management. Brainstorming sessions during the study and design phases of the project provide a great opportunity for introducing ideas and gleaning reactions. Reviewing the results of employee interviews performed during the study phase is another chance to introduce ideas. Throughout the life of the project the project manager must maintain a meaningful dialogue with user management. The project manager must *listen* and be alert for concepts and ideas proposed by the user that can be fed back as more complete proposals for action based on the *user manager's* ideas.

One important key to success in working through user managers is to give credit to the users, wherever possible, for ideas and actions that they originate. The project manager will receive adequate recognition for the successful implementation of the new system. He should not be stinting of giving credit to others (and incidentally gaining their increasing cooperation).

There are two primary functions in which project managers and systems analysts interact directly with user personnel (workers). These are during the study phase for interviewing and during the implementation phase for training.

The management techniques and motivating factors that have been discussed find ready application in both of these areas.

It is appropriate to discuss some of the management and behavioral aspects of interviewing and training at this point.

The project manager has the responsibility for training analysts on the project team in the techniques of interviewing. Such training will avoid problems that might arise during the interviewing process and assure better results from the interviews.

One must first recognize that there is a transient motivation for the respondent to participate in the interview. Such motivations might include: respondent likes to talk, interview is a break from routine, respondent likes to show off knowledge of the job, the boss ordered participation in the interview, respondent feels that it's part of the job, or respondent wants to contribute to the improvement of company procedures. All of these motivations limit the time that the respondent will contribute and/or the quality of information that the respondent will provide.

The interviewer must find some way of continuing the motivation of the respondent to maintain a high level of interest in the interview. The interviewer must convince the respondent that:

• The respondent is free to express opinions without being judged by the interviewer or management.

• The interviewer respects the respondent's ability to provide the information desired.

• The two have a common basis for understanding each other.

• The interviewer is capable of constructively using the information supplied.

These attitudes can be cultivated only through preparation in advance of the interview. The project manager should review with the analyst the significant features of the system and require the analyst to prepare a written guide for the interviews before they are conducted. The guide should contain a statement, in the analyst's words, of the objectives of the interviews, and a list of the questions that must be asked to achieve the objectives. The project manager should review the guide before it is used.

Each interview develops in a slightly different fashion, so the guide cannot be followed verbatim. However, the analyst must make an effort to obtain answers to all questions during the course of the interviews.

Any appearance of arguing with a respondent, demeaning the intelligence of the respondent, or using the respondent's ideas without suitable recognition will prejudice subsequent interview results and destroy the validity of the interviewing process. Ronald DeMasi has constructed a table of actions to be taken by an interviewer in response to problem behavior on the part of a respondent.[13] (See Figure 3.) These

Respondent Behavior	Interviewer Action
1. Appears to guess at answers rather than admit ignorance.	1. After the interview, cross-check answers that are suspect.
2. Attempts to tell the interviewer what he presumably wants to hear instead of the correct facts.	2. Avoid putting questions in a form that implies the answers. Cross-check answers that are suspect.
3. Gives the interviewer a great deal of irrelevant information or tells stories.	3. In friendly but persistent fashion, bring the discussion back into the desired channel.
4. Stops talking if the interviewer begins to take notes.	4. Put the notebook away and confine questions to those which are most important. If necessary, come back later for details.
5. Attempts to rush through the interview.	5. Suggest coming back later.
6. Expresses satisfaction with the way things are done now and wants no change.	6. Encourage him to elaborate on present situation and its virtues. Take careful notes and questions about details.
7. Shows obvious resentment of the interviewer, answers questions guardedly, or appears to be withholding data.	7. Try to get him talking about something that interests him.
8. Sabotages the interview by noncooperation. In effect, refuses to give information.	8. Ask him, "If I get this information from someone else, would you mind checking it for me?" Then proceed on that plan.
9. Gripes about his job, his pay, his associates, his supervisors, the unfair treatment he receives.	9. Listen sympathetically and note anything that might be a real clue. Do not interrupt until he has poured out his gripes. Then, make friendly but noncommittal statements, such as, "You sure have plenty of troubles. Perhaps the study can help with some of them." This approach should bridge the gap to asking about the desired facts. Later, make enough of a check on his gripes to determine whether or not there is any foundation for them. In this way, you neither pass over a good lead nor leave yourself open to being unduly influenced by groundless talk or personal prejudice.
10. Acts as eager beaver, is enthusiastic about new ideas, gadgets, techniques.	10. Listen for desired facts and valuable leads. Don't become emotionally involved or enlist in his campaign.

Figure 3.

actions provide an outline of methods that may be used to avoid demotivation of respondents.

An interview should close with three actions designed to build confidence in the respondent: a last chance to add anything that has not been covered, permission for the interviewer to return with future questions, and an offer to allow the respondent to review the interviewer's report.

One reason why interviewing methods are so important is that the interview provides first contact between the analyst and the worker. A good interview can condition the worker to an acceptance of change, provide a favorable image of the systems analyst, and create a bias in the respondent *toward* the new system. A bad interview can reverse all these and make implementation of the new system much harder.

The interview also provides the first opportunity to do some subtle training. The process of training user personnel should be approached with consideration of four ingredients:

1. Who should be trained?
2. Who should do the training?
3. How should training be done?
4. When should training be done?

First, training should concentrate on those individuals of the user staff who appear to have the greatest facility to coach others. The identity of these people should become apparent during the early stages of training. Frequently, but not always, they will be the more experienced users. If the level of staffing is to be reduced as a result of implementing the new system, avoid too early a selection of employees to be terminated. The training process may help to identify the employees who should be retained.

Second, some project managers delegate the task of training to the less experienced analysts. Less experienced analysts may assist with training, but this task is so important to the success of the project that only those analysts with prior exposure to training, a thorough knowledge of the system, and a good rapport with user personnel should be responsible.

Third, training should be done in small groups. About fifteen is the maximum number of students that can be given intensive instruction by an experienced teacher. Six to ten students is optimum because it permits teacher attention to each student and provides enough students for interaction to take place. In addition to classroom training using visual aids and text material, which is the standard method, Leslie Matthies has put together a list of training options that may be used.[14]

These include reading, lectures, technical sessions, local seminars, in-house systems courses, seminars in major centers, visits to other systems departments, manufacturer's schools and others.

Fourth, training should take place as close to the time that it will be used in practice as possible. This timing allows students to retain as much of the training information as possible at the time they start actual work on the system. It also may be used to create an enthusiasm for the new system—a motivational "high" that can carry over into the first few weeks of operation of the new system. Employees should be instructed that any difficulties experienced with the new system should be reported immediately for attention and that such difficulties are normal at this time and should not be discouraging.

Negotiating Skills

Negotiating skills, necessary for success in both intragroup and intergroup relationships, have been largely ignored until recently. It was assumed that successful negotiation was a matter of luck and personality, something like winning at poker.

During the last few years some systematic attention has been given to the art of negotiation. Almost all the major authors on this subject stress two facets of negotiation that lead to success, *motivation* and *preparation*.

Chester Karrass views negotiation as a game for which one can prepare by developing certain traits.[15] He indicates that several studies have shown that the following traits are the most important for a negotiator:

Planning skill

Ability to think clearly under stress

General practical intelligence

Verbal ability

Product knowledge

Personal integrity

Ability to perceive and exploit power.

Gerard Nierenberg relates negotiation to the satisfaction of needs (using Maslow's need hierarchy), and stresses preparation, accommodation, and attitude modification.[16]

Preparation should include the following steps:

Establishing objectives

Choosing the negotiating individual or team

Defining the subject matter for negotiation

Collecting all the facts available

Analyzing issues and positions.

Nierenberg points out that the successful negotiator changes the climate of a negotiation from a confrontation or win-lose situation, to a climate of accommodation in which creative alternatives are proposed. This can be done through the following steps:

• Recognize the shortcomings of and the alternatives to a win-lose approach.

• Understand defensive and supportive climates.

• Engage in joint fact finding.

• Get mutual suggestions of creative alternatives.

• Involve everyone on both teams.

• Be ready for spontaneous, problem-oriented courses of action.

The cooperative attitude engendered by these steps is essential for the project manager, since his task involves selling systems ideas, obtaining management approvals, obtaining project funding and resources, setting project schedules and priorities, and a host of other situations that involve negotiation. Each of these situations differ in content and in the individuals involved. Philip Crosby has established some "Laws of Situation Management" which seem to apply well to many situations.[17] These are:

1. The primary concern of management is survival.

2. A person's loyalty is a function of how much he feels he is appreciated.

3. The amount of accurate information an executive possesses concerning the status of his operation varies inversely with his position in the organization.

4. The effectiveness of any program depends upon the amount of participation delegated.

5. The less systematic support a decision-maker receives, the better decisions he will make.

6. Pride goes before all.

7. A job can only be as successful as the means applied to measure it.

8. People are more important to situations than things.

9. Improvement is the only practical management goal.

10. Nobody really listens. (Unless they feel personally affected.)

In summary, there are two basic elements to successful negotiation.

Preparation. Before negotiating one should:

• Gather all appropriate information regarding the subject of the negotiation *and the individuals on the other team.*

• Establish the real goals of the negotiation and what can be given away to obtain those goals.

• Analyze the other team's personal strengths, weaknesses, wants, and motivations.

• Try to presell some of the members of the other team before the negotiation starts.

Motivation. During the negotiation one should:

• Approach meetings on the basis of cooperatively creating alternatives rather than win-lose.

• Play to the satisfaction of the other teams personal wants, motivations, and pride.

• Identify and concentrate effort on the key decision maker on the other team.

Summary

The analyst/project leader is a manager in training. The transition from analyst to manager is made more difficult by the need to actively participate in both the analysis and management functions simultaneously.

This section provides some insight into management theory and illustrates practical techniques derived from behavioral research that the project manager can utilize to improve effectiveness.

The information provided here should be used for self-evaluation and as a checklist or guide to the actions upon which his performance as a manager will be evaluated.

Personal management skills deal primarily with people and situations rather than things. The bibliography provided with this section can be used to enhance the project manager's knowledge of the management field. The skills themselves will only develop through use.

Footnotes

1. Stogdill, R. M., *Handbook of Leadership*, New York: The Free Press, 1974. p. 30.
2. Herzberg, F., Mausner, B., and Snyderman, B., *The Motivation to Work*, New York: Wiley & Sons, 1959.
3. Argyris, C., *Personality and Organization*, New York: Harper & Row, 1957.

4. Maslow, A., *Motivation and Personality*, New York: Harper & Row, 1954.

5. Stogdill, p. 419.

6. French, R., "Management and Motivation," *Managing the Systems Analysis Function*, F. Greenwood, ed., New York: AMA, 1968.

7. Weinberg, G. M., *The Psychology of Computer Programming*, New York: Van Nostrand Reinhold, 1971.

8. Cribbin, J. J., *Effective Managerial Leadership*, New York: AMA, 1972. p. 113.

9. *Ibid.*, p. 117.

10. Fried, L., "Hostility in Organization Change," *Journal of Systems Management*, June, 1972.

11. Reference to this study is found in Douglas McGregor, *The Professional Manager*, New York: McGraw-Hill, 1967.

12. McClelland, D. C., et al., *The Achievement Motive*, New York: Appleton-Century-Crofts, 1953.

13. DeMasi, R. J., *An Introduction to Business Systems Analysis*, Reading, Mass.: Addison-Wesley, 1969, p. 38. Reprinted with permission.

14. Matthies, L., "How to Pick the Top Training Methods," *Peopleware in Systems*, Cleveland: ASM, 1976.

15. Karrass, C. L., *The Negotiating Game*, New York: World Publishers, 1970.

16. Nierenberg, G. I., *Creative Business Negotiating*, New York: Hawthorn, 1971.

17. Crosby, P. B., *The Art of Getting Your Own Sweet Way*, New York: McGraw-Hill, 1972.

Discussion Topics

1. What features of a job or a potential employer would make them attractive to an applicant for an EDP position?

2. Can consultants be used to the advantage of the EDP manager? How?

3. What are the potential dangers of using consultants and how can they be minimized?

4. What benefits can accrue to a company from using consultants?

5. Why are people threatened by change?

6. Do people with technical backgrounds make good managers?

INDEX